MANAGERS TALK ETHICS

MANAGERS TALK ETHICS

Making Tough Choices in a Competitive Business World

Previously published in hardcover as
Tough Choices: Managers Talk Ethics

BARBARA LEY TOFFLER

WILEY

John Wiley & Sons, Inc.
NEW YORK • CHICHESTER • BRISBANE • TORONTO • SINGAPORE

Copyright © 1986, 1991 by Barbara Ley Toffler

Published by John Wiley & Sons, Inc.

Library of Congress Cataloging-in-Publication Data:
Tough choices.
    Managers talk ethics : making tough choices in a competitive
business world / [compiled] by Barbara Ley Toffler.
        p.   cm.
    Originally published under title: Tough choices.
    Includes bibliographical references.
    ISBN 0-471-54262-8 (paper)
    1. Business ethics—United States. 2. Decision-making (Ethics,
3. Executives—United States—Attitudes.   I. Toffler, Barbara Ley.
II. Title.
[HF5387.T676   1991]
174'.4—dc20   91-11325

To Chuck, with respect and love

PREFACE

When I first began the project that ultimately became *Managers Talk Ethics: Making Tough Choices in a Competitive Business World*, originally published in hardcover as *Tough Choices: Managers Talk Ethics*, it was with a modest goal: to write an article—or maybe two—identifying and describing the kinds of problems that managers in North America call "ethical." The few years I had spent thinking about and participating in activities related to business/management ethics had convinced me that there was a significant discrepancy between what scholars were writing and teaching about ethics in the world of commerce and what people working in organizations, particularly managers, were experiencing as ethical concerns. A brief exchange between two participants at a San Francisco conference on the topic supported this view. A prominent philosopher, author of a number of books and articles in the field, confronted a senior executive from a major corporation with the question "Do you people ever read any of the books we write?" The immediate answer was, "No, I don't. Because I don't think you people have any idea about what we do." Several similar exchanges, plus my own experiences working in both large and small business organizations, persuaded me that it was imperative that somebody listen to the folks in the trenches and learn what it was that troubled them ethically. And so the decision to conduct in-depth interviews with practicing managers.

But it was after the interviewing, during the analysis stage, that this book took on the shape that it has. Two things occurred:

First, as I was attempting to extract categories of problems—or just to make lists of problems—I discovered, quite simply, that I couldn't. And the reason that I couldn't was that every story I had been told fit into a number of different categories. For example, the "Cambodian woman" story near the end of the Tom Benjamin interview can be categorized as a personnel problem, a concern about fairness, a case of stealing, a problem of forgery, a harassment situation, a case of potential race or gender discrimination, a compromise of honesty, and probably a few other things. So, in fact, by developing a typology as planned, I would be maintaining the status quo, trimming the reality to present an outsider's interpretation of the problem rather than reflecting the practitioner's experience. And the fact was—and is—that one of the challenges managers face in resolving ethical dilemmas is that it is so difficult to figure out just what the problem is. And when one cannot figure out what the problem is, it is usually hard to solve it. The second formative event occurred as I was reading the transcripts of the tapes for the first time. Over and over again I would enthuse to anyone within earshot, "Listen to this, just listen. Everyone should hear how managers talk about ethics—they're so so articulate, so real!" One of my listeners—my husband—finally said, "Well, why don't you write a book that lets those voices be heard?" And so, *Managers Talk Ethics*.

But one should not write a book just to let the voices of some segment of society be heard (although that practice is not uncommon). If some particular words, or ideas, or perspectives are being presented, there must be some purpose behind it. In this case the purpose was twofold. First, as indicated, was to make available to the thinkers the "real stuff" from the doers. Second, was to provide all of us—thinkers and doers—the material from which we could understand what kinds of problems become ethical, how these problems arise, what organizational factors and what characteristics of individuals are critical, and ultimately what can be done to prevent ethical dilemmas from arising and how they can be resolved when they do occur.

What has turned out to be most striking to me, four years after this book first appeared, is that it is the voices themselves and not the variables (organizational factors, individual characteristics, kinds of problems, etc.) that have had the greatest effect on the people the book has reached and, especially, on my own work. Prior to conducting this research, I believed that "doing ethics" in an organization meant conducting a generic program—cases, exercises, etc.—and allowing participants to figure out how to apply the learnings to their own circumstances. But after doing many such programs—often up to a dozen or more in a single company—I recognized that after that initial feel-good glow of almost any new intervention, many attendees were left with a vague disenchantment. One reason was obvious. Most programs were directed to middle management, the "I'm caught between a rock and a hard place" group, who felt frustration at the fact that these programs focused on them as decision makers vis-à-vis their peers and subordinates, but left unaddressed the stresses and constraints resulting from the decisions and directives of their superiors. More significantly, however, their discomfort took on the same tone as the senior manager at that earlier ethics conference: "Why don't you stop telling us what to do for just a minute, and listen to what is troubling us?"

Maybe I had never done so because I had somehow uncritically bought the imperious statement of a former academic colleague that "managers don't know what they are thinking or saying. We have to tell them!" *Managers Talk Ethics* taught me that not only do managers think clearly and speak articulately about what they do and how they feel about what they do, but they have a "genuine ethical sensitivity," as Peter Steinfels reflected in his May 1987 address to the National Federation of Priests Councils, in which the voices of the *Managers Talk Ethics* managers served as his data. It is interesting to note that Steinfels suggested that if, as it appears, managers have lost a religious conception or "biblical language for framing their work, in no small measure that is because the speakers and teachers of the older languages of ethics and Scripture have not been good listeners and learners in the face of the modern American economy." (Do none of us listen to each other, or is it particularly members of the institutions that keep our economy going to whom we are deaf?)

So with the support of some courageous senior executives who wanted ethical performance (corporate and individual) to be one measure of their success—and some equally intrepid senior and middle managers and lower-level employees—I began to "do ethics" by engaging the voices of the members of one large financial services institution. There were individual interviews, there were four- to six-hour group sessions; detailed notes were taken (no tape recorders were used); ideas were captured, the participants' own words were recorded. When it came time to "analyze" the data, I didn't. I identified several themes (e.g., dealing with employees, managing competitive pressures) and within each theme listed direct quotations from the hundred or so people who had been part of the project. These organized quotations were then fed back to a senior management ethics group—as well as to all the participants—to begin the process of understanding and, where necessary, changing the way ethics is part of this company's organizational strategy and individual employee behavior. Further details of the unfolding of this effort are not necessary, although they were exhilarating for all of us. Nor can I point to some glorious manifestation of ethical insight on the part of the particular organization, other than to say that I am told that many in the company believe that ethics has become a significant part of the fabric of the firm. And let me hasten to add that this process is no new invention; it grows out of my learnings in an exceptional Organizational Diagnosis course in graduate school in the 1970s. This project, however, marked the first time I had used this process in the ethics arena.

What is significant is that this process affirms the reality that the language and experience of the members of any institution— private sector, public sector, not-for-profit—are the core fibers that will bring ethical vibrance to that institution's tapestry of successful performance. There are, now, several more organizations that have undertaken projects similar to the one discussed above. The outcomes are manifested in many different ways. One common result, however, appears to be a chipping away at that ever-cited obstacle to effectiveness, "a failure to communicate." It is becoming acceptable to talk about ethical concerns, downward to subordinates, upward to superiors and leaders. The next challenges lie in building ethical language bridges across organizational, national, and international boundaries, a process we can at least begin if we can just keep talking.

BARBARA LEY TOFFLER

Boston, Massachusetts
April 1991

ACKNOWLEDGMENTS

I am indebted to the managers who participated in this project. Their openness in talking about the feelings and beliefs that most of us have learned it is safer to keep to ourselves, their enthusiasm for, and commitment to, the intellectual matter with which we were grappling, and the generosity with which they gave of their time not only made the intention of this study a reality, but also enriched my life enormously. My hope is that in return I have presented their words as they intended them to be heard.

My deep appreciation goes also to the organizations that employ these managers. Each company, with guarantee of anonymity, supported the project, provided access to personnel, and, recognizing the sensitivity of the subject matter, asked no feedback or other return. That trust made possible the open and honest contribution of the participants.

This book has benefited from the thoughtful comments of many colleagues at the Harvard Business School. Kenneth Andrews, Louis Barnes, Michael Beer, James Heskett, Linda Hill, Paul Lawrence, Jay Lorsch, and Quinn Mills reviewed the manuscript and provided valuable ideas and insights. George Lodge and John Matthews read endless drafts, questioned and challenged me, but always offered encouragement and support. I am deeply grateful to them.

I wish to thank Dean John McArthur for his commitment to the study of business ethics and, very specifically, for helping me find the time necessary to finish this project. My appreciation in that regard, as well, to Gordon Donaldson. The research was generously supported intellectually and financially by the Harvard

Business School's Division of Research and its director, Raymond Corey.

Many people contributed valuable assistance to the production of this book. John Mahaney, my editor at Wiley, kept the creative fires burning when they threatened to dim. Barbara Feinberg not only brought her exceptional skills as an editor to the shaping of a sometimes unwieldy manuscript, but also buoyed my occasionally flagging spirits. I am indebted to Carol Gerrior, who organized and managed the process of bringing scrawled yellow sheets to presentable manuscript form. My special thanks to Christine Mattson, who willingly and graciously offered extra support whenever it was necessary. Rose Giacobbe and her staff in Word Processing did a masterful job of typing many drafts of the manuscript, often under great time pressure.

I am fortunate to have been supported throughout this endeavor by dear friends. Judy Bodie, Joline Godfrey, Judy Grumbly, Linda Hill, Diana McClure, Janice McCormick, and Rose Zoltek have provided sustenance, affection, and good humor. Rebecca Hartman was an ever cheerful, extra pair of hands for which I am grateful.

Like so much of my work, this book has been enriched by Madeline Heilman and Richard Hackman, who continue to share with me the respect for people and ideas that was so important a part of my Yale experience.

My deepest thanks and love to my family, who endured the disruptions and volatile emotions that accompany the writing of a book. My parents, Clarice and Ted Ley, have always had faith that I could achieve whatever I set out to do. My children, Sam, Aaron, and Judith, have, with unstinting love and support, taken the time to make me believe that what I am doing matters. My "other" children, Laura and Catherine, with their energy and enthusiasm, have added immeasurably to my work and my life.

Finally, it is to my husband, Chuck Powers, who introduced me to the discipline of ethics, who taught me to think of ethics as a source of energy and action, and who has been my mentor, my colleague, and my friend, that I dedicate this book.

BARBARA LEY TOFFLER

CONTENTS

CONTENTS

Charles Warren

" . . . If you're in a position of jeopardy with your management and if you're not doing something that's illegal, it's difficult not to want to play ball."

Jeffrey Lovett

"I was really acting almost like a spy. . . . It's taken me almost two years to get over it."

Wendell Johnson

" . . . The guilt trip is over. He performs or he's fired. Except it won't be that simple. It's just easy to say."

Jackson Taylor

"Our biggest concern was our customers; and the issue was our implied commitment, what we had led them to believe."

Ronald Harris

"These guys steal technology from each other all the time. Nobody else would have your concern!"

CONTENTS

Frank McGraw

"This is the kind of ethical thing you get into. It's not black; it's not white. You're not responsible legally; but you are responsible. The question is, what are you responsible for?"

Peter Lathen

"There is no danger to anyone but people are putting up their dough, and they're not going to get the results they want every time."

William Robertson

"To me it's immoral, but that doesn't mean it's immoral in terms of what big business does."

Robert McDonald

"The 'anonymous letter' bothers the hell out of me because I don't really like to lie."

James Gordon

"The company, because of the lack of structure, ends up chewing up a lot of people."

CONTENTS

I would insist that we must start from the recognition that there is something peculiarly puzzling and problematic, peculiarly arguable, about the whole phenomenon of morals. Not everyone, naturally, feels this, but even if one does not feel it the record shows it to be so. So much is unclear; so many different views have been taken—and not only, of course, about what is morally right or wrong, but about what it is to be morally right or wrong. . . . How, when one meets a moral issue, does one recognize it as such? . . . One thing that in my view is of the first importance is that we should begin more nearly at the beginning than is commonly done, and determine how we propose that the subject-matter is to be identified.

G. J. WARNOCK
Contemporary Moral Philosophy

An abstraction has its natural and proper place in reasoning; so does its contrary, which is the mind's openness to a great range of largely unexpected observed features of a situation all of which are allowed to influence the response. Kant's account of practical reason was an insistence on the abstract will, which in virtue of its rationality would not be engaged by the multiplicity of concrete features that complicate particular situations. The opposing school of moralists, utilitarians, associate rationality in moral reasoning with scientific method, therefore with verifiable judgments of right and wrong, and therefore with a general criterion or test that yields definite results in particular cases. Therefore a primary abstraction is required . . . that leaves out of account . . . those features of situations which are not mentioned in the utilitarian calculus. The agent can feel secure with his rational method. He has eliminated the worst uncertainties of living. . . . Much that is puzzling, exceptional and difficult about those practical questions which are called moral issues has been cleared away for the utilitarian by a policy of abstraction.

If I were to defend . . . the case against abstract thinking in many matters of moral judgment . . . I would do best to tell true stories, drawn from direct experience, of events which have actually involved difficult decisions.

STUART HAMPSHIRE
Morality and Conflict

I am not a survey social scientist. I claim no definitive conclusions about what any "group" feels or thinks. I don't even claim an exclusive say about what the limited number of children I've gotten to know "really" think. As clinicians know, patients possess within themselves many truths. Different doctors elicit different patterns of those truths—and often enough see different people in the same person. One can only insist on being as tentative as possible, claiming only impressions, observations, thoughts, reflections, surmises, speculations, and, in the end, a "way of seeing." The limitations of this approach must be stressed again and again—no percentages, no statistics, no all-out conclusions. But there are a few rewards, too—those any doctor knows when he or she feels newly educated by another human being.

ROBERT COLES
The Political Life of Children

MANAGERS TALK ETHICS

INTRODUCTION

The topic of business ethics* has long intrigued and challenged management educators, philosophers, corporate managers, and the general public. Despite the attention paid to the subject, however, there has been minimal agreement about what "business ethics" is and what values, standards, and beliefs are or should be important. And despite the fact that many would agree experience is the best teacher, most definitions and descriptions of ethical concerns in business have come not from managers themselves but from professors, politicians, and the public. Business managers, primarily, have been invited to comment on those thoughts. For example, managers are frequently polled to determine what they would do with a specific problem that the investigator defines as ethical. Rarely are managers asked to volunteer their ideas about what constitutes an ethical problem for them.

Raymond C. Baumhart, S. J. set a stage for research on ethics in business with his work "How Ethical Are Businessmen?," published in the *Harvard Business Review* in 1961. Most of his article focused on analyses of executives' responses to a range of questions grouped under the general categories "What would you do if . . . ?" and "What do you think about . . . ?," which used brief cases and examples of practices recognized intuitively as having some ethical content (such as the giving of gifts to secure a contract). One section of the study did ask the participants about ethical experiences they had had, such experiences defined specifically as conflicts between economic demands and ethical demands. This phrasing not only did not elicit from the business people what it was that constituted an ethical experience for them, it conveyed the message that ethical considerations, whatever else they might be, were concerns that stood in opposition to economic considerations. Implicitly, then, being ethical meant sacrifice on the bottom line.

In 1977, Brenner and Molander reported a 15-year follow-up to Baumhart's study. Again, the "What would you do" and "What do you think" categories dominated, and, again, executives were

---

* The words "ethical" and "moral" (or ethics and morals) will be used interchangeably in this book. This is consistent with my intention to examine the range of factors managers see as moral or ethical. It is also consistent with some, but not all, philosophical definitions.

not asked about the ethical problems they experienced but only if they had had conflicts between economic and ethical demands. Research by Carroll (1975) and Purcell (1977), and numerous others over the last 25 years, has followed similar survey methods. This work has yielded information concerning what managers think *about* issues already identified as having an ethical dimension. It has not explored the important questions of what managers themselves perceive to be ethical concerns, why they see them as such, and where, in their perceptions, these problems come from.

More critical, when outsiders define the domain of ethical business activity, they focus on *behaviors*—the giving or taking of gifts, the misrepresentation of data, discrimination in hiring—and they declare, unequivocally and appropriately, that that behavior is wrong. The implication they then draw is that this wrong behavior has occurred because the actor intended to do wrong. This focus on *intention* leads to the assumption that to be ethical, managers simply must be made to want to be so. Intention, however, is only a trigger to action. Implementation of action requires another ingredient—*capacity*—the ability to carry out an intention. For managers to carry through on their good intentions, organizations and organizational members must provide the conditions under which those intentions can be brought to action. Only through first-hand reports of what is experienced as ethical concerns on the job and of the processes affecting the creation and handling of those concerns can managers, organizations, and those outside who would judge them understand what is essential to produce ethical practices in business.

The absence of such first-hand reports—and the need for them in order to expand both knowledge about business ethics and ethical business practice itself—prompted the development of this study. Its critical point of inquiry was to learn what managers say that ethics in business is for them. These practicing managers do not describe systematically every ethical problem that can occur in a business situation, but their situations represent the kinds of events and the circumstances surrounding them that raise ethical red flags. Further, these experiences exhibit common characteristics of both individuals and organizations, which suggest basic conditions that must be met to allow ethical managerial performance.

THE ORGANIZATION OF THE BOOK

There are, then, two purposes to this book. The first is to present in a public forum the voices of managers talking about their work, the values they bring to that work, the kinds of ethical concerns they have, and their feelings about them. The second purpose is to explore the nature of those ethical problems and how they come about, and to identify the organizational conditions and individual characteristics and actions necessary to allow and assist ethical business behavior.

Following this introduction, "Ethical Situations at Work" begins by looking at the formal definition of "ethical," comparing it to the connotative meanings of the word expressed by managers in this study, and noting the implication of this lack of definitional consensus. This part then looks at the characteristics of the problems managers call ethical—first noting the categories of managerial practice in which these problems emerge, then addressing the elements that lead them to attach the label "ethical" to a problem, and finally describing the form that these problems take. Also discussed are the differences between issues (the way ethical problems are framed at the organizational policy level) and dilemmas (the way those problems occur for the individual manager). This comparison highlights the discrepancy between intention and capacity to focus on the factors which challenge the implementation of ethical managerial decisions.

The next part, "The Managers Who Talked Ethics," introduces, in a brief, demographic overview, the people whose interviews appear in this book. The first 18 interviews are organized around two themes: ethical problems that concern the relationship between the organization and the individual and ethical problems that deal with conflicts within the individual. Any organization, by the complex design necessary to create and maintain its form, and by the culture that emerges within it, shapes the kinds of problems that occur and influences what its members can do and how they do it. These are the conditions giving rise to the frequently uttered phrase, "That's the way we do things around here." While the relationship between the individual and the organization can and should be mutually beneficial and productive, often the organization creates roadblocks for the individual and impedes her chosen course of action.

In the next part, "In their Own Words," the first ten interviews deal with ethical problems in the organizational/individual relationship. Mike Williams launches this group with his tale of being sent to deal with a loan loss cover-up in a foreign branch of his bank. His story identifies the organizational factors that contributed to the occurrence of the problem as well as those which limited his capacity to act in as ethically effective a manner as he would have wished. Mike Williams is followed by three managers—Harold Lightner, Charles Warren, and Jeffrey Lovett—all of whom talk about organizational impediments to their implementing an ethical course of action. In Harold's unhappiness at being a pawn in an organizational restructuring, in Charles' decision to "fudge" the numbers, and in Jeffrey's anguish when he was asked (or so he believes) to spy on his boss, we see played out the ethical consequences of limited participation and individual choice.

The next interview, with Wendell Johnson, demonstrates a different kind of organization/individual interaction. Wendell finds himself caught between two conflicting directives, each of which reflects values held by the organization. He is constrained by organizational policies and, at the same time, left adrift by his institution's apparent unawareness of the situation. Jackson Taylor and Ronald Harris pick up this theme of an organization's lack of awareness and responsiveness. These two managers, however, are not constrained by organizationally dictated limits to their ability to choose a course of action. They are, in fact, set afloat in an ethical sea by their organizations' lack of necessary and appropriate action.

These first seven interviews, then, reveal the lines of conflict drawn between the person and the institution, with an imbalance of appropriate organizational direction and individual independence contributing to ethical difficulties. If the organizational/individual relationships were the key contributing factor to ethical problems at work, however, we should find fewer such concerns when the individual is also "the organization," that is, when he is the one who is defining the policy and procedures upon which to act. But, as the next three speakers—Tom Benjamin, Carol Miller, and Mark

Hoffmann—demonstrate, even when a manager defines the environment, he may be setting conditions which will later create ethical challenges. For example, Tom Benjamin points out that when he pronounced that "hanky panky" within his department was unacceptable, he did not anticipate the arrival of a dynamic and attractive woman consultant who would stir some feelings in his own heart.

Evelyn Grant leads off the interviews sounding the second theme: people dealing with their own conflicts within a work setting. Often ethical problems at work are not related to conflict or confusion between the individual and the organization, but instead have something to do either with an individual's conflict of values, of needs, of commitments to stakeholders, or with an individual's inability to figure out what the ethical course of action is when these competing claims arise. In such cases, "the way we do things around here" must, at best, support and provide mechanisms to assist the individual, or at least play a neutral and nonobstructive role. Evelyn Grant begins this thematic unit, as Mike Williams did the first, by talking in some detail about her organization and addressing ethical problems she has experienced. She and Ronald Harris (Ronald Harris and Harold Lightner appear twice in this book), whose interview follows, each talk about two situations with which they struggled. In one, each describes reaching a decision to behave according to the dictates of their consciences—in a sense, regardless of consequences—both also fairly sure that their organizations would stand behind them. For each, the second situation was one in which the "right" action was less clear. Both talk about using their organizations to assist them in sorting through the complex issues either to make a decision (Harris) or to implement a decision painfully arrived at (Grant).

The three managers who follow—Frank McGraw, Peter Lathen, and Bill Robertson—could be called the wrestlers. In these cases, the organizational factors relating to their problems are adequate. For each of these men, however, a feeling of "Should I be doing more?" drives him to explore his own relationship and obligation to a key stakeholder. For instance, Bill Robertson's company's provision of a satisfactory disability policy does not mitigate his concerns about the psychological needs of an employee.

The final three interviews in this section bring us full circle: they help demonstrate how, out of the ethical wrestlings of individuals, come the policies, procedures, rules, and norms that can become "the way we do things around here." In some situations, the manager may be unaware of setting a norm or a practice, as, for example when Bob McDonald uses an anonymous letter "ploy" to protect an informant. In other situations, a manager may be fully aware that his action could set a precedent. Jim Gordon discusses that possibility when he talks about "altering" a policy. In yet other circumstances, as with Harold Lightner and the bomb threat, a manager will use the challenge of an ethical dilemma to make a statement or set a policy or practice which can become part of the organization's culture. In each of these interviews, then, the manager begins to shape the conditions with which others will have to cope.

The part titled "The 'Public' Manager and the Private Person" presents the final three interviews in the book. These three "full biographies"—Robert Smith, Arnold Rowan, and Richard Manzini— are offered in evidence of the coherence of beliefs, commitments, and actions within the professional and personal lives of the American corporate manager.

"Creating Capacity: Shaping the Way Things Are Done," the conclusion of the book, is addressed to the manager in the two roles that she plays: that of "the organization," a person who, in some ways, influences the way things are done and who is either in a position senior to some other individual or agent of the organization to outside stakeholders; and that of "individual," who sits in a position subordinate to some others and who must respond to the way things are done in the company. This part emphasizes that ethical dilemmas in the workplace, the conditions that cause them and affect the way they are handled, are not discrete parts of the practice of management. They are of a piece with the values, the design, the strategy, the policies and procedures, the systems and process, and the people who must interact effectively to produce quality products or services, growth and satisfaction for employees, and a commitment to responsible and ethical action for all who are touched by the institution.

ETHICAL SITUATIONS

AT WORK

The word "ethical" will appear repeatedly throughout the book. According to the definition found in *Webster's Seventh New Collegiate Dictionary*, it means "relating to what is good or bad, and [having to do] with moral duty and obligation." ("Moral" is defined as "relating to principles of right and wrong.") And in fact, "ethical" has become a label we attach to situations which produce some sense that a wrong might be or has been done. Attaching labels frequently implies that we assume not only that we know what we mean, but that others mean the same thing when they use the label. This is often not the case. When managers in this study were asked for a definition of the word ethical, they exhibited different understanding of this common label:

"Ethics are eternal verities of right and wrong."

"They [ethics] are really rules—rules of behavior."

"Integrity is what it means; it has to start from within [the individual]."

"The most appropriate meaning of ethical is: conforming to the standards of a given profession or group. So any group can set its own ethical standards and then live by them or not."

These statements represent the four categories of personal definitions offered: basic truths, rules of behavior, the integrated unity of an individual's character, and institutional (or cultural) codes. Although the common thread of these definitions is that "ethical" has something to do with right and wrong, good and evil, virtue and vice, there is no agreement on the substance of right and wrong, its source, or on the universality of application.

"Ethical" derives from the Greek word "ethos," which means both "character" and "sentiment of the community"—what we might call culture. The dual meaning reflects the four categories presented above; it also reflects the definition of ethical with which I undertook this project. For me, ethical has to do with a general conception of right and wrong in the attitudes and actions of individuals and the communities (institutions) of which they are a part. I did not, however, give my definition to the participants. The definition each offered held for his or her interviews. That these people were not working from a common definition of ethics is compatible with the approach this book takes; connotatively, they and I were all talking about the same thing. Our definitions were not completely congruent but were more in the nature of circles of meaning that overlapped at various points. How managers defined ethics certainly affected how they perceived and handled problems. Such differences, however, did not impede our understanding of each other.

This approach seems to accept that there can be different notions of right and wrong. However, this book is built on a basic assumption that there are principles such as honesty, promise-keeping, doing no harm, which are held by most people, at least in the Western world. This assumption allows us to make statements like "that's unethical" about a given action, with which most of the general public would agree.

One final comment on the use of "ethical." There are two common uses of this word: one to refer to a problem that implies a right versus wrong solution, for example, when we talk about facing an ethical dilemma; and two, to refer to a "right" choice or action ("she did the ethical thing")—or obversely ("she behaved unethically"). As in ordinary discourse, the word will be used in both ways in the interviews and comments that follow them. In each case I believe the meaning is self-evident.

Ethically questionable situations in business most frequently cited by the public are either practices involving outright illegal activities such as the application of personal expenses to contract budgets, the stealing of company products, or practices which compromise a recognized corporate code or policy like gift-giving, or practices that result in physical harm to a person or group like producing a gas tank vulnerable to rear-end collisions or dumping of toxic wastes into a local river. These common examples suggest that situations concerning ethics in businesses are those dealing with the breaking of laws and rules or with the causing of physical harm, and are situations in which the individuals involved are offered a clear choice between doing right and doing wrong. The data from the managers in this study, however, suggest that ethical concerns in business are more pervasive and complex than is generally recognized. In fact, *ethical concerns are part of the routine practices of management*; they are characterized less frequently by legal issues than by *concerns about relationships and responsibility*; and while they deal with right-and-wrong decisions, they *frequently involve factors that make the right and wrong less than patently clear.*

AREAS IN WHICH ETHICAL PROBLEMS ARISE

The design of this study allowed managers to think, during a three- or four-week period, of two ethical situations in which they had been involved. With the exception of one individual who said he had never had an ethical problem,* every manager had little difficulty identifying such situations. Significantly, however, many managers expressed concern that their situations did not conform to the a priori assumption about what business ethics is, that is, laws, rules, physical harm, and thus were not "important" enough to share. Many seemed to feel that unless they had a minor Watergate, a case of international bribery, or at least a hefty dose of white-collar crime, the world was unlikely to be interested in their problem. One manager of a 450-person division began our meeting by saying he had been up since five in the morning trying to think of "good" cases, but that he had "had a hard time because it came down to the fact that the ones I had trouble dealing with had to do with employees and peers—people. I asked, 'What are the decisions I have to make?' and they were all around employee working situations." At our next meeting, this manager said his wife wondered why he had not talked about a "major" issue, like the company's policy on trade with South Africa. His response, echoed by manager after manager, was, "I don't make the decisions about South Africa; I do decide on things that will affect my people."

The 33 managers in this study described 59 situations which they felt had an ethical component. These incidents fell into three major categories:

Area	Number of Cases	Percentage of Total
Managing human resource processes and personnel	39	66.1%

---

* Two years after collecting these data I received a call from that manager to recount an ethical problem he had, at last, encountered.

Area	Number of Cases	Percentage of Total
Managing external constituents	10	16.9
Managing personal risk versus company loyalty	7	11.9
Other	3	5.1
Total	59	100.0%

Managing Human Resource Processes and Personnel

Most frequently cited as a source of ethical concerns were those activities dealing with (a) performance evaluation and resultant hiring, firing, promotion, and demotion decisions; (b) designing and administering personnel policies and systems, for example, disability policies, reward systems; and (c) managing relationships on the job. These problems occurred at all levels of the organization and were not specific to particular functions. The interviews in this book provide examples of these concerns, especially those with Wendell Johnson and Evelyn Grant.

Managing External Constituents

The situations noted second in frequency were those that dealt with two groups outside the organization to whom the organization had obligations and upon whom it was dependent: customers and suppliers. Problems discussed ranged from the specific—"What is our responsibility to a supplier upon the abrupt discontinuation of a product?"—to the general—"What is the appropriate cost/quality balance to best serve the customer?" These problems arose in specific functional areas like purchasing, sales, and quality assurance, where the managers' tasks related to the outside constituency group. Frank McGraw and Peter Lathen, in their interviews, offer examples.

Managing Personal Risk Versus Company Loyalty

A small number of people talked about situations in which they felt the threat of personal loss if they did not comply with a "company" expectation. These situations included pressure from a superior to act against one's own values or beliefs, making a personal sacrifice for the good of the company, and managing the work/home conflict. These problems were not function-related and generally were not level-related. It is clear, however, that managers at higher levels in the organization felt more able to change the situation from pure win/lose to one of more balanced outcome than did lower-level managers, who often talked of having "no choice." Some examples in the interviews are Charles Warren and Jeffrey Lovett.

* * * * *

These findings support the notion that ethical concerns in business are part of the routine practices of management. They are *not* problems set apart from the rest of management. Ethics is intertwined with personnel, finance, production, and every other part of business management activity.

ELEMENTS OF ETHICAL SITUATIONS

After identifying ethical situations they had faced, managers were asked why they called those problems ethical. Four elements emerged from the interviews as key to why managers identified particular problems as having an ethical dimension: people, competing claims, intervention, and determining responsibility. While these elements can and often should be talked about in relation to each other, they are sufficiently different to be described individually.

Element	Components
People	Relationship
	Commitment
	Proximity
	Harm
	Inevitability of causing
	Response of the harmed
Competing claims	Between two or more personal values
	Between personal value(s) and value(s) of others

Element	Components
Competing claims (*continued*)	Between means and ends
	Between two or more individuals or groups to whom one has an obligation
Intervention	With value agreement
	With value conflict
Determining responsibility	

People

"Having to do with people" sounds both trite and general: general because it really doesn't tell us specifically what "having to do with people" entails, and trite because it seems the matter of pop music and media advertising. (Of course, frequently, the reason things become trite is because they express a general truth.) But as managers talked about their concerns in dealing with people and why they felt that "people" contributed to a situation's being called ethical, two aspects emerged.

The first is *relationship*. As managers expressed their concerns about people, it became evident that they did not really mean nameless, faceless people but specific individuals, known to them, who knew them, and with whom they had some kind of contract— formal or informal, written or psychological, role-determined or personally determined. In other words, individuals with whom they had a relationship. The notion of relationship has several parts. One is commitment: an explicit or implicit set of obligations that allows the parties to the relationship to hold trustworthy expectations about what the other will do. Managers make commitments to their subordinates, their bosses, their coworkers, to suppliers and customers. They depend on reciprocal commitments from those people to get their own jobs done.

A second part of relationship is proximity: a degree of nearness that makes the commitment felt. Although proximity is usually thought of in spatial terms, psychological proximity is also a characteristic of relationships. We all have relationships with people, family members for instance, with whom we are not necessarily physically proximate. But some of what maintains the relationship is a proximity by verbal contact (phone calls) or written communication (letters and cards). So, too, do managers describe the proximity that contributes to the ethical quality of relationships, whether the proximity be adjacent offices, a daily or weekly phone call, or a monthly report. What seems to be at the heart of the proximity concern is, first, that it affects the managers' sense of responsibility ("if I am near to a situation, I may have, or be thought to have, the capacity to do something about it"), and second, managers will get direct and reasonably immediate feedback on the effects of their actions. Feedback is important. Most people would agree that the pain of making and implementing difficult decisions of any kind is increased by the anticipation of direct feedback from the affected parties. One CEO said that he was more keenly aware of an ethical dimension in dealing with the plateaued career of a senior vice-president than in making policy decisions about the company's involvement in South Africa. The reason he offered for this difference was that he would have to face the reaction of his vice-president, with whom he had a relationship, whereas there was no immediacy of contact with South Africa and those affected by the decision.*

The second element is *harm*. Harm as an ethical dimension is more frequently triggered by managers' concern for people than by the need to adhere to a principle that says "Do no harm." For managers, causing harm can mean a number of different things. It can mean doing something that threatens the life or physical well-being of another person; but it can also mean causing emotional or psychological distress, or even simply doing something that will be less satisfying to another person than what that person would have desired.

Although there are some situations in which decisions resulting in the potential for life-threatening or physical harm are posed for managers, more frequently they find themselves in positions in which the possible harm is of a lesser nature. In these cases there are two critical factors that appear to affect the labeling of a situation as ethical. One is the *inevitability* of causing some harm. The pos-

---

* It is interesting to note that whenever an intuitively "ethical" example was needed, interviewees almost always mentioned doing business in South Africa— and these interviews took place in 1983.

sibility of managers wending their way through the many needs and demands placed on them without causing some discomfort somewhere is close to impossible. Similarly, many of the necessary actions managers are required to take must, by their very nature, cause harm. Telling an employee that he or she is unlikely to be promoted is one such action which managers frequently cite as an ethical situation because it causes harm (unhappiness, loss of self-esteem, etc.). But, if you look beneath this genuine concern, the second factor appears: the response of the person harmed. Managers wish to cause no harm out of a fear of being disliked. As one interviewee put it, "One of the biggest problems in management is cowardice. It's very difficult to sit down with someone and really criticize him—fairly and honestly criticize him. You want to be liked."

Competing Claims

Competing claims—being "pulled in two or more directions"—was frequently cited as an identifying feature of ethical situations. Competing claims appear in a variety of guises: conflict between two or more personally held values, conflict between personal value(s) and the value(s) held by another person or the organization, conflicts between basic principles and the need to achieve a desired outcome (a means/end conflict), and conflict between two or more individuals or groups to whom one has an obligation.

Conflict between two personally held values can be exemplified by the painful dilemma of a manager concerned about a troubled employee. On the one hand, his concern about caring, about the importance of helping others, may propel the manager to investigate the difficulty by asking questions or calling the spouse or taking some other action. On the other hand, if the manager also believes in respecting others' privacy, which may compel him to take a hands-off approach, the manager may find himself torn between competing personal values.

Suppose, then, the manager decides his values of caring predominate and he very carefully and respectfully asks the troubled employee what the problem is. If the employee holds privacy as critical and responds, "Mind your own business," the manager is dealing with an interpersonal value conflict. To carry it one step further: suppose the company has a policy saying that every alcoholic employee must attend the company alcoholism program or be terminated. If the manager thinks his employee's problem is, in fact, alcohol, but he has no evidence and cannot get any without invasion of privacy, and if, as well, the manager has questions as to the appropriateness of such a policy, there is now a conflict among the manager, the subordinate, and the company.

The conflict between a basic principle and a desired outcome can be exemplified by the manager who considers lying to a subordinate about why she was not promoted to allow the subordinate to save face, a common example of compromising a principle to achieve a "good" result.

The final area of the conflict of competing claims has to do with obligations to two or more stakeholders. Whether trying to get the best deal for the company while being "fair" to all suppliers, or adjusting policy for a needy employee while rejecting the demands of other employees, in balancing work and family commitments, the pull of multiple obligations signals "ethical" to managers.

Intervention

Many managers consider a situation ethical if their decisions and actions result in their intervening in the lives of others, or if they perceive their own lives are being affected by others' intervention. In many cases, the kinds of decisions and actions they refer to are things like making personnel decisions about subordinates, canceling contracts with suppliers, and speeding up production at the behest of a boss. These kinds of activities are part of their normal managerial roles and support the notion that when managers talk about the ethics of intervening in others' lives, they are saying there is a core ethical dimension to their professional work.

The notion of intervention has to do with an emotionally charged word—control. When managers talk of intervening in others' lives, they are really talking about who is in control, who makes the choice about what is done. Most people want control, at least of the things that matter most to them. And most people have a fear of or frustration with situations which are beyond their power to manage. Thus the notion of intervention or control works in two ways. Managers see situations in which they intervene in people's lives as ethical. They also see as ethical, situations in which they are rendered impotent by other people or by their organizations.

Intervention can have two substantive forms: when there is agreement about what ought to be done and when there is conflict. Intervention with agreement occurs, for example, when, as the parent of a teenage driver, we insist on an early curfew because of drunk drivers on the road. Both parent and teen agree that the danger is real, but both recognize the parental intervention as controlling the behavior of the youngster who would prefer "to make my own decisions about what to do." That situation is substantively different from an intervention accompanied by a conflict. The parent who sets limits on a teenager based on the parent's assessment that the teen's friends, who the teen thinks are great, are a bunch of bums, is both imposing beliefs and controlling behavior.

Determining Responsibility

The final "marker" of an ethical situation interviewees identified concerns responsibility, a subject treated in depth later in this section. For the moment, however, a few points can be made.

The question of whether or not a manager has a responsibility in a situation is critical from two perspectives: Should she do something? Should she *not* do something? First of all, if a manager does have a responsibility and fails to act, she is committing a breach of obligation. The manager also may be allowing circumstances to occur which may produce harmful or other negative results for other people and/or the organization. The manager who has the capacity to prevent an injury on a faulty machine, but who says "It's not my job," might be considered by many people to be acting in an ethically questionable fashion. However, many managers would ask, "How *does* that manager know if she has a responsibility or not?" Similarly, the manager who leaps into the fray inappropriately where she has no responsibility can slow down production, intervene in others' lives, and affect a number of outcomes in detrimental ways. Repeatedly the question, "How do I know *when* I have the responsibility to act?" signals an ethical concern for many managers.

That managers do experience as ethical those problems having to do with people, with competing values, with intervention, and with determining responsibility, further supports the assertion that ethical concerns are present in a high proportion of routine and not-so-routine managerial activities. And it challenges the notion that business ethics is primarily concerned with the breaking of laws and rules and the causing of physical harm.

THE FORM OF ETHICAL PROBLEMS

As managers talked about ethical problems in their work, it was clear that what they were describing were *dilemmas*, situations in which they were faced with a difficult choice and where no clear-cut right answers existed. These dilemmas contrast with the way ethical concerns are usually voiced at the organizational level, both in the writing of formal policy and in the informal expression of company values. At the policy level, ethical concerns are appropriately expressed as *issues* where the right course of action is prescribed. Recognizing what constitutes that difference is critical to understanding managers' ethical concerns at work.

As noted earlier, when the general public is asked to identify ethical problems in business, the following are among the examples offered: product safety, affirmative action, bribery, fair treatment of employees, worker safety, doing business in South Africa, environmental pollution. When managers in this study were asked about ethical problems they had faced in business, no single word or phrase was ever offered in response. To identify the problem, every individual had to tell a story. For example:

> Bill, a young vice-president, was sent by his firm to make a last-ditch, all-out effort to turn around a failing overseas plant. On arrival, Bill's assessment of the situation was that critical to a successful turn around was a hard-driving, committed effort on the part of the disillusioned work force. So Bill's most pressing problem was motivating his people. But, he said, "One of the ethical crisis points was arriving in Country X and trying to figure

out whether it was proper or not to give a 'win one for the Gipper' speech to all the employees about what a bright future they had with our organization, when deep down I wasn't at all sure that that was the case. One of the possibilities was that I would have to close the whole thing in a year or less and send everybody packing.

* * * * *

Carl, a white senior manager, has a personal commitment to beefing up his company's affirmative action practices. Among his most talented employees is Ann, a young black woman. An avuncular type, Carl encourages his people to discuss their career concerns with him, and prides himself on offering sound counsel. Recently Ann came to him to talk about an exciting job available in another organization for which she was considering applying and for which she was highly qualified. She wanted Carl's advice about whether or not to go for it. Uncertain as to whether to encourage Ann's personal development or to support his own campaign by building a solid body of high caliber minority employees, Carl had not, at the time of our interview, come up with an answer for her.

The questions that immediately come to mind—for example, what is the financial picture of the overseas plant and the parent company's commitment to it? what are the possibilities for Ann of advancing in Carl's organization?—make evident that even a brief version of the stories they told does not do justice to Bill and Carl's dilemmas. But they allow us to make some comparisons between issues and dilemmas by looking at six comparative characteristics.

CHARACTERISTIC OF ETHICAL ISSUES AND ETHICAL DILEMMAS

Issue	Dilemma
1. Is easy to name	1. Is hard to name
2. Is acontextual: stands outside specific setting	2. Is embedded in a specific context

(*Table continues on p. 22.*)

Issue	Dilemma
3. Agreement that the issue is ethical	3. Disagreement as to whether or not the case in point is ethical.
4. Addresses the claims of a single stakeholder.*	4. Addresses the claims of multiple, often competing, stakeholders
5. Addresses the right and wrong of one value	5. Addresses multiple, often competing values
6. Assumes that individuals can do the "right thing" if they want to	6. Assumes that individuals want to do the "right thing" but a) do not know what it is, or b) do not have the capacity to do it

* Individual or group who has a "stake" in what happens.

1. The first characteristic deals with the ease of naming, or identifying, the ethical problem. As noted, it is relatively easy to come up with the "names" of ethical issues. However, identifying just what an ethical dilemma is can be more difficult. For example, Bill's problem could be called a motivation problem; it could be called a case of fairness to employees; or it could be termed a plant closing issue. Similarly, Carl's apparently affirmative-action problem is also a case of career counseling, and of honesty. In both cases, other names could be applied. But in both cases, as with every experience recounted in this book, no single word or phrase reflects the complexity of the dilemma.

2. The second differentiating characteristic, following on number one, is that an issue is acontextual, while a dilemma occurs within a specific set of circumstances. One quality of an issue formulation of a problem is that it allows clear focus on the conceptual notion without the necessity of responding to situational variables that can contaminate the logic. An individual facing a dilemma, however, does not have the luxury of clearing away the situational debris and attending solely to the resolution of the issue. Although company policy may strongly support affirmative action, that policy does not tell Bill what he ought to do in the situation with Ann.

3. The third differentiating characteristic is whether or not the label "ethical" would be assumed, generally, to apply. In the case of issues, it is almost tautological to say that there is general agreement that the label "ethical" is appropriate. Ethical issues are called such because everyone agrees, intuitively, that they are. But a dilemma perceived by one manager to have an ethical component may, in fact, be seen by another as being without ethical content. Bill labeled his overseas plant experience as having some ethical content. In trying to prime the thoughts of the only manager who had no ethical experience to relate, I told him Bill's tale. His immediate reaction was, "That's not an ethical problem, that's just a problem of motivating your people." The quotation from Warnock at the beginning of this book, expresses this very point. The characteristics of dilemmas generally make it difficult to generate agreement about what is ethical, and they contribute to the difficulty in managing them.

4. The fourth characteristic focuses on the individuals or groups who will be affected by a decision and who have needs and preferences about that decision. The way an ethical issue is formulated directs attention to the concerns of a single, "primary" stakeholder. Plant closings focus on the terminated workers, affirmative action on those discriminated against, and so on. This focus is essential for a company to develop a policy stating what it believes. A dilemma, however, involves not only the primary stakeholder but also other individuals and groups who will be affected by a decision. Whatever Carl decides will affect not only Ann but other employees—black, white, male, female—the company, Carl himself, and possibly the community and other companies in the industry.

5. One of the reasons issues called "ethical" bring agreement with that label is that they are framed to respond to the common denominator in all the definitions of ethics: something to do with right and wrong or good and bad. Issues are essentially single-value concerns in which the right and wrong of the value is specified. Bribery is wrong; affirmative hiring of minorities is right; fairness to employees is good; polluting the environment is bad. However, in a dilemma an individual must act on more than a single value so that the problem is rarely one of simply choosing right over wrong. In a dilemma, the opposite of one right is often another (and maybe several) right(s). For example, in Bill's situation he is dealing with two (if not more) competing values: it is right to do everything he can to turn the plant around; it is right to be honest with the employees. So the fifth differentiating characteristic is that issues address the right and wrong of one value, while dilemmas involve multiple, often competing, values.

6. The final characteristic can be called the intention/capacity dimension. The formulation of an ethical issue, and its presentation in policy or code, assumes that individuals *can do* (have the capacity to do) the "right thing" if they want (i.e., if they have the intention) to do so. By its characteristics, an ethical dilemma is not amenable simply to good intentions. Regardless of how well-intentioned the manager, the "right" course of action is often not clear. And even when a best decision is made, the complexity of organizations and of the individuals working in them can deny the individual the capacity for what he believes is the right action.

* * *

To understand how everyday, routine circumstances could allow ethical dilemmas to occur, we must look at a number of determining factors in an organization, and in the individual's perception of his relationship with the job and the organization, that were identified by the managers in this study as critical.

ORGANIZATIONAL FACTORS

Organizations provide two broad categories of information that shape and communicate precepts which guide the organization. The first is written down in policy manuals and rules or procedures manuals. The second, often called the "culture," refers to values explicitly or implicitly espoused, and encompasses the understanding of "the way we do things around here."

Policies, Rules, and Procedures

Nowadays, it is considered almost *de rigueur* for a company to have a code of ethics neatly bound in a little green or blue or red book and usually referred to by company members as "the green (blue, red, etc.) book." It is also becoming increasingly common for new employees of a company—at every level—to be given a copy of the ethics booklet upon entry into the organization and to be required to sign a statement indicating that they have read the material and will uphold the values and practices espoused therein. But the evidence in this study suggests the existence of an ethics code and pledges of compliance with that code do not necessarily represent an awareness on the company's part of how ethical concerns arise for its employees; nor are they an effective commitment by the organization to finding ways that allow employees to act with integrity and to solve ethically complex situations. While codes and compliance statements may be some indication of company commitment, they are frequently viewed as that and nothing more. At worst they are seen as some sort of protection against charges of illegality. In fact, many corporate codes of ethics equate "ethical" with "legal," since many codes advise uncertain employees to "check with Legal" if they have any questions.

Nonetheless most managers reported that the presence of policies, rules, or procedures that either tell them what to do or back up their decisions makes dealing with ethical situations less painful. Policies and rules "tell" managers in what they will be supported, and where, in the eyes of the organization, they will be seen to be transgressing. Rules and procedures guide managers towards how they should deal with specific situations. Well-developed and appropriate policies, rules, and procedures can help managers shake off the paralysis an ethical problem can produce and can ease fears about personal accountability. But the presence of policies, rules, and procedures has a downside. Guidelines of any sort can lead to laxness on the part of managers in making an effort to understand the dilemmas before them and to seek the best outcomes. It becomes easier—and acceptable—simply to go to the rule book and follow instructions. Also, as is evident in some of the interviews, some policies and practices, either in the way they interact or in the way they are implemented, can have effects that were not intended, and produce unexpected outcomes with ethical overtones. Further, policies, rules, and procedures can result in a dissipation of responsibility and accountability and a discounting of the importance of the moral and managerial judgment of the individual.

The Organization's Culture

The values and operating style of an organization ("the culture") have a potent effect on what managers identify as ethical concerns in their work and on how they go about handling those concerns. Not only do values and styles affect the identification and management of ethical problems, they often are the cause, quite unintentionally, of ethical dilemmas that arise; that is, some organizations have a set of beliefs and/or a way of doing things that can result in managers resorting to ethically dubious tactics simply to get the job done. Take, for instance, the company that encourages austerity by its employees but which is part of an industry or is operating in an environment where lavish entertaining is a norm. Although thriftiness and controlled spending are in themselves neither good nor bad, for managers in that austere organization whose bottom line—and personal career success—depend on their ability to compete with others in that industry, austerity—labeled "good" by the organization—is in conflict with the reality of the environment. And that conflict can create ethical dilemmas. A manager who ultimately falsifies expense vouchers or transfers budget items may be desperately trying to do the job while conforming to unsupportive organizational beliefs.

Sometimes the things an organization values conflict with each other. For example, one company had built its reputation on quality in its products and impressed that commitment to quality upon its employees. At the same time, survival in an increasingly competitive market drove the company toward saturation of the marketplace as rapidly as possible. The manager charged with overseeing quality of a not-yet-first-rate product, found an ethical dilemma on his doorstep when confronted with pressures to maintain the company's quality image while getting the product out the door. Similarly, a company professing to value its employees' integrity, and vowing to stand behind their decisions, while at the same time demanding that these decisions conform to company dictates, can tempt its employees to behave in an ethically questionable manner.

Another aspect of organizational culture that appears to be critical to both the emergence and management of ethical dilemmas is top management's responsiveness to employees' ethical concerns. Several managers reported being rebuffed, if not threatened with "career disadvantage," when they raised ethical concerns with superiors. For example, one manager found no ear willing to listen to his concerns about being asked to "alter" data on an internal report; another raised questions about the ethics of a decision-making process affecting his career in which he had been given no opportunity to participate. In both cases, the companies' messages were, essentially, "We don't talk about those things around here." Although the companies in these two cases have ethics codes and policies, and publicly demand ethical behavior on the part of their employees, their cultures frequently do not support the expression of ethical concerns by those same employees.

Organizational Systems

Another factor that can create ethical dilemmas for managers and affect their handling of such dilemmas is the design and implementation of personnel and information management systems. Although these systems are put in place to enable managers to achieve the goals of the organization by implementing policies, rules, and procedures, too frequently they impede the necessary activity or, in the worst cases, encourage ethically questionable behavior to meet the system's requirements. For example, one manager reported the frustration of working with a management information system that erroneously kept spewing out the demand for more product. The decision to hire more workers to fill the "need" resulted in the firing of the new hires when the system was finally untangled some months later. The manager who had fought the personnel addition felt the company had acted unethically toward the new people and the local community. And the only answer to why the company had acted in that way was, essentially, "the system made us do it."

The Way We Do Things Around Here

If every problem that arose in the course of doing one's work were considered unique and unprecedented, the world would come to a standstill. The multitude of decisions to be made, the pressure of deadlines, and the similarity and frequency of most day-to-day activities demand that out of the policies, rules, procedures, values, and style of our organization we build a way to manage our work lives and relationships to get things done. And what we, the organizational community, build is a "way we do things around here." This way to do things can range from writing and distributing memos in triplicate between offices located in the same corridor ("Why do you do that?" "I don't know, it's the way we've always done things around here!"), or always identifying the cause of an industrial accident as "worker carelessness," to responding by letter to every customer complaint, or knowing how to get the duplicating machine fixed without going through a prescribed series of phone calls and requisitions.

These implicit norms, procedures, and beliefs are essential to the conduct of business and to individual sanity. However, they can also become mechanisms for stifling creativity, for discouraging the questioning of old practices, and for disregarding the "not so usual" situation. When practices become so ingrained that people forget why they were established, or neglect to anticipate any but the expected outcomes, the way is laid for ethical problems to arise.

INDIVIDUAL FACTORS

The Manager's Perception of the Job

One of the factors affecting how people experience ethics at work is their perceptions of themselves in their jobs. These perceptions focus on the task requirements, role perceptions, the availability of choice, and the utility and appeal of the job.

Task requirements of the job.   Although no organization designs jobs to include unethical tasks or activities, sometimes the tasks or activities required by a job have the potential to create ethical dilemmas. Take, for example, the product manager who has no formal authority over the functional personnel whose talents must be coordinated in a timely and effective manner to move a new product from design through production. In few cases will the job description specify how the job is to be done; usually the description just states what must be done. It is generally recognized that a good product manager knows how to use influence to motivate and to respond to the needs and styles of different people. But it is not hard to imagine a product manager, under deadline pressure from a highly competitive marketplace and faced with recalcitrant team members, using ethically questionable tactics to get what he needs from his people.

Look at a common situation. One of the frequent descriptives of management jobs—"evaluate performance of subordinates"—can create the potential for unethical activity under certain conditions. For example, to combat inflated evaluations (where everyone is rated "excellent" so the manager will look good or get a larger percent of the merit pool), many companies are instituting a forced bell curve evaluation distribution. Such a distribution requires a certain percentage of a manager's subordinates be rated at the bottom, whether or not they deserve to be. As one manager said, "To do my job as I'm expected to, some of my people just don't get a fair shake." On the opposite side, managers in companies which believe the sign of a good manager is a good subordinate find themselves tempted to rate some employees as effective who are mediocre or, in fact, even incompetent.

Another task requirement aspect of the job that affects, particularly, the handling of ethical dilemmas is the degree of autonomy and flexibility managers have to do the job. (This issue will be discussed in detail in the section "The Availability of Choice.") For example, recall the problem of the sophisticated, computerized system that resulted in the hiring of extraneous personnel. The inability of the manager to question, challenge, and change information he knew to be wrong led him to participate in an activity he felt was unethical, that is, hiring people who were terminated once the system error was discovered. His job description allowed no other recourse. The way that jobs are designed can have a critical impact (positively and negatively) on how ethically effective a manager can be.

Explicit and implicit roles.   In an organizational context, the word "role" usually refers to the activities, responsibilities, and level of authority specified by the formal job description. As managers talk in detail about what they do on the job, however, they describe an "implicit" role, which is different from the "explicit" role of the job description. They talk about implied responsibilities and about activities they see as part of their roles that are neither written nor formally verbalized. Moreover, they recognize they are not alone in holding implicit expectations for themselves in the job. One of the definitions of "role" applied by sociologists is "a set of expectations, held by anyone, for a position or person" (Biddle and Thomas, 1966). Most managers are aware that others with whom they work—superiors, peers, subordinates (not to mention those outside their work sphere like family members, friends, etc.)—hold implicit beliefs and expectations for what the manager's job entails. The presence of multiple role expectations has been recognized for many years as a cause of stress. (See, for example, Toffler, 1981.) But it takes on additional significance when we consider the possible effects of many different role expectations on the creation and handling of ethical concerns. Differences in beliefs about what a job entails can lead to different interpretations of events and of the role of the manager in relation to those events.

Take, for example, Dan, a promising young assistant manager whose formal responsibility brought him in contact with the community where he became well-liked. As a result, his boss's boss, who had once held Dan's position and performed it highly effectively by becoming active in community affairs, encouraged Dan to reach out by sponsoring, on behalf of the organization, dinners and other events for community groups and charities. Dan's immediate boss, however, not only had less concern about the community, but was under intense organizational pressure to cut back the department budget. When Dan's budget was cut by 20% while his boss's boss was urging increased community spending, Dan found himself caught between conflicting role expectations. His painfully arrived-at solution to ask a secretary to redirect expenses for a community dinner to another department's budget netted him a two-level demotion with a comparable salary decrease.

Differing expectations can even result in different assessments of whether or not a situation is considered ethical. For example, managers in matrixed organizations may expect that confidentiality of certain information be maintained with each of the superiors to whom they report. However, one of those superiors may interpret the manager's role to involve stronger loyalty to him and therefore expect the funneling of some information from the "other side." The point is not whether it is right or wrong to pass along certain information, but whether managers and their superiors see the manager's role in different ways. For the superior, the sharing of information is "part of the job"; for the manager, it may be an "ethical dilemma."

The Availability of Choice.   Choice boils down to a simple issue: Am I free to choose what I will do, or must I do what someone else wants me to do? This question of choice is a central concern to managers faced with dilemmas initiated by a superior. Partly because of our cultural beliefs about obeying authority, with the "punishments" we anticipate for not doing so, and partly because most organizations do not offer mechanisms—and protections—for questioning or challenging authority, many managers *feel* as if they have "no choice" when directed to act by a superior.

I have emphasized the word "feel" because we should distinguish situations in which there really is little or no choice for the manager, because organizational sanctions are severe and/or the claims of other stakeholders are strong, from those in which there is the opportunity to choose an action, but where the manager thinks that he has no power to do so. Let me pause for a minute to talk about what I mean by "having no choice." Obviously, in almost any organizational situation one can think of, managers do have choices about whether or not they will act and what they will do. But in many situations, the consequences of not following directives are sufficiently severe—loss of job, loss of promotion possibilities, and such—that an observer would agree that a manager in such a position has no choice but to act as directed or risk some major consequence. I would like to forestall an argument that the individual of sound moral fiber will recognize the painful choice and take the moral route, that is, refuse to act if such action does not meet his or her moral standards, regardless of the consequences. As most of us are aware, there are other stakeholders, such as family, whose needs affect managers in such situations, so what the appropriate stance of a moral manager ought to be may become a matter of dispute among decent people. So there are situations in which a manager under a superior's orders can say, "I have no choice."

That type of situation is different from those in which managers think they have no choice. While I do not want to go so far as to suggest that such people will blindly follow authority believing they must regardless of the consequences, many managers do take a superior's directive as a "must do" without considering that they can question, challenge, or creatively carry out (do it in a way that feels "right" to them) such orders.

Both concerns around the choice issue are very important in managing, generally, and even more important in managing ethical situations. Certainly the implementation of well-planned corporate strategy with carefully executed, logical, tactical steps requires that individuals not exercise "choice" whenever they feel like doing so. But, organizations that culturally demand rigid adherence to authority, or which provide no means for questioning it, and managers who feel they must walk in lockstep with whatever they are told to do, contribute to the creation and inadequate management of ethical dilemmas.

When we talk about choice, and the willingness to challenge authority, we are also alluding to the question of personal risk. Risk can vary from that of incurring the temporary wrath of co-workers to that of losing a job. Most managers recognize that taking action in what they consider to be an ethical situation holds some downside risk for them. And most managers are willing to take some risk. But individual personality, family circumstances, and other things do affect how much a person is willing to put on the line. Managers who are sole breadwinners of families with young children, or who are about to put three kids through college, for instance, are likely to be more wary of diving into a tough situation than their young, unattached associates. Of course, there is a risk attached to choosing not to choose, and that is the risk of painful conscience at having allowed an ethically questionable situation to pass unchallenged.

Dependency on or utility of the job: the stakes. Managers view their jobs from a number of perspectives: they are concerned with how much the job meets their inherent interests, how much the content of the job gives them satisfaction; they are also affected by the degree to which the job is useful and/or the degree to which they feel dependent upon it for security of employment. Managers' perceptions of these factors can affect the way they handle the ethical concerns that arise in their jobs. If the job is so specially engaging that it would be painful to lose it, or if the job is perceived to be critically important to the development of the manager's career, or if the loss of the job is a threat to her financial security, the stakes attached to any action can become uncomfortably high. When stakes are so high that potential loss is great, managers often gauge and weigh the consequences of any action to a point that can produce either of two unproductive outcomes: paralysis or unethical behavior.

This is not to suggest that the highly committed, totally "engaged" manager is likely to be less ethical or more paralyzed than her more casually involved colleagues. Managers who love their work, find it challenging and engaging, and happily anticipate coming into the office are the people most of us believe would be above reproach. But a fear of the loss of a job she values, for whatever reason, can make it particularly difficult for a manager to act responsibly in a situation with potentially threatening consequences.

Likes and dislikes. All managers—like all of us—find some parts of the job great fun, very challenging, highly intriguing, or simply easy to do. And all managers—like all of us—find some of their required activities boring, routine, uncomfortable, or just plain unpleasant to do. While there is nothing inherently significant in this, it is important to consider how the positive or negative feelings about an area of their work may allow ethical situations to develop and may affect managers' abilities to resolve them effectively.

Of the many ethical problems discussed by the managers with whom I spoke, 32% related to performance evaluation and its consequences (hiring, firing, promotion, or demotion). And the same theme—and often the same words—usually followed the tale: "I hate giving negative feedback"; "I'm a coward, I don't want to tell someone he's doing a bad job"; "This is the only part of my job that I don't enjoy." On the opposite side, of course, people are likely to work harder at things they enjoy to make sure they come out right.

Personal Background and Characteristics

How managers react to dilemmas—ethical and other—is certainly affected by factors in their background and by personal charac-

FACTORS AFFECTING THE EMERGENCE AND MANAGEMENT OF
ETHICAL DILEMMAS IN ORGANIZATIONS

Organizational Factors		Individual Factors
Policies, Rules, Procedures		Manager's perceptions of job
		Task requirements
Culture	*Responsibility*	Explicit and implicit roles
		Availability of choice
Systems		Dependency/utility of job
		Likes and dislikes
"The way we do things around here"		Personal background and characteristics

teristics and traits. A manager raised by a successful, domineering
father may react to authority differently from one whose parent
struggled in an assembly-line job. The manager who attended a
racially torn inner-city high school may look at affirmative action
from a different perspective than the manager from the all-white,
all-girls academy or one who attended ethnically and racially balanced summer camps. And the executive whose father began a
punishment, for what both agreed was a transgression, by telling
his son he would spank him with a stick, and then sending the son
out to find the "right size" stick (and, ultimately, *not* spanking
him), may handle subordinates differently from the one whose
parents' punishment was banishment to his television and comic
book-filled bedroom. The section "The 'Public' Manager and the
Private Person" will deal in greater detail with the personal background of the manager.

Responsibility

Responsibility is a critical concept related to management decision
making, and particularly to ethical management decision making.
It is the link between the manager, job, and the organization.
Although we might comfortably say that managing means taking

responsibility, no manager is responsible for everything. Good managers must know *when* and for *what* they are responsible. Generally recognized are three kinds of responsibility: role, causal, and capacity (Hart, 1961; Simon, Powers and Gunnemann, 1972). Understanding them is critical to understanding how the organizational/individual relationship creates and resolves ethical dilemmas.

Role Responsibility

The notion of role responsibility first appeared in the discussions about task requirements of a job and explicit and implicit roles. Simply stated, role responsibility is all of the activities and obligations specified by one's *formal* role. Although confusion about what a role is (from implicit role expectations) may exist, role responsibilities can be held, generally, to mean those activities stated in the job description. In the course of getting their jobs done effectively, however, managers frequently find that a particular problem may not come under their formal responsibility, and yet something tells them that they may have a responsibility to act. That is where causal and capacity responsibility come in.

Causal Responsibility

The basic notion of causal responsibility is simple: if one has caused harm or a problem, one has the responsibility (ethically) to correct or attempt to correct it. For instance, if a supervisor sends a subordinate to work on a machine that the supervisor knows to be broken and the subordinate is injured, the supervisor is "responsible" for the accident and therefore, theoretically, responsible for dealing with it. Straightforward as the notion of causality may seem, the experiences of many who work in organizations of all kinds belie that reality. Frequently causality is not clear. For instance, a manager gives a subordinate an assignment but does not provide the resources for the subordinate to complete the assignment successfully. If the subordinate fails, whose responsibility is it?: the manager who failed to provide the resources, or the subordinate who failed to find a way to get the job done? The philosophical notion of causal responsibility would lay the "blame" at the feet of the supervising manager. The experiences of many in organizations would suggest the opposite. One of the problems with the concept of causal responsibility is that most situations are too complicated to assign clear causality. Causality is simply assigned if I punch you in your nose and break it. I am responsible. (Although even there I might be tempted to say that you "asked for it.") But in management situations, causal responsibility frequently gets intertwined with role responsibility. The manager who gives an assignment without providing resources or access to resources might well respond to an accusation by insisting that the subordinate's job (role) was to find the way to get what was needed to get the job done. If personal causal responsibility is redefined as someone else's role responsibility, the role occupant may be forced to choose between acting unethically or being seen as derelict in taking responsibility. The responsibility issue becomes even more complex when the notion of capacity is added.

Capacity Responsibility

"This is a job for Superman!" "Let them eat cake!" Two sides of the capacity responsibility coin. Capacity responsibility says, simply, that one has a responsibility to deal with a situation if one has the capability of doing so. Implicit in that statement is the assumption that if one has the capacity to handle a situation, one, unlike Marie Antoinette, must be willing to accept the responsibility.

Take a nonmanagerial example. Suppose you are standing at the water's edge and you see a person drowning 100 yards from shore. You do not know how to swim, there is no boat nearby, the only life preserver has a 50-foot line attached, there is no telephone, and so on. Do you have a responsibility to save the drowning victim? The answer must be no, because you do not have the capacity to do so. If, on the other hand, you were a swimming champion, the situation would be different. You might be presumed to have the capacity to take responsibility; the more critical question would be whether or not you were willing to assume it.

Capacity responsibility is the most subtle of the three forms of responsibility, especially as it is played out in organizations. On the one hand, an assumption of capability when none exists can have disastrous consequences. The manager sloughing off causal responsibility for a subordinate's failure might, in fact, have been operating under the belief that the subordinate had the capacity for action. While it is reasonable to assume that a competent manager would have a good sense of subordinates' capabilities and the resources available to them, organizational pressures on the manager can lead to a misperception of or even blindness to the real situation. The manager who charges a subordinate with the task of wooing potential customers in an environment where lavish entertainment is the norm but limits that subordinate's budget, assuming the subordinate will somehow have the capacity to accomplish the task anyway, may be creating fertile ground for unethical behavior on the part of the subordinate (e.g., charging dinners and theater tickets to another account or writing up false travel vouchers).

On the other hand, the use of real capability on the part of all members of an organization can be a very productive force, and one that can counter potentially unethical activity. It does require that the organization and its leadership allow employees the flexibility to use their capabilities. Take the simple example of the worker sent by a boss to work on a broken machine. Regardless of whose fault it may be (boss or worker), unless something or someone intervenes, an injury is likely to occur. Suppose a coworker on the shop floor knows that the machine is broken. That coworker did not break the machine or assign someone to work on it, so he has no causal responsibility; his job description specifies no activity in relation to the broken machine or even that part of the plant, so there is no role responsibility. But that coworker knows of the problem and has the capability of telling the worker, the floor supervisor, or someone that the machine is dangerous. Therefore, he has capacity responsibility to prevent an injury.

Of course the use of capacity responsibility raises a number of questions about the consequences to individuals of assuming such responsibility. Although we would hope that the responses would reinforce such behavior, sometimes the reactions can be negative, ranging from the coworker's angry "mind your own business" to the supervisor's punitive action for "interfering" with production. The ongoing debate about whistle-blowing is really an argument about the exercise of one kind of capacity responsibility and is very much a microcosm of the pros and cons of assuming responsibility outside of one's appointed role. Depending on the environment in which it is operating, the taking of capacity responsibility can create ethically sticky situations or provide energy and creativity toward their resolution.

THE MANAGERS WHO

TALKED ETHICS

Thirty-three managers took part in this study. They were neither randomly selected nor chosen by specific characteristics to represent various segments of the corporate world. Although the initial plan had been to recruit a representative group of different ages, sexes, and educational backgrounds, from a variety of functions and levels in organizations of different size and from various industries, the concerns of many companies (or at least of their representatives who were my contacts) about participating in an "ethics" study or having their employees do so required working with each company to develop a recruitment plan that was congruent with the company's style.

After initial discussions to assure the companies that my plan was not to dig for dirt or to show any company in a negative light, but rather to learn what ethics was for some of their employees, two organizational concerns about recruitment emerged. One was for employees to know the company was firmly behind the project and that their participation would not be seen as going behind the company's back. The second was for employees to have the freedom to refuse to participate, without fearing "consequences" if they chose not to take part. Depending on what was most bothersome to a company, I used either of two patterns.

When a company was primarily concerned that employees feel no organizational sanctions for not participating, I used a volunteer technique. A brief memo from a vice-president or human resource director was attached to a detailed memo from me. The cover memo simply indicated that the company thought this project worthwhile and employees were invited to call me directly if they were interested. The second design was what could be called "By special invitation." In these cases, the human resource director or vice-president selected individuals he or she thought would be "interesting" to me and invited them to meet with me, either individually or in small groups, and learn more about the project. No one who was tapped declined the invitation to participate.

What were the trade-offs? On the positive side, the voluntary approach provided participants with anonymity in the company. Nobody needed to know they were participating unless they shared that information. (Although frequently asked if others in a company were involved and if so, who, I did not give out that information.)

Although this approach gave me the chance to do some selection within the volunteer group, the negative side was that it severely limited my selection options. There was no way I could say, "I really need some younger folks" or "How about someone from quality assurance?" Of course, another concern with the volunteer group was that they had some specific feelings about ethics—some predisposition to participate in a study of this kind—that would bias the findings. During the course of the interviews I asked volunteers why they wanted to participate in the project. The range of responses suggests that this was not a group of "goody two-shoes" as one or two cynical colleagues suggested, but rather, if there were a bias at all, a group of individuals who were intrigued by research and thought it would be "fun" to participate.

The invitational approach had the opposite trade-offs. On the positive side, it gave me the opportunity to ask my contact for a participant in a particular category. On the downside, though, there was the risk of bias on the part of my contact (or "the company") as to who would be "right" for the study or who would represent the company in the "appropriate" way. Also, of concern, was the fact that no one who was asked to participate felt anonymous, despite my assurances of disguise in whatever came out of the project. At least one person—my contact—knew each invited participant and, in those companies in which I met with small groups, several people knew of a person's involvement.

Fortunately, there was a balance of voluntary and invitational approaches, so if biases are present in the data they, too, are balanced. Moreover, in the course of six hours of one-to-one discussions conducted, as these were, over several weeks, predispositions and planned poses and presentations tended to be worn away by the intimacy of the interview situation.

In terms of the characteristics of the group, the recruitment procedures yielded a remarkably representative sample. Of the 33 participants in the study, 28 were male, five were female; 32 were white, one was black. They ranged in age from 25 to 64 and in level from first-line supervisor to CEO. On the whole, the group had been with their respective companies for a fairly long time, 17 years on the average, with the range being ten months to 37 years. The average time they had been in the particular job in which they were interviewed was four years, although the range was from brand new (one fellow changed jobs during the course of the study) to 25 years. The group members put in long hours at work from 45 to 70 hours per week, averaging about 55 hours.

At the time of the study, 82% of the participants were married; six of those individuals had been married more than once. More than half of the spouses, 56%, worked outside the home. And 82% of the participants had children.

FAMILY BACKGROUND

A majority of these managers, 53%, grew up in suburban communities or small towns. Twelve percent were from urban backgrounds and only 3% grew up in rural areas. Fifty-eight percent of their fathers and 34% of their mothers had attended college, while 16% of their fathers and 25% of their mothers had completed grade school only. Although fathers worked in a variety of occupations, 38% were employed in some form of sales or business management. Professionals (doctors, lawyers, dentists) accounted for another 22%. Other occupations included farmer, maintenance man, and United Nations finance officer. Of the 38% of the mothers who worked at some point during their children's early years, 6% were in nursing, another 6% in accounting, and other occupations included service station owner, jeweler, seamstress, and teacher.

Five of the participants grew up as only children; nine were raised in families of more than three. Ninety-four percent of them had completed college and 67% had a graduate degree: 33% had MBAs, 24% other masters degrees, one individual had a law degree and another a diploma from a business school executive education program. Fifty-two percent of the group—all male—had served in the military, 41% of those in the navy and 29% in the army.

RELIGION

Because people instinctively tie ethics and religion together, the interviewees' feelings about the role of religion in their lives constituted a relevant concern. Of the 33 managers in the study, 50% were Catholic, 38% were of a Protestant denomination, and 9%

were Jewish. When asked how important religion was in their early years, three people did not respond, but 60% said it played a very important role as they were growing up. Only two people said it was of little importance. The response, however, was noticeably different when they were asked the importance of religion in their lives at present. Six of the managers did not answer the question, and of those who did, only 22% said it was very important, while 30% said religion had little impact on their present lives. These responses suggest that religion was a critical factor in these managers' development of a sense of self in the world. Religion, for them as children, prescribed what they did, who they associated with, and how they saw themselves. Typical comments were "I was sent to Catholic school because everyone went to the nuns," "I had a bar mitzvah and went to confirmation class because that's what everyone did," and "Like all little WASPs, I went to church." Religion's impact was more cultural and traditional than spiritual. Certainly there were managers who talked also of the spiritual influences of their religious upbringing, but those influences were not frequently apparent in their management of ethical situations on the job.

ROLE MODELS AND INFLUENCES

Since for many people the values they have and the ways they think about ethics as adults were shaped by people they admired as children, the interviewees were asked who had influenced them as they were growing up. The persons most frequently cited were teachers, usually from elementary school. After teachers, fathers were considered important role models. The third influential role noted was the high school athletic coach. These three roles accounted for 70% of the responses given (several people named more than one person), although mothers, clergymen, grandparents, and others were mentioned.

Teachers, fathers, and coaches seem to have exercised their influence in different ways. Teachers (and, as noted, primarily elementary school teachers were identified) served as surrogates for "society" in that they were the first adults encountered outside the home who rewarded and punished expressed values and behaviors.

And not only did the managers as children learn appropriate values from elementary school teachers, they also experienced with them a beginning sense of competence and an awareness of how their capabilities could contribute to family and community. Fathers were seen more as role models, people to be admired, people to be emulated, people from whom acceptance and respect were sought. Athletic coaches, in particular high school football coaches, brought forth the most spontaneously enthusiastic responses from those who cited them as influences. They were seen as models and teachers of fairness and sportsmanship. They were also remembered for the values and skills demanded by team membership with which they imbued their students, and which those students, as adults, found critical to their success as managers.

THE INTERVIEWS

Each of the managers participated in three two-hour interviews. In the first they talked about their jobs and the people they worked with; they discussed their organization, its values, and how people learned "how we do things around here."

At the end of the first session, participants were asked to prepare for the second interview by thinking of two situations in which they had been involved which they believed to have had an ethical component to them: one situation they found relatively easy to handle and one that was fairly difficult to resolve. The phrase "ethical component" was carefully chosen to encourage participants to scan an array of problems they had encountered in the course of their business lives that might not have initially struck them as an ethical concern but rather as, perhaps, a financial or a personnel problem, but which, when they thought more about them, might have seemed to have had an ethical part as well. They were also asked to consider what led them to call the two episodes ethical, and what made them more or less difficult to manage.

In the final session, each person talked about his or her family background, school and other formative experiences, religion, major influences in life, and present family commitments. Each manager also completed a biographical questionnaire.

Although the interviews were structured around formal interview schedules (which appear in Appendix A, along with the questionnaire), the sessions themselves were freewheeling, with the managers following ideas and trains of thought triggered by either the questions asked or their own initial responses to them. The process that went on over time, as the participants became more relaxed, and as each of them and I developed trust and a sense of comfort in our relationship, was an unlayering one; a framework of an experience would be offered and then slowly developed and elaborated upon; a brief thought or feeling would be expressed that would be explored piece by piece.

What follows now are interviews with practicing managers; the interviews are followed by comments. These comments are not intended to provide a detailed analysis. Since the major purpose in this book is for us to listen to and hear the words—and through them the beliefs, attitudes, and feelings—of these managers, the analysis of an outsider both compromises the goal and denies the real purpose of the study. The comments do offer, however, some selected thoughts—my own impressions—of specific things I was brought to consider by each of the managers with whom I met.

The names of all individuals in the interviews have been changed, and details of their organizations disguised (e.g., location of branch offices). For further information about the process of editing the interview tapes, please turn to Appendix B.

"IN THEIR OWN
WORDS"

MICHAEL

WILLIAMS

Vice-President and Group Head
Forty-nine years old

" . . . Stop that SOB from giving away
any more of this bank."

I am in charge of the Far East Group which is principally a support group for our overseas units in the Far East and Australia. It is also a training ground for young credit officers on a fast track to an overseas assignment. Besides all of that we actually run a business in this group which is very important to the profitability of the Far East division and very important to our correspondent banking relationships worldwide. It is called an Acceptance Participation Program. It is an idea that did not exist three and a half years ago until I thought of it. In October 1982, Congress, in their wisdom, decided that it was such a good idea that it was enshrined in law. That was nice and flattering, but unfortunately it then cut everybody else into the action so that the market we had to ourselves we no longer have to ourselves. We have such a long head start, however, and we've built up such a loyal following of foreign correspondent banks that are instrumental in this arrangement, that we are still way ahead of the pack. It has earned this bank literally millions and millions of dollars, and will continue to do so. So I have the pleasure of running that marketing program and am making a great deal of money for the bank which will more than pay for my services for the remainder of my career. It's a bit of a thrill from that standpoint in the sense that I was an entrepreneur and innovator; I created a new service, a banking service. That's one of the thrills of the job I now have. The other thing I like, from a more personal standpoint, is that because of my years with this bank—as you can tell from the wrinkles and the gray hair—I have a sense of continuity and an insight, a feeling, for how senior management think, how they are liable to react, so that I can champion the cause of the Far East division. I feel my role is productive, I feel my role is challenging, and I feel it is important; therefore, I love my job. I also like working with junior credit officers and seeing the transition from "the world owes me a living" point of view, the pampered academic approach, to the mature loan officer who is ready for an overseas assignment and who realizes that his pay comes from the bank and is given to him because of his performance, and because that performance involves duties that he may not want to do but that need to be done. So I enjoy teaching aspects of it as well. I try to make myself available. I do not have an office. I sit right out in the middle. I want to see them operating; I want to know what they're doing. And I want them to feel free to come to me if they don't know how to handle something. But I want them to come to me only when they've thought through what it is they want to discuss with me. I don't want them to panic. I'll belittle them if they do that; if they haven't thought it through. I will not give them the answers sometimes. I'll simply tell them how to get their answers. I don't do their work for them. I'm not gearing them to be prima donnas because in an overseas assignment there's nobody to look to. You do everything, not only credit, but also administration, operations, tax problems, financial reporting questions, policy questions, procedure questions. There is a lot of guidance, a lot of steering, and a lot of job evaluations. We talk about leadership, technical ability, communication, interpersonal relationships, entrepreneurialship, flexibility, and so on.

This career is not completely fulfilling for me, so I have to supplement it with different kinds of achievements in my personal life. Those achievements involve building things that will be here longer than I will, that I can reach out and touch, like the phone company. I'm into cement, brick, hammer, saw, that sort of thing. That's how you have a balanced feeling in a business like this.

I think, generally, that the greatest frustration I have is the fact that this organization is understaffed. It always has been. We've never had enough people to do comfortably everything that had to be done. That was true when I first came to this bank 29 years ago and it is still true. This is a service business. Computers do not provide service, people provide service. There seems to be a tendency to forget that.

This is a bank filled with characters, people who are rather unforgettable individuals. It's a very unstructured organization. There is very little in the way of policy and procedures that's written down. And what about arms shipments to foreign countries? Do we have a policy on that? Virtually every bank does. The answer is "no." We will look at arms deals, but we won't always approve them. If they're offensive arms, we will not finance them. If they're arms for police protection, riot control equipment, and such things, we will. It sounds like a policy, but it isn't a policy. You can't find it written anywhere. That's the point. In fact, often the philosophy here is that no policy is better than a policy, that we ought to consider every opportunity on the basis of its own merits or demerits. Nothing should be cast in concrete; let's be creative; let's be entrepreneurial; let's create an organization in which that kind of creativity and entrepreneurial ability can work, can cook. And despite the fact that we're a much larger bank today than we were when I came here, we've managed more or less to preserve all of that. There are still disproportionate numbers of banking services taken for granted today, which are part of the landscape, that started here.

Even though we're all for creating individual achievement, we also are a team. We have to be. We learn from each other by just working together and talking with one another. Since there aren't any rules and regulations published and disseminated throughout our world, the only protection we have—or that senior management feels it has—is the personal knowledge of the individual it has assigned to any post and any position of authority. Our chairman wants to know me. He wants to have seen me on my hind legs saying "This is what I believe in, this is what I think is right and what I think is wrong." It's a highly personal organization, and the judgments of management about the capabilities of people are critical to our success or utter failure in any undertaking.

As I said, our institution has an unstructured environment with unwritten rules and regulations. In order to ethically perform in this organization, a lot is left to chance. The person who is executing whatever the action is has to be aware of the general philosophy and the rules of the game that have been established for the organization. Our management takes a certain amount of pride in the fact that little is written down because they don't want us to be an organization that does things by the numbers. I would say that in an organization like ours, we probably have a better chance of erring from the corporate standards of conduct than in a more highly structured organization where all of these things are set out in black and white. But I've seen no real evidence that this bank is in violation of its own standard of conduct any more than any other bank. In fact, if anything, we err on the side of adhering to these standards, maybe because we realize that we have to be aware of them since they are not generally promulgated. Sometimes things work out exactly opposite to how you would expect them to work out, at least in this institution. A perfect example of that is our credit approval process. At most major American banks there are discretionary limits, that is, the ability of a lending unit or officer within that unit to extend credit without going to a higher authority or approving body is limited. In the case of a bank, it's usually an approving body, not an individual, simply because banks seem to gravitate towards committee actions. Generally speaking, our managers in the field, even at the most senior level, including the division head, have a discretionary limit of no more than a million dollars, which, with the kind of wholesale business we're doing, is very small. They have to send those credits back to me, the reports have to be prepared and presented to a committee, then approved, and then they go to the chairman's office for final blessing. (Doesn't this sound terribly time-consuming and cumbersome? It does, of course.) Whereas, the fellow who is competing with us — let's say the head of corporate credit for Citibank in Tokyo—may have a discretionary limit of $20–25 million. He can do the business on the spot. But often we get there faster with the answer. Why? The reason is that our people in the field are a little more cavalier about presenting credits because they know they're going to have a second opinion. If they've missed something that's critical, that's key, somebody else is going to pick it up. Whereas the fellow who's sitting in Tokyo for Citibank, who has got $25 million discretionary limit knows full well that if he blows it, it's all on his shoulders. He can't point the finger at somebody else. So he is probably a little bit more cautious about exercising that discretionary limit.

Credit is a discipline. I suppose that our approval process reflects that more than the approval process in other institutions where they may be prepared to take a certain amount of loss every year. We are not. We don't have those kinds of resources. That's a luxury that a larger bank can afford; we can't. And philosophically it bothers us because it really is not good credit. The idea of providing complex services involving expensive computer systems other than the fundamentals needed for the bank, and having a room that's a mile long with clerks shuffling papers and banging rubber stamps and the rest of it—that, to our management, is not what we are all about. Part of that relates to our philosophy of lending and our approach to lending. The result is that we have suffered less from credit problems that are so prevalent today than our counterparts. I guess it's working, even though it sounds cumbersome. And we are still gaining ground, from a marketing standpoint, so I guess it's not a bad policy.

I was a branch manager overseas. One thing you have to face up to when you are lending abroad is that in some countries every potential borrower maintains at least three sets of books. He maintains a set of books for his banker, a set of books for the tax collector, and a set of books for himself which tells the real story. There are very definite inconsistencies. Ordinarily it is in direct proportion to the rate of inflation in a country. Where you have high rates of inflation and, therefore, devaluation of the low currency, this three-tiered bookkeeping system is designed to (1) cover up flight capital transactions, and (2) reduce taxes to a minimum. Let's take an example. Say I live in Argentina. The rate of inflation, let's say, is 200% per annum. My peso value is deteriorating by the minute. I have a number of ways open to me to protect the value of what I have obtained. I can put it into real estate, but I can only go so far in that. Or I can put it into other assets which have a tendency to retain their value or appreciate, such as diamonds, stamps, or other storehouses of value. Or, I can get my pesos converted as quickly as possible to a hard currency which does not devalue at a very fast rate, such as U.S. dollars. But in many countries that is illegal. No one is supposed to have foreign assets. But the point is, they do. That's what I meant by flight capital: money that flows out of the country. What you hope is that you will get close enough to those kinds of customers that they will show you the set of books with the real dollars. They won't do it ordinarily—and they may never—but they certainly won't do it the first time you do business with them. Well, if you don't see the numbers, and we always start with the numbers, how in the world do you evaluate what the worth of this enterprise is, what kind of protection it has, what kind of expectation it has for repayment of its debts?

In a country such as the United States, where books are audited by reputable people who cannot be bribed, there are generally accepted accounting standards so that when you're looking at Ford Motor Company's and General Motors' balance sheets, you're looking at essentially the same things. That is not so in most of the rest of the world. Now that has got to bother a U.S.-trained banker. And it does. Still, you want to deal with this fellow, even though initially he is only showing you the picture he wants to show you. What do you? Do you say "No. Unless you can show me the real books I'm not going to deal with you."?

So overseas I made it a rule to live with the situation. I required all my lending officers to receive a narrative description from the owner of the company or a principal officer of the company as to what the operations of the company were, what the general state of sales were, and so forth. Then, in view of that narrative, I wanted each lending officer to take the numbers, the balance sheets, and the profit and loss statements that had been presented, and proceed to determine whether or not those numbers made sense in the light of the way the customer had described his business activities. If they did make sense, then I felt that at least the customer was being consistent; he was intelligent; he knew how to create numbers that fit his story and a story that fit his numbers. Therefore, the chances of the tax authorities coming in and seizing his assets and leaving nothing for the bank after they had assessed him for back taxes, interest, and penalties (which they would do and which would leave the bank in a very poor position) were small. I insisted that the narrative and the numbers make sense, and that we not deal with anybody who didn't realize that a financial statement actually was a reflection of the story. I'm not sure whether that's an ethical consideration or not. But it turned out to be a good policy because our loan-loss experience in that country quickly declined. The ethical issue here, the overriding ethical issue was, and is, and always is in international affairs, "Do I want to deal with a person who is obviously a sham and a fraud, who is presenting fraudulent information?" That's the problem. He is cheating his own country, and we are assisting in all of that. In our own country, with our own citizens, the expectation is that we will be absolutely lily-white in dealing with our customers. Abroad, that rule is bent. I think it is practical and realistic, and for a bank that wants to succeed internationally, it's essential in my view. It really is not inconsistent. Why should we worry whether a citizen of Brazil or Argentina is minding his p's and q's as far as his own country is concerned? Why should we worry? I don't think that is our responsibility as a U.S. bank. Sure you can talk about our being a good citizen of a country, of our host countries. I think we are. We definitely bring a number of benefits.

Now you can say that in addition to being a good citizen the bank ought to be concerned about the issues of poverty and the disequilibrium of the distribution of wealth. But let me tell you—the bank stands for one thing, which is always in its best interest, and that is—no change. Don't rock the boat. Let's keep things going as they have been going, whether that's right socially, morally, ethically, whatever—whether that's right or wrong. Let's not make waves because radical change is not in the best interest of the bank, generally speaking. So what do we do as bankers? We promote the status quo. Young people come in here who have worked in the Peace Corps, and they say, "I'm involved in the Poverty Program and I was going to be a social worker but now I think I'll go into international banking because I'll have an influence with . . . " and I say, "Wait, wait, wait just a minute. You mean you think you're going to promote the welfare and advancement of mankind and fairness in this world by being an international banker? No way. You're kidding yourself. We are not do-gooders. We're money lenders, financial intermediaries. And social progress is not necessarily in our best interest as a lender, because if the parties in power, many of whom are our customers, are thrown out or exiled or shot, we don't get repaid."

Actually, the biggest ethical dilemma I have had was an internal one. I was deputy head of the Latin America division at the time. We had gone through a period of rapid expansion without enough people to cover all the slots. At that time the U.S. economy was in a little bit of trouble and the bank was not eager to hire additional people. So some of the new branches that opened in the early seventies were understaffed. We tried to do it on a shoestring. In one country we took a fellow, Ralph Quinn, who was three or four years away from retirement and we made him the branch manager. He had never been a manager before and he had no credit background whatsoever. We gave him an operations person, but no credit person, despite the fact that he had asked for a credit person. I want to make that clear at the outset. But the answer he got from the division head was, "Ralph, we just don't have anybody at the moment.

But, Ralph, you've worked for this bank for 40 years"—which he had—"you can do it." Sort of blind faith. We sent him on his way and he got the branch up. He opened the shop at a time when a lot of other banks were going into that country, and when there was unbridled enthusiasm about the economic future of the country. There had been eight years of sustained growth, and nobody could see the end. That is the worst possible situation in which to be lending as a new bank without lending skills and experience.

I soon suspected something was wrong because I would say to Ralph, "Well Ralph, we haven't had any credit reports yet. You know there is a requirement at this bank that you must provide a credit report within 30 days of extending credit." None of this approval process we have now was in place at the time. We were far more laid back, far more informal. Anyway, most of Ralph's loans were a million dollars or less, so they did not have to be approved by anyone. Ralph's answer to me was, "Gee, it's a new branch. We don't have very many people and we are so busy putting good assets on the books that I don't have time for a report." This went on for about a year. Finally I sent one of my associates down there to look into the credit side. Now Ralph was very clever. He knew how this bank operated and he knew how to cover things up. Basically what he did was to keep my associate out of the credit department and the loan department. He took him out to lunch. Then he would drive him out to a project we were financing and show him around. This fellow had his picture taken—I've still got the pictures—with his arm around the general manager, a big smile on his face, plunk in the middle of a project that ultimately "went south." He came back with a report that everything was fine. Well, I didn't believe it, but he had seen it and I hadn't.

About six months later I really became concerned because I began to hear some names, names of borrowers who I knew were not good. At that point I talked with the head of the group and said, "I really have bad feelings about this operation. Ralph's reporting super profitability, but I just sense that something is wrong." The group head said, "I agree with you. Let's put together a credit examination and go down there and go right through it." They did it. At that time, Ralph had a portfolio of $90 million in loans, and the auditors classified $20 million as being substandard or doubtful.

That's a big, big slug. Then, of course, the head of international banking and the head of the division went down. Good old Ralph had been with us for 40 years, and he had performed in the jobs he had before this last one very well. He was an exemplary employee. He had lots of friends in this organization. But as they used to say in the air force, if you don't understand the problem it's probably because you are part of it. And in Ralph's case, he definitely was a major part of it. They knew they had to get somebody down there to stop the insanity. But they did not want to can Ralph since he was only a year from retirement. So they went through the internal telephone directory to try to pick out the name of a person who Ralph respected, liked, could get along with, who would not be perceived by Ralph as a policeman. They came up with my name. So, you can see it coming. They decided they'd leave the problem, Ralph, at the head of the unit and try to control it through the number two guy, me. Now here's a moral judgment. The head of international banking talked to me, and I remember the words of his charge to me. He said, "Mike, I want you to do everything that is humanly possible to usher Ralph out to a normal retirement with dignity. And in the meantime, you stop that SOB from giving away any more of this bank." I said "All right. I don't like it. I think you're putting me in the middle. But I'll do it on one condition, and that is, if it becomes absolutely intolerable and impossible to achieve what you've just asked me to do, I want the ability, the right, to pick up the telephone, to call you personally, and to tell you that. And I want you to swear here and now, that if I tell you that, you will immediately get rid of him." He said, "All right. That's fair enough. But I don't ever expect to get that telephone call." I said, "I hope you won't. It will be only if I'm going down for the third time."

Well, I survived. I was scared to death. I walked in—there were no credit files, there were no financial statements, there were no comments, there was no information on the borrowers at all, except in the loan department which billed for the principal and interest. There had been no credit discipline whatsoever. We knew we had problems, but we didn't have enough information to know what kinds of problems we had. By this time Ralph could not believe that anything was wrong. He would not admit it. I don't blame

Ralph for getting into this situation. We asked for it. Clearly, the responsibility for setting up a situation in which this kind of disaster could happen was ours. No question about it. What I blame Ralph for is for covering up. We had overdraft banking down there. If you had checking, we would approve a line of credit for overdrafts. You do it by writing a check on funds you don't have in your account. That automatically becomes a loan. So what would happen is this: when a customer did not pay, Ralph simply charged his overdraft and, therefore, it would not be past due because it was a current overdraft. He just transferred the problem from one spot to another.

And he had a major drinking problem by the time I got there. He was a spunky little man. We had 90 or 100 employees down there of whom maybe two or three knew what they were doing. They were local people, and Ralph had great loyalty to and from his local employees. He had spent much of his life in the country and was beloved there. In fact, when he left upon his retirement, the government awarded him its highest honor, which people like Dwight David Eisenhower have received. He spoke the language perfectly, he acted like a native, he related to them totally. He would have been wonderful if only he had had some seasoned person to back up all this marketing fluff with some substance and to make the credit decisions for him. Often I would say to him, "Ralph, why did you make this loan?" And he would say, "I liked the cut of his jib." Great. We're in the jib business now! I remember, it wasn't easy.

The first thing I did was to set up a credit committee since there was no credit approval process. I put the people I thought were knowledgeable on it as well as some of Ralph's favorite people, so that he couldn't say that his side didn't have any inputs into these decisions. He said, "What do we need it for?" And I said, "There's a memo here from International saying that every local unit should have a credit committee. So I'm just complying with that." That was an easy way to start. I remember some credits on which we disagreed. He had his side and I had mine. The credit committee meetings were at three o'clock in the afternoon. Ralph would go to lunch at his favorite restaurant where he had his own table. He would have six or seven drinks and come back to the meeting loaded. I can remember him standing on a cocktail table and saying, "If you don't approve this credit, I'll punch you right in the mouth." It got to that. And I'd look at him and I'd say, "Ralph, your first shot better be a good one, because I'm a hell of a lot younger and a lot bigger than you are." And that would calm him down.

We finally got some controls on extending additional credit. That stopped any new nonsense. Then the problem became one of finding out what kind of problems we had from old extensions of credit. That was more difficult. In that case I asked him to cooperate with me and give me whatever papers he might have in his desk drawer. He wouldn't. So I had to work around him. I formed a problem loan group. We had to reconstruct all the files. Actually, reconstruct is not the right word. We had to create files, information, financial statements, spread sheets, the whole thing. I had to send my loan officers out to the customers to say, "We understand you have a problem. Can you tell us what it is because we notice you're not paying us anything." We had to cover two and a half years of banking business and reconstruct it or construct it to try to find out why the credit had been extended, what had been extended, what kind of extension of credit it was, why the customer wasn't paying, and ultimately, what we had to do to try to collect. We had to get lawyers involved in those situations in which we had to bring suit, and we ran into other problems because we found the legal system there was fraught with nepotism.

Well, we did construct all the necessary information. We did develop plans of action with regard to all the problem loans. And we did implement controls. So we really had a professional branch running by the time I left. It was very difficult. I had no one to talk to. That was also frustrating. When I came back to the home office from time to time, no one wanted to talk to me about it. No one ever asked me what went wrong, or what it was like, or how I planned to solve the problem. I had lunch with a senior officer about three months ago. He said, "Mike, I've been meaning to ask you—what the hell went wrong down there?" I said, "Where the hell were you when I was there and needed somebody to talk to?" He looked at me. You know. He got it. He didn't argue with me. But that is what this bank does. It's a very personal bank. Basically, he had been saying "I have confidence in Mike Williams; he's going to fix it up." That's scary, because that's how we got into the problem in the first place. Then it was "I have confidence in Ralph Quinn. Let's open the branch."

We do have a great deal of freedom. There is a great emphasis on personal credibility which is why I think we work so hard at hiring good people and why we work so hard at training them to become bankers. The price we have to pay, occasionally, is a situation like the one with Ralph. When everything was all said and done it probably cost us $14 million. That, in the overall scheme of things, might be a small price to pay for preserving this unstructured environment. We're not judged on how many transactions we process correctly on a computer. We are judged by how fast and professionally we react when people need us. Our most important resource in a service industry or business is people. If you recognize that, and you recognize the individual limitations of people, then I think you come out with the view that the way we are can be potentially dangerous. How do we compensate for that? By balancing our management. Balance. If only we had recognized that Ralph wanted to prove, before he retired, that he should have been number one years ago. He was trying to prove something. With people in that stage of their career, who haven't been number one before, for goodness sake don't make them number one the last two or three years of their career. They are likely to be out to prove something. Recognize a person's limitations and plug those limitations with somebody who offsets your accounts and balances them.

So Ralph retired. Every year he comes back to the bank's annual meeting. For a person who has put in a lot of years of loyal service it is amazing the degree of loyalty he gets back. That's the kind of organization I want to work for because I may boot it at some point. Who knows?

Did we learn from that mistake? I don't know. That's been a question that has been bothering me all along. However, when I had that lunch with the senior executive I did tell him what I thought the fundamental problem was, what mistake had been made, and what we could do in the future to avoid that kind of mistake. He did listen, and he did say "I think you're right." Maybe he had already realized it, but at least I had a chance to express my views. The other thing that concerns me is that nobody has said anything to me about it. It does bother me. I am not sure if the job I did was valued. I did not do it alone, obviously, but frankly, I did a fine job. I did everything that I was asked to do. But being involved in an internally well-publicized mess like that, you wonder if you have been identified with the problem or with the solution. You wonder if that kind of an experience has done your career any good.

After I had been down there about two years, the head of International called me and said, "You've done the job I sent you down to do and I understand you're not particularly happy there. I think I've got an opportunity for you here at home, where I understand you prefer to be." And I said, "Yes. I think that's correct." I think he was sincere about it, and I think I did have a good opportunity here. I'm happy about that. But there is a nagging question that I have in the back of my mind. It has been made pretty clear to me that the only way I can advance myself now is by going overseas. I am not prepared to do that. Not at this stage. So I am moving out of International. And I ask myself, "If I'm such a Captain Billy Whiz-bang in International, why aren't they offering me something in International right here at home?" In other words, I wonder if I have been tainted by the experience. I think maybe I have been and now I have to get rid of that. I think making a move now is smart. I'm going into the domestic side. In this organization, the people who pull the strings are generally domestic people. In my whole career I have never been involved in the domestic credit side of the bank. That's another reason why all this makes sense. When I was offered the chance to come back here I could have said, "You're right, I do want to come back. I don't like it here. But as far as I'm concerned, I haven't turned the profitability of this branch around. I'd like the opportunity to do that." I think he was disappointed that I didn't say that.

There are some scars, obviously, as a result of this experience. Why wouldn't there be? It was not a pleasant experience. But it does, I think, address some moral, ethical issues that reflect the philosophy of this bank when it comes to its people.

We talked about older employees and the dilemmas they can create. If you give them a responsibility that seems higher than they have had previously, what they often try to do is prove that the bank made a mistake in not giving them this opportunity sooner. The Ralph story is not the first such problem we have experienced here. It's like Bob Newhart's routine on the retirement party. "Forty years of loyal service and what have I got to show for it? A lousy watch!" But I think you lose sight of your objectives — to raise your kids and keep them clothed and fed, and have a vacation now and then, and buy a nice car, and live in a decent house.

I don't even think about retiring. There are people my age who have already built their homes on a lake somewhere, and they talk about whether or not they will take early retirement. I don't know if I am avoiding the inevitable, but I just don't think about it. I don't want to think about it. I enjoy working around the house, but I also enjoy coming into the bank every day and having a place where I can serve a useful purpose. Whether I need the money or not is immaterial. If I could afford to do it for nothing, I'd still do it for nothing, I think.

COMMENTS

Organizational Factors

Mike describes his organization as very unstructured, with little in the way of policy or procedure written down. He suggests that the value to the institution is that individual creativity and entrepreneurial activity are brought to bear both in the development of products and services and in the finding of solutions to tough managerial situations. These company values make demands on senior management, as Mike puts it, to "have personal knowledge" of every individual assigned to a position, since there are, ostensibly, no requirements, guidelines, or codes to control or at least shape the behavior of employees, and since creative problem solving (which can have a number of very different meanings depending on the values of the solver) is encouraged. In addition to a loose structure and minimal formal rules and policies, the company also values lean operation, that is, operating with the least number of people necessary to get the job done—and maybe even one or two fewer than that. There is much that is admirable and conducive to productive activity in the value framework that Mike describes, but it is not clear that this set of values is congruent with the charter of a large financial services operation. If this company were described simply by its values to a reasonably sophisticated listener, who was then asked what type of organization was being discussed, the answer would very likely be a small, entrepreneurial, high-tech firm. But *this* organization is a large company with domestic and international units charged with investing the capital of others through a responsible lending system to produce growth for investors, borrowers, the community, and the bank itself. With a charter like that, it is not difficult to imagine that minimal structure and staff might easily lead to managerially unsound and ethically questionable situations. Look at the Ralph Quinn case.

Ralph Quinn at the helm of the new Latin America branch bank was an ethical catastrophe waiting to happen, not because Ralph was a "bad" or unethical person (although he ended up doing some unethical things), but because he did not have some of the basic knowledge and skills required for the job into which the bank placed him. The question, of course, is why would a reputable institution place an unqualified person into a position of such responsibility? The reason is clear: making Ralph branch manager in Latin America was a decision driven by the values of the organization of which, in the abstract, it is justifiably proud. First of all, the bank cares about its people. Ralph has given 40 years of loyal service and so should be rewarded for it. In other institutions the next step would be to check his qualifications. But this bank values "personal knowledge" on the part of senior management as the best measure of competence for a position. The fact that "good old Ralph" had been with the bank for so long and was known by everyone became the surrogate for any careful evaluation of ability or qualification. Since the institution had few written policies and guidelines, there were apparently no set of qualifications specified for anyone applying or selected for the position of branch manager. Or, if there were any written requirements for the job, the valuing of loose structure allowed the decision makers to comfortably disregard them. The problem, of course, was that, whether or not the bank wanted to write them down, the job of branch manager required certain skills and abilities at managing both employees and customers. The corporate system that valued flexibility and minimal formal policy resulted in the selection of a branch manager who was almost destined to either (1) fail, or (2) be forced to find some way to appear to do a job which he did not know how to do. Now Mike tells us that Ralph was well aware that he did not have the necessary skills in credit risk assessment and that he had asked for a credit person to work with him. Here the bank's value of leanness compounded an already precarious situation. A credit person on top of a branch manager in a small, new operation was too "fat" for this company. So by its values, those same values that might have been essential for the development of an exciting new computer in Silicon Valley, the bank created an ethical time bomb in its new branch office.

There is yet another aspect of the corporate value system that contributed to the situation. It is apparent that the bank believes in caring for and rewarding loyal long-term employees. That value is one that most people would like to see more of in our culture, generally. However, the desire to reward Ralph's 40 years of faithful work by offering him an undreamed-of opportunity without understanding the psychological implications for him of that offer, may have unintentionally created a painful, ethical problem for Ralph, rather than providing the intended reward. The caring extended as far as providing the opportunity, but did not consider what was necessary to enable Ralph to meet that opportunity successfully. One of the saddest aspects of this situation is that it reveals many good, if not completely wise, intentions gone awry. Certainly the bank did not cause Ralph to behave unethically, but it did create a situation in which unethical behavior became one of the possible coping responses.

I am not suggesting that a loose structure, a lack of formal, written procedures, and a tendency to run lean are "bad" values that can produce unethical behavior in employees. What I am proposing is, first, that an organization's values may be more or less appropriate for the kind of work that it does (e.g., handling other people's money with somewhat lackadaisical procedures may not be an appropriate match) and the lack of congruence may create an environment in which ethically questionable behavior becomes a mechanism for bridging the gap. Second, I am suggesting that an organization's values may be sound, responsible, and, even, admirable (e.g., caring for employees) and may still, in their implementation, produce unethical results.

Organizational values affect not only the emergence of ethical dilemmas but also the ways in which managers can cope with such dilemmas. While we do not have Ralph's first-hand testimony, we can infer that the very culture that produced the dilemma for him (the dilemma being the necessity of extending credit without knowing how to assess credit risk), also facilitated his managing that dilemma in a highly questionable fashion. First of all, we are told the credit approval process that presently exists was not in place at the time of Ralph's appointment. Of course, Mike notes, most of Ralph's loans were under $1 million and so would have been approved locally anyway. Nonetheless, the system provided no backup. However, Mike does say that credit reports on each new loan were expected back at the home office within 30 days. Although no reports were forthcoming from Ralph, no one felt the need to check out the situation until one full year had passed. We can debate whether or not it was the fault of one individual (Mike or someone else) that the problem was not investigated earlier (and we will look at that issue when we discuss individual factors and responsibility). However, the laidback, informal style of the firm permitted—and even encouraged—Ralph to handle this dilemma as he did. Having been with the bank for 40 years, he had to have known that no one was likely to check up on his credit approvals. And with the enthusiasm and excitement he must have felt at holding this unexpected managerial position, Ralph probably assumed his borrowers would pay their loans, later if not sooner. In addition, the overdraft banking procedure which allowed Ralph to cover up nonpayment of loans was apparently administered in the bank's casual style with no limits or mechanisms of accountability in place.

Now what about Mike himself? One of the strongest factors in Mike's experience of managing the Ralph Quinn affair was the organization's responsiveness—or lack of responsiveness—to Mike's concerns about handling the ethically loaded problem he had been given: how to allow Ralph to retire with dignity, while both blocking further credit activity on his part and cleaning up the mess already made. Mike tells us he recognized the potential pitfalls, catches, and double binds in the situation and requested corporate back up (the removal of Ralph) if he found himself "going down for the third time." The group head's response that he doesn't "expect to get that call" throws the dilemma squarely on Mike's shoulders. It may be the group head's inability to respond to Mike's request was a result of that "we know you can do it!" culture espoused by the bank. More likely, the reason is that the bank, at least as personified by the group head, is caught in a conflict between its concern for the respect for long-time, loyal employees and its need for fiscal responsibility. Unable to manage those competing claims at the organizational level (the group head is saying in essence, "Don't make *me* choose"), the dilemma is pushed down to Mike. The effects of organizational nonresponsiveness are compounded for Mike by his perception that no one back home is willing to talk to him about the Quinn problem. By the group head's overt refusal of assistance, and his colleagues' covert unresponsiveness, Mike was unable to test ideas, play out scenarios, or get the usual feedback most people need as they think through a difficult problem. Mike got the job done, although not without a lasting sense that his career may have suffered because he was associated with the "problem" and not with the "solution." If it is true that Mike's career has been damaged, or even if that is only thought to be true by Mike and others in the bank, the message sent to all members of the organization about what happens to people confronted with an ethical dilemma may not be as positive as the bank would wish. If the message is "You're on your own," the legitimate resources and avenues of recourse for the manager may be acutely limited, forcing solutions that may be ethically, managerially, or personally less than satisfactory.

Individual Factors

One is initially struck by the role confusion surrounding Mike. Who is he and what should he be doing? Mike's formal position at the time was deputy head of the Latin America division. In that position we can assume that he had oversight responsibilities for branch banks in Latin American countries, and that managers of those branches had direct or indirect reporting relationships with him. All of a sudden, because he is seen as someone Ralph respects and might listen to, Mike is dispatched to Ralph's branch, not as deputy head, not as Ralph's boss, but as "number two guy" under Ralph. There are no formal task requirements to this new position; there is likely to be incongruence among the role expectations for Mike held by the head of International Banking, by Ralph and his staff, and by Mike himself. It appears, in fact, that there was no formal position into which Mike was stepping. Of course, at this stage we might describe Mike as enjoying the luxury of role flexibility. However, while the role may have been flexible in terms of what he did and how he did it, Mike was operating under a difficult command from the head of International: "I want you to do everything that is humanly possible to usher Ralph out to a normal retirement with dignity. And in the meantime, you stop that SOB from giving away any more of this bank." This command not only created an explicit and implicit set of task requirements, it also put Mike in the position of having to achieve two potentially conflicting goals.

To make matters more strenuous for Mike, he had a 20-plus-year investment in the bank; his career had been built there; at his age and with his past fine performance, his hopes for continued advancement were high. Mike had a lot at stake going into the situation. A failure to either clean up the credit mess or move Ralph along to dignified retirement might diminish the reach of his career. And regardless of how much it may draw on skills, abilities, and areas of interest, no one (and we can assume that that includes Mike) likes cleaning up someone else's mess. So individual factors of role, interest, and personal risk added difficulty to the challenge laid at Mike's door. But, again, it was not these individual factors alone that created a tough arena in which Mike had to perform. It was those factors in concert with the organizational factors—values, style, lack of structure, limited responsiveness to the ethical concerns of its managers—that made the task so painful and ultimately left Mike, despite his successful completion of the task, feeling scarred by the incident.

Responsibility

When we talk about placing responsibility on a person, or group, or organization, the intuitive reason for doing so is to locate blame.

"Who is responsible for this mess?" "Who got us into this?" The reason for fixing the blame, at least ostensibly, is to identify who should be doing something to correct the situation. Of course, often the reason for blame-calling is simply to clear oneself of suspicion rather than to move toward mending the damage. This notion of responsibility was referred to earlier as causal responsibility. In addition we introduced two other concepts of responsibility: role and capacity. The purpose of introducing these notions is not to blame or point fingers, but rather to look further at the relationship between organization and individual in both the emergence of ethical dilemmas and in their management. Frequently, as we have already seen and will see repeatedly in this book, factors within an organization (or subsection of an organization) provide an arena in which an ethical dilemma can arise for a manager. By our taxonomy then, the organization (or subsection) might be said to have causal responsibility, and by extension ought to be responsible for fixing the problem. However, it is the nature of the way organizations work that when problems arise—ethical and nonethical—the responsibility for managing them falls on either those whose role it is to handle the situation (with the assumption that with role comes capacity), or on those who have the capacity to do so. The problem that can occur is that "the organization"—as embodied by someone who assigns the responsibility for dealing with the problem (e.g., the head of International)—sees the capacity as inherent in the individual, and neglects the part the organization must contribute to creating capacity. Too often organizations fail to see that their responsibility is to provide the resources and support to enhance the capacity of their members to manage ethically.

In Mike Williams' case, the bank had pretty clear responsibility for creating a situation in which Ralph could either (1) fail or (2) choose an ethically questionable coping mechanism. Ralph chose the latter. Even as it became evident that credit reports were not forthcoming, the assumption of responsibility remained focused on Ralph in his role of branch manager. The only problem was that role or no role, Ralph had not the capacity to remedy the situation (particularly as he got in deeper and deeper). When it became apparent that the person who by role should be taking care of things couldn't, the bank (represented by the head of International) did not step in to assume responsibility (despite being a causal agent), for instance, by removing Ralph from his position. Its concern with Ralph's retirement precluded that action. So the bank turned to Mike, who had neither caused the problem nor was officially responsible for mending it, on the assumption that he had the capacity to handle the situation. And, as it turns out, he did. That he suffered a sense of isolation and the lasting perception of being "identified with the problem and not the solution" might be interpreted by some as simply the breaks of the game. I would suggest that the struggles he went through with Ralph and the strain he felt were the result of his operating on the margins of his capability, and had the organization taken the responsibility to provide the support and resources to enhance Mike's capacity, the outcome might have been more satisfying to everyone. In fact, the bank was fortunate that in Mike they had a man of integrity and capability, since the arena they staged for him held some similar hazards to that which they had set for Ralph.

HAROLD
LIGHTNER

Director, Manufacturing Personnel
Fifty-three years old

*"Another alternative was 'Oh, yeah
—I can just sit here and do nothing.
Let's see how it plays out. I'll just sit
in my job and act passive, and it may
or may not happen!'"*

I'm in my seventeenth year with this company, so I've been around for a while. Prior to coming here I worked in a number of large companies. I hadn't been with this company very long before I recognized it was a very special kind of place. I based that on my experiences here versus those I had at the same point in time in other companies. And I still believe that today, I still believe this is a very special place to be, even though it isn't the same kind of a place it was 16 years ago. For example, 16 years ago our primary challenge was growth, unlimited horizons, and my major concern was how do I absorb and assume and carry out all these responsibilities that I have or that I expect to get? Now we're on a plateau for the next leap forward, and it is different. But I still think it offers the same set of conditions. This is still a good, rewarding place to be. The thing that impressed me the most was that you were important as an individual. You were here, you were a person, and it was important to have you here. They were interested in your opinions, and they expected a hell of a lot out of you. If you carried it out, you were reassured and you were supported. And if you deviated a little bit, they weren't hesitant at all to come up and say, "Just a minute here," rather than wait a year to tell you about it. That's important to me. That's how I was treated, that's how I believe most members are treated, and that's how I've tried to treat others. You have your place and it is important. You do count.

Right now I'm senior personnel manager for manufacturing. In my position I report jointly to the division vice-president for personnel and the group vice-president for manufacturing. I've been here for about a year and a half. Prior to that I was the division manager of the plant engineering division. The reason for the change was the corporate decision to decentralize plant engineering, which did away with my job. This position is really a staff assignment, whereas the other one was heavily line oriented. So there was an adjustment for me to go through. Let me talk about that situation; it was one of the most complicated and difficult I've ever been in. As I said, I was the division manager of plant engineering. One day I received a call to report to the office of the vice-president. I had no knowledge of what the heck it was all about. I suspected that maybe the roof leaked and I was going to get a chewing out.

I could tell when I entered the office that it was going to be a heck of a lot more than that. And as it turned out, it was. What it was, was his telling me about a decision they—maybe he—had made. They had decided they were going to decentralize plant engineering, plant engineering being the department I was responsible for. He went briefly through the rationale for why that was important, and really didn't give a lot of specifics about why the judgment had been made or how this thing would be played out. It was kind of a shock. In retrospect, it really shouldn't have been this big a surprise, but at that point in time it was not the way I had played out the scenario. So I sat there a little bit dumbfounded. He had all the right words, and he tried to make me feel good about it— that I was not to take it personally, that it wasn't a reflection of how I did my job, it was just a broader decision of how the company was going to be organized, and how they wanted to run things around here.

As I thought about it, there were four things that came to mind. One was "Shoot, I can just pick up and leave. I can pick up and find another job here in the company, or I can leave the company, and do my thing someplace else." That was an alternative. Another alternative was "Oh, yeah—I can just sit here and do nothing. Let's see how it plays out. I'll just sit in my job and act passive, and it may or may not happen." Another one was that there were a heck of a lot of questions about whether that was a good decision or not anyway. There was a lot of resistance to it, among the members of the division, and also by the employees' organization. So the thought went through my mind, "If I want to stay in this job, and work against that decision, there's the chance I might be able to keep it from happening." And then the fourth one that crossed my mind was "Think about what that directive is, in a broad context, and see whether that's a good business decision, and if it turns out it's a good business decision, and if it doesn't harm the members of the organization, or the discipline, or the operation in any mean-ingful kind way, although it might be a severe price for you to pay, you're the best person to do this. You're to manage through this change." And I think for me that was the nub of it. It was a personal hurt. It was going to be a significant price for me to pay, because it was a job I thoroughly enjoyed, that I got a lot of job satisfaction from, and that I figured still had some potential for growth, both for me personally and for the organization as well. I struggled long and hard with just walking away from it. The thing that goes through your mind is "Good Lord, after having worked hard at this thing for 10 years, if that's the only appreciation they have for the contribution that I, as an individual, have made or the operation has made, the hell with them."

The decentralization of this organization was placed within the larger context of the bigger organization in the sense that we were going from a functional organization to one that was more business oriented. So, from a broader framework it seemed to make a lot of business sense. For me personally the future wasn't very well laid out or explained. They were kind of vague about things like "You're a good person, you don't have to worry. Something will work out; something will come up. It could be here or it could be there. Have faith, and it'll be OK." And I was being asked to help effect the complete decentralization, which was the movement of individuals from one central organization into a number of line organizations.

Most people could identify with the rationale for why it seemed to make long-term if not near-term sense. But dealing with the emotions of individuals in terms of what they felt they would have to pay was the difficult part. It's like losing your security. You belong to an organization and you're comfortable with the environment; you've developed symbols of security around you. So I was being asked to deal with all of those anxieties as well as the mechanics of how does the head count change, and who reports to whom? At first I thought the company was well prepared for this, and had clear vision about what it meant for them. That wasn't the case either. It would be a case of not only trying to have the group specifically affected by it, those who were being decentralized, try to understand why it was an appropriate action, but also helping the receiving divisions, the groups that would receive these new people have a clear picture. What could they expect, how were they expected to behave in the future? So I was in the middle of two points of view, if you will.

Part of my personal hangup early on was that a decision of such magnitude could be made without my involvement in it. It's tough to have the decision made and then to have to be the key to its implementation when you have not been involved in the early stages of it. That bothered me. Actually, no specific time frame was given to me. It wasn't the kind of thing which they saw as a 10-year thing, but there wasn't any specific timetable established. I walked away with the feeling that if I wanted to take on the assignment they would be comfortable with my developing the time frame. Without anything being said the sense was "In two years we'd like to have this thing accomplished."

But I felt I wasn't appreciated and that I'd been taken for granted. I think I could have walked away from it and not suffered at all in the environment. I think the corporate hierarchy, or the organization, or my peers, could have said "My God, that's fine, that's a choice that he had." And I don't think they would have necessarily held that against me; I don't think professionally I'd have been hurt by it. So it was a case of looking at myself and saying "OK, you have your needs; let's put them aside for the moment, and let's think about the other needs that are around you. What is the balance among them?" For my own self-satisfaction at the moment, I think walking away would have been the best thing. There was a lot of hurt. I didn't particularly look forward to the process of taking apart something I had devoted a hell of a lot of time and attention to building. So for me it was kind of a conflict: what's good for Hal versus what only may be good for Hal within the larger context.

For me, the whole thing turned out to be an ethical question because I think I could have sat there and done nothing, and worked counter to the operation, and not necessarily been hurt by it. Certainly I could have resisted it. But that would have been only an attempt to satisfy my own personal needs. I felt I had a larger obligation. I thought about the responsibility I had to the organization that I had led for the 10 years, and that if, in fact, this change was going to happen (and I was convinced in my mind that it was), I thought I had a responsibility to see us through it. It's kind of like, if you want to live with the good, you have to also accept the bad for awhile, the personal bad. I'm convinced that managers are going to be confronted with more situations like this. The situation is representative of managing conflicting claims. Everyone can't have everything, so it's a matter of trying to assess the needs, and balancing between those things that may or may not be in conflict. In a growth situation, not everyone can have everything, but there's a little bit for everyone. But if you're managing on a downturn, there just isn't enough to go around for everyone to be satisfied. What we need to do is balance things to make sure no one is dramatically hurt by it.

I did talk to some other people about my dilemma. Most of the advice I got was "It's going to happen, Hal. You could resist it if you want, but that's not really wise." I don't know that anyone said "Jeez, Hal, you really ought to stay there." I think that most of the advice I got was "If you can feel comfortable doing it, then stay by all means. But don't think you're honor-bound to do that. If you have a better opportunity at the moment, then you ought to take it." Of course, three or four people said "Go get them, Hal." I didn't actually struggle with the decision long enough to look for anything else either inside or outside. I suppose I came pretty quickly to the point of view that what I was going to do was accept what I was told. There seemed to be a good feeling about me, so I figured what I ought not to do at this time was worry about my own personal career, and somehow everything would be OK. All my professional life had been in this discipline, and it sounded like the company was going to de-emphasize the discipline I was in. At my age, and the stage of my career, starting something new is hard. So the potential I had in the organization was significantly greater than anything else I could conceive of. There was no personal gain by my resisting. But I think what I came to was the responsibility that I had for the people in the organization. I sat and considered the reason I was in the position I was in. It was really because of them and the support they had given me over the course of 10 years. It seemed to me that I had an obligation now, and the obligation was to somehow lead the organization to make the kind of contribution in which the results were going to be as positive as they could be on the organization and on them as individuals. And I really couldn't walk away from that, I just couldn't do that.

When there was resistance to the change, I could use my own situation as an example, or as a model, for describing to the individual or individuals what they might be going through. I think that was most helpful. There's only one instance I can think of where it didn't work, and I had to lose my patience, and almost demand we move forward because we couldn't afford to delay any longer. But most of the people in the organization recognized that what I had gone through, early on, was in essence what they were going through now.

There's certainly a large consideration today for increasing the involvement of all of the employees in major decisions, and I would support that wholeheartedly. I think when you do that you get a much better product, and you get employees who get a greater sense of satisfaction. It eliminates all of the unknowns. It's terrible to have a decision made that affects you, and not to have all of the data, especially when it's a change. You don't start thinking of all the positive things, you start thinking about all the negative things. You start second-guessing yourself, and unless it's said directly, you say, "My God, there must be other reasons why we're doing this." So I think involvement is the way to go. I think a lot of people are like me. I generally will find 10 reasons why it isn't such a good idea, if it doesn't happen to be mine. On the other hand, if the decision is one that's sound, and there is a basis for it, I think most people will react initially with 10 reasons why it isn't a good idea, but eventually they'll come around and accept it, or even improve upon it. Oftentimes that happens. They'll bring variations to the original decision that will make it even better. And to me that was a part that was missing in this situation; the one ingredient that was missing in the whole process. Not that we should not have done it; clearly that isn't the case. But we might have done it differently, and we might have done it better, and we certainly would have done it with greater satisfaction on the part of those who were involved. And that includes me.

COMMENTS

In this situation Hal's first awareness of an ethical concern grows out of a personal hurt. A major decision about an organizational restructuring which will drastically change his job has been made without his even being consulted, and he feels angry and powerless. The anger does not trigger an ethical dilemma for him, but rather it gives him a sense of having been dealt with unethically by his boss. And the core element that drives his perception of unethical behavior is the relationship Hal feels existed between him and his boss. Where the problem turns around and poses a dilemma for Hal is when he "changes" roles and thinks of his responsibilities as a manager to his subordinates. Because of his disappointment with his own boss, he is keenly aware of the relationship—and the obligations it entails—between himself and his subordinates, and the responsibility he feels to "the organization that I led for 10 years." There is some desire for retaliation (to leave or to "go get them") that sharpens his ethical sense. But Hal, like many managers who find themselves caught between superiors' demands and subordinates' needs, uses his perception of the ethical compromise of the former to respond ethically to the latter.

CHARLES
WARREN

Manager, Manufacturing
Forty-six years old

" . . . If you're in a position of jeopardy
with your management and if you're not
doing something that's illegal,
it's difficult not to want to play ball."

I am responsible for the engineering management for the introduction of new products. Our goal is to introduce the product on time, at cost, and to make sure it does what the customer wants it to do. So we are responsible for working with the design group and other organizations to plan for the introduction of their new products. We decide what facilities are required for manufacture, what those facilities must do, and how they should be laid out on the shop floor; we then order those facilities and work with other organizations to have them purchased and installed. Finally, we have to get them up and running.

At the present time, I have four managers reporting to me, 70-some engineering people in total. We have to identify all the detail things that have to happen in order to successfully manufacture the product. We have to make sure everything that's needed gets ordered, and then follow up and follow up and follow up, and make sure things get done. In general, we look for the other organizations to manage their job and get it done. When things are going to be late, we then have to get everybody together and say, "All right, now what are we going to do to keep the thing on schedule?" In some cases, it's impossible and we have to push the manufacturing schedule back, which may then require a response on the part of another organization to collapse the installation time so that even though we may ship three months late, we may still be able to make the eventual service date to the customer. Some of the other functional organizations are reluctant to tell us when they have problems, they feel that "Gee, if we hold off, we'll be able to fix it, before somebody finds out." That kind of thing. I think basically, however, we have a very good working relationship with the other organizations; everyone really tries to pull together.

In this job you have constant pressures hanging over you with respect to trying to meet schedules and dealing with the problems associated with the products with which you're involved; you feel that this whole thing rests on your shoulders, and you've got the responsibility for making sure all these things get solved. In some cases there isn't that much you can do, and you worry a little about how those things will be perceived. The old story of the king—kings in ancient times used to kill messengers bearing bad news, and if you're in my position, you're in the position of bearing bad tidings and less frequently in a position of bearing of good tidings because, in general, you manage by exception and you only have time to bring up the problems that have to be dealt with. So indeed, you feel a lot of pressure. If you're not careful, it can be easy to let some things get away from you.

I don't find the atmosphere here to be as open and supportive as the organizations I've been involved in in the past. I'm not quite certain as to the source of that, but there was, I think, a much more open atmosphere elsewhere that made it possible to raise problems and discuss them and work out solutions, or at least make people privy to what was going on so they could pose alternatives to what was being proposed by management and have them listened to. I would say things here tend to be a lot more autocratic, and there's a perception that it's a lot easier to get "killed," if you will, than in previous environments in which I have worked. And communication is not quite as open as in previous organizations.

From my perspective, you're dealing in a situation of business ethics whenever you are forced to do, or even asked to do, something that makes you uncomfortable, something that goes contrary to what you feel to be right or ethical. Of course, in many cases you find ways to rationalize your behavior and try to make the situation appear to be acceptable so you can live with it. You can rationalize things in many ways, like leaving a few words out here and there or whatever. Maybe you don't tell quite all the truth. I think generally you have to rationalize or irrationalize things to live with them; I imagine most people have to do that, some way. There must be certain individuals that just out and out lie, and it doesn't bother them. But most people have to rationalize things. I consider myself to be a Christian, and in those instances when I am in trouble, I pray and ask for assistance and sometimes that assistance is immediately forthcoming. In some cases the situation with which I have been asked to deal has changed or that particular dilemma has gone away. In other cases, I think I have gotten some guidance that I then put into action with the faith that it was the way to go. I would have no problem with saying to my boss we ought to deal with something differently or we ought to say something differently. But I suppose in those instances where I have raised something with my management, and the decision has gone contrary to what I believed, if it's not grossly unethical, then I feel in some way it's out of my hands, it's gone beyond me at this point. I don't really have control any longer in that situation. In that kind of case, I consider that I had taken it as far as I could take it. You can take things so far and recognize it's not going to do any good to take it further.

We aren't required by our management to do things that really bother us from an ethical standpoint. I had been part of an executive training program where we went through a number of case studies that touched on ethical situations. These cases were based on actual incidents, and a lot of them were almost life-shattering experiences resulting in the firing of individuals or in legal actions. They were far beyond what I've been exposed to here. I haven't had anything so difficult to resolve, but I can think of situations that raise questions I would call ethical. But they are the kinds of questions that can be more easily rationalized and dealt with. There have been instances when, in certain situations, management above me has lied, outright purposeful lies, primarily to other individuals within the company with respect to commitments that had been made. Now in these cases, you know it's a lie, but, and it's kind of a quick reaction, you know immediately you are not going to bring out the truth. I guess you can end up being in several different situations when that happens. Maybe you are in the position where all you have to do is be quiet and it goes by. Or maybe you are forced to cover up for what has been said, or to provide backup for what has been said. I guess I have done all three of those things. But again, it's one of those instantaneous kinds of things where I feel the jeopardy to me, personally, could be very great were I to go contrary to what was being said by the boss.

I'm not talking about anything that involves legal matters or anything like that which would have any outstanding consequences to the company. It's more trust among individuals that's destroyed in these kinds of instances. Tails are being pinned on donkeys that will then get pinned somewhere else. So we're not talking about a consequence where you would agonize and not be able to sleep nights because you thought you'd been party to something illegal. But it is a situation that may cause you to do something you're not comfortable with. I find it difficult to remember the specific instances, but I know I have had several instances of this type, over the years, which I have had to deal with. It has to be almost an automatic response in that kind of an instance. I guess your first thought is self-preservation. But from that point on you have a lack of trust with that particular individual, and you know he's willing to lie about what he's doing. You don't really trust him from that point on. You may, in fact, then document things that must go through him, things that could be associated with you, to cover your . . . I may tend to be too honest. Nobody appreciates a Boy Scout, and I think some people could suffer by being too honest.

We have certain shipment commitments where we have to get so many "whatevers" out per week. It became clear in our reporting that we could look a lot better were we to fudge a bit in stating when something was actually shipped. Now, this is just in-house reporting on how things are going and my tendency was to say "If we don't ship by the deadline, we don't ship." My management's view was to make things look a little better, and there were ways of doing that. So I would present my information about where things stood. And then I would be told, essentially, what to indicate we did ship and what we didn't ship, in order to look better. Well, I was, in a way, party to it. I was presenting things as they were, and somebody else was fudging information, although I might have benefited in some way by it. Production statistics looked better than what was actually the case. And I was partially responsible.

I felt it was out of my hands, that the decision was made by management higher than I, and that I wasn't going to blow the whistle. I wonder, myself, did it really matter all that much? The people were still getting their product by means of expedited shipment; we were still able to get the product to them within approximately the same time frame as if it had been shipped when we said it was shipped. So the customer was still getting the product in the appropriate time frame; we just had to do some fudging to get it to come out that way. I get the impression there are other organizations in other areas doing the same thing; people can make things look better than what they actually are by some creative manipulation. But I suppose, then, there are the consequences. Consequences could be great if you got caught doing that. And you do think about that. You think about who they will think is really responsible for having it done. But I guess, again, if you are in a position of jeopardy with your management, and if you are not dealing with something that's illegal, it's difficult not to want to play ball.

I suppose if you were constantly missing your dates and things were constantly going out late, there could, indeed, be consequences to your upper management and to you as a result of those targets not being met. And, of course, there can be various reasons why those dates are not met that do not relate to what's going on in your specific area. They may relate to factors that are beyond your control, but are within the control of the upper management; they may be rectified over a period of time, and you don't have to fudge anymore. But until you get to that point, it's nicer to look better sooner.

I try to be consistent in my dealings no matter what I'm involved in. I don't feel I can be any less ethical here at work than I am at home. I try to conduct myself in the same manner, no matter what. I think I become uncomfortable with things that other people wouldn't think twice about. That leads me to believe that maybe I'm almost too honest in comparison to other people I work with. I know there have been instances where I prayed for guidance to show me the proper direction to go. I guess that's where I turn when I feel really in trouble.

JEFFREY
LOVETT

Manager, Engineering
Thirty-nine years old

"I was really acting almost like a spy.
. . . It's taken me almost two years
to get over it."

I find myself defining an ethical situation as one in which I am put into a position of having to do something that internally I don't feel good about doing; an episode in which I have to subordinate what I consider to be right or good to some other good that is in conflict with what I believe. I have been in one situation that has left an indelible mark on my life. The company offered me a position in a field office. This office was a significant distance from corporate headquarters. The manager at this local field office was a somewhat arbitrary individual, manipulating people and events so that the amount of revenue had grown but the amount of profit coming out of the office was really very minimal. The manager who hired me, Bob, was two levels above me. He had hired me to go in there to start to straighten out one portion of the local business. I did not know I was being forced down the local manager's throat or that I was not going to be accepted by the other managers in the office. Basically, my subordinates accepted me, but because the local manager had previously been managing these people, my ability to manage the subordinates was constantly being challenged by him. And who had the final word? He did.

When I was offered the position I was very excited about it. It was a quantum increase in responsibility. I was gung ho. I was fired up. I wanted to do some really neat things. I'd gone from a planning position to a managerial position to a major marketing position, and then I went to this office. So I was moving fast.

I had some theories of the way I wanted to run the office, and it was clear that my style of management and the style of work that had been established by the local manager were inconsistent. When I was hired Bob said, "I want you to set up the office, Jeff. It's been a really difficult situation there. You're going to have some difficulties because people have certain behavior patterns." So I expected certain things.

About eight or nine months after I started, I had a meeting with Bob, who said he had some suspicions about what was going on in the local office, but because he was so far away, he couldn't prove any of his accusations. He needed somebody on the inside. I said to him, "Is this what you really want me to do?" And Bob said, "Yeah, we can't handle it any more. We have no control over the office. Help me." And I said I would because I really felt it was in the best interest of the office and the company. Bob was straight; I believed him. I wouldn't have done it unless I felt the support system was in place in case things were to crash around me.

In fact, the local manager had so ticked me off by this point that I thought, "Why sure, I'll get that son of a bitch. I'm ready to go for him too. He's given me so much aggravation. He's made my life unbearable. If Bob wants it, then I'll support him." I think I truly did believe it would be in the best interest of the office to put another person at the helm. I didn't like the guy personally and I thought he was doing a disservice to the people in the office.

I spoke with Bob constantly. When I talked with him I told him everything that was going on in the office, and how I felt things were being run, and that I felt very uncomfortable. And I said, "Look, I'm putting it on the line with you. I'm really acting almost like a spy." I don't think I used that exact word. "Clearly," I said, "I'm reporting to you. I'm assuming you're going to support me when things get rough." And Bob said, "Oh, don't worry about it. It's now May. By October or November this whole thing is going to be out of the way, and I'll take care of everything." Well, clearly what happened in October or November was that the person who got swept away was not the local manager, it was me. The local office had put me in a position where it appeared I was stealing. They couldn't prove it but there were a lot of innuendos. And Bob said, "If you were in my office, I would have fired you already."

I had asked him for support all along, help me with this, help me with that. So I felt like the grunt in the armed forces where you have the general sitting back in Washington calling the shots. I was the one in Vietnam getting shot at and if I got blown away, well, it's just somebody else who bit the dust. So I was in a position of limited control. The question was, what was I going to do about it? There were a lot of things I could have done and I said to myself, "You know, in the final analysis, I'm a stone in the path of a boulder." So I decided I was going to take the licks and not elevate the situation. It would have resulted in a constant finger pointing session and clearly I was not wanted there. So the ultimate decision was to get the hell out as fast as I could and go back to where I belonged. I had been in a position of doing something for Bob, literally spying on the local manager, but when it came time for

Bob to support me—nothing. And I had followed him all the way. I stuck with him; I helped him. When it came time for helping me to solve the issues, then there was no response; he just wanted to let it slide to the point where I bore the brunt of whatever the resolution was. I was left to burn. And essentially it wasn't a decision of mine; it was somebody else's decision. I didn't really think, "What am I going to do?" Really it wasn't much of a decision.

The whole thing came to a head when they did a review of me. It was time for me to be reviewed by my manager. I flew up to Bob's office for the review. There were some problems with it, but generally they were pretty well satisfied. In order for me to get my salary increase, the review had to go to the local manager. He wouldn't sign off on it. He didn't like the review. And nobody told me. The review had been sent to the local manager in July. I didn't find out until September that he wouldn't sign it and wouldn't give me the money. Then Bob suddenly says, "You're doing a terrible job." Meanwhile, I'm not getting any feedback from the local manager. So all of a sudden I'm finding myself in a position where I have to defend myself to Bob and pit myself against the local manager. It was really becoming a battle at that point. I hadn't gotten my review, I was due money; it just wasn't working out. I was pushing it and pushing it and pushing it. And Bob probably got ticked off and finally said, "I won't put up with this any more." The only thing to do was to transfer me back to corporate headquarters. Bottom line. And that's what happened.

There's a whole bunch of issues that are on the periphery. The local manager never made the effort to help me and my family feel at home in this new locale. He invited the other managers to his house. Nobody ever helped me when I came to the local area; I had to handle it pretty much myself. And when I left the field office, I arranged my move without their support. I wanted to succeed. That's an internally driven motivation. If I do something I like to do it right; I like to be a professional. I came out of this situation crushed. It's taken me almost two years to get over it. I saw myself coming out of it about two months ago. Before this incident I was a fighter. I really was. And slowly but surely I'm getting my spirit back again. I always used to say "Goddammit, I am right and I'm going to go for it." That's the way I was before. That whole experience caused me to doubt myself in terms of my capabilities to manage people, to manage ideas, manage concepts, and to have good ideas and good concepts. So, not only was it an ethical situation in terms of doing something I found contrary to my basic belief in doing business, but it had a profound effect upon me professionally and personally. I threw in the towel. This whole situation was creating an incredible problem with my personal life. Prior to this I had a very balanced view about professional versus personal life. But during that time when I came home, I was a son of a bitch. I had so much built up anxiety, so much built up hostility, because I wasn't getting satisfaction from anyone. Nobody would help. Every day was like they were taking another chunk out of me. At the end, I gave the last pound of flesh I could give. I had no room to fight any more because the person whom I'd expected to support me when I had no pound of flesh was also gone.

My ethical dilemma was that I was being forced into doing something I felt was not the right thing to do. I should have said to Bob "If you want to deal with him, deal with him. I've got my job to do." But the fact that they held onto my performance and my salary review compelled me to do what they wanted me to do. I was so far away from any other support system. I guess I could have said "I'm not going to do this." But I didn't. I didn't. To some extent I wanted to do it even though it was ethically wrong because I wanted to get rid of the guy. He'd given me an untold amount of aggravation. I felt it was bad for the office. So I had done a rationalization that it was OK to be sneaky and get rid of that guy because the end justifies the means. The office will be better if we get rid of the guy even if it's done in an unethical manner. But I did feel I wasn't dealing with the requirements of my position. I was dealing with some political stuff. My job was not to do that. I had a definition of what my job was. But, as I said, I rationalized it to some extent because I felt the end justified the means. And I had a certain personal vendetta involved in this. But when I found I didn't have the support system, the ethical value of what I was doing caused me to say "You know, you compromised yourself and now you're in the bed, chief, and now you're going to have to sleep in it for a while." And it really caused me to say "What did I do this all for?" Maybe it was a bad decision. I'm not even sure it was an ethical decision. I'm trying to understand it. But I didn't like doing it. It made me very uncomfortable. If my manager had a problem with this local fellow, he should have dealt with it. I was essentially told to compromise my ethics for somebody else's greater good. And that's my responsibility, because I went along. I have to accept that I willingly compromised my ethics.

It was a greater good. There's nothing wrong with that. It's still a balancing act. But when the company, at the end, almost lets you hang out to dry, then all of the ethical issues surface. "What am I doing? Why did I do this? Why did I sacrifice myself internally?" It's the hardest thing to recoup on something for which I'm getting no return. In fact, I was getting negative reinforcement for doing what I thought was good. It's difficult to talk about. I had a lot of psychological problems. I didn't have to go for therapy, but I did a lot of deep thinking. "What am I going to do? What have I done? Have I ruined my career? Am I ever going to be able to get a decent job again?" Things like that. But I enjoyed working in the company. I haven't talked about this in at least a year and a half because I began to get paranoid about it. When I came back I said, "I'm going to have to leave the company." And another manager who knew me said, "Don't worry about it. Put it behind you and you can make the best of the situation." The final decision to get out of the situation was really made for me, but the decision making that went on prior and afterwards was really the hard part. My normal weight is about 152–153 pounds. When I came back I weighed 139. I looked like I came out of a concentration camp. I looked like death. I had a lot of problems sleeping, smoking cigarettes. I didn't drink; I never reached that point. It was a very traumatic part of my life. I'll never forget it and I'll never forgive that manager.

It was a tough situation. I knew what the situation was and I did make a value judgment. I made a bad call. I really made a bad call. And it came back to haunt me. Maybe if I had been more sophisticated, I would have realized the evil in the situation when it was first presented to me—that I really didn't get positive vibes from that local manager, and if there was anybody I needed to get positive vibes from it should have been him. I learned a lot from the experience. What I learned I think gives me enough of an understanding of life, not necessarily of that specific situation, to be able to stand back and stick my finger out and say "The hell with you. I'm not putting up with that shit." I couldn't do it then. I don't know why but I really couldn't. And what was even worse was that I knew I had put myself into that situation. The closer I got to it the more I realized: you share part of the blame for what you now endure.

In retrospect, I should have met with all the individual managers first to talk to them about how they saw my role. Now I understand that when you're being asked to take a position you should talk about peoples' expectations for you, and how they see you communicating, what they would like to see you achieve. And you work out something of a contract with the individuals. I never did that. In retrospect that's part of the learning experience. When you work for somebody you develop that on the front end, before you get into a situation where you can't walk out. If I learned anything, I learned that when somebody makes a commitment to you, put it in writing. It's not just the matter of covering your ass. It's that when somebody puts it in writing it generally means they're willing to back it up. There's something about putting something on paper. Going back and saying "You told me to do this" still has no value. But when somebody's willing to put it on paper, it generally means they're going to adhere to it. It's all a matter of communication. One of the primary causes of something going wrong, even ethically, is the fact that you didn't communicate clearly.

In that situation, I had a choice; I clearly had a choice all along. I could pack up my family and leave. I always had that choice. But I'm the type of guy who likes to stick it out. I don't like to give up. And maybe my manager knew that too, that I was a very tenacious individual. He may have played upon that too. "He wants to succeed. I know this type. I can squeeze him but he'll still produce." I would like to take him aside and say "Do you have a couple hours? I'd like to hear your perspective." The problem is, I think I know what he'll say. "You screwed up. You screwed up. We did what was in the best interest of our company. It was all for the greater good."

I think that it was an isolated incident, based upon all the history and all the people I knew. I really do believe it was an extreme situation. I think it had a unique set of ingredients: personalities, situation, job, time. And I'd have been a different person if I'd been just a couple years older and I'd had some kind of life experience to compare that against. Some solution or thought process that I could have carried over to apply there. Everybody around me was more sophisticated than I was.

When I look at an ethical problem, I'm really saying that something is against my moral or ethical grain and I try to be a lot more objective about the decision or the action being asked of me. I want to find out if it really is an ethical question and if I am being asked to do something I can't or shouldn't be doing. I have to be prepared, when it is truly an ethical issue, to say "I do not feel comfortable doing this," and refuse to do it. Even if somebody says it'll mean a million dollars for the company, if I feel strongly about it I have to be prepared to say "Get somebody else to do it." If they say "Nobody else can do it," I say "Sorry. I have to live with the action." So, in the future, I will treat things differently. Most definitely. And I feel I have a responsibility to those I'm interacting with. I don't want to compromise myself.

I just did an assessment of my MBA program. They asked me all kinds of questions about the applicability of the courses I took. I learned a lot in the program, but very little to help me in my job. They don't tell you how to deal with people. What they talked about, generally, in the case studies were financial issues. Understanding what the business decision is. Managers don't have business issues all the time. They have people issues: motivating people, doing performance reviews, communicating with people, learning how to manage conflict. The interpersonal part of being a manager. I've got all my books up here—consumer behavior, basic finance, and all that stuff. I loved it and I learned a lot. And I use it when I deal with marketing issues. But in order to get a marketing issue to come to pass I have to sit down and negotiate with somebody. And that's what I didn't get out of school.

Ethics is often thought of as a philosopher's issue. But philosophers don't have to develop those behavior patterns that help you resolve problems. They can sit there and ponder their navels for 40 years because nobody is holding them accountable for a decision.

COMMENTS

The distress that Charles and Jeff experienced, and the situations that produced it, are typical of what one executive has called the "Move It!" philosophy of management: down the hierarchy comes the word to get the job done, or the product out, or the troublemaker canned, or whatever—no questions asked, just do it. These two episodes are also typical of the kinds of situations in which (1) we, as observers, are quick to question the integrity of the actor ("he really could have refused to do it if he wanted to"), and (2) we, as targets, tend to rationalize our own decisions to comply.

Charles talks about types of dilemmas in which he has felt it appropriate to let a management lie go by, or to back it up, or cover it up. And he discusses the practice of "fudging" shipping dates in a weekly in-house report because his management wanted things to "look a little better." In his present environment, Charles feels that a dissenter can get "killed," so questioning an order or an ongoing practice can be dangerous to one's job or career. Now Charles does not say he simply complies, whatever the command. What he says is that he raises his objections and asks his questions, but if the decision goes contrary to his beliefs—-and if it is not illegal or "grossly unethical," he feels it is out of his hands, that the choice is not his to make, that he has no control over the situation.

Charles does not comply in these situations without considerable discomfort. It is his sense of himself as a religious and decent man which allows him to rationalize things so he can "live with them." Charles' experience is a painfully common one. (We can assume, in fact, from the "Move It!" philosophy, that Charles' boss is acting on a directive from his boss, who is acting on orders from his boss, etc.) The critical question is: How does a manager say "no" to something that goes against his values and what he believes is ethically right and not suffer what may be very real effects on job and career?

Many managers to whom I have posed that question in a variety of settings over the last year or two has staunchly stated that the person of true moral integrity would just say "no," regardless of the consequences. Some few have come closer to what I see as reality by suggesting that unless the organization, by policy or informal procedure, supports its managers' refusals to compromise personal values, and prevents negative consequences from being levied for such action, they, too, would likely comply as long as "it really doesn't matter that much" (in Charles Warren's words).

Situations like Charles' are very complicated. When does "doesn't matter that much" cross the line to "does matter?" What about the erosion of trust that accompanies these episodes? In the best of all possible worlds every person would stand up for her values. But in that same best world, organizations would create environments in which that integrity could be practiced without unnecessary sacrifice and in which the phrase, "I had no choice" would not be a necessary rationalization.

Jeffrey Lovett's situation offers a different perspective on the choice/compliance issue. For Jeff, the painful episode he relates began when he was asked by the man who hired him, Bob, to report on the manager for whom he (Jeff) would be working. Jeff's early perception of the situation was similar to Charles' view of the shipping date alteration, that is, that a superior was directing him to "do something that internally [he didn't] feel good about doing," but that he, essentially, had no choice. Part of the tacit understanding in these psychological contracts between commanding superior and complying subordinate is that compliance will yield some "protection" of the subordinate from unpleasant consequences. (Although Charles does say that if the situation became known, he would have been held responsible.) But in Jeff's situation, the psychological contract was broken and Jeff suffered reputational effects and severe personal pain. It was out of the effects of the broken contract that Jeff was driven to review the situation and redefine the initial relationship with Bob. Most important, Jeff's redefinition of the problem changed his notion of choice. As he says repeatedly—he did have a choice in the action he took. Unlike Charles, he comes to believe he had been driven not by fear of career consequences but by a desire for rapid career enhancement which he believed compliance might bring him, and that he would not have suffered in his career development; he simply would not have moved as fast.

There is a critical difference in implication for future behavior between Jeff's and Charles' reactions to their situations. Neither manager feels pleased with himself for acting as he has. But Jeff, one can assume, is more likely than Charles to examine carefully a future similar situation and actively to seek alternative solutions. The reason is that Jeff believes he had a choice about what action he took: He could have said "No." Consequently he feels responsible for some part of the episode and its outcome, and so recognizes his capacity to manage an ethical dilemma. Charles, on the other hand, states that he had no choice, that the matter was out of his hands, and thus he had no responsibility for what was done and no capacity to alter it. Without a sense of some capacity to act, he is less likely in the future to feel capable of taking on an ethical challenge.

WENDELL

JOHNSON

Manager, Field Engineering
Thirty-six years old

" . . . The guilt trip is over.
He performs or he's fired.
Except it won't be that simple.
It's just easy to say."

My official title is field engineering manager. Basically, my role is to manage an organization of about 25 people. The functions of my organization are key to our parent organization, customer services. When the product breaks, CS goes out to fix it. When customers need help in tying the product into their systems, or when a sales-person needs help in selling the product—that's customer services. My organization was created to be the buffer between the field where all the selling and servicing is going on, and engineering where products are being developed. As a result of what we do, we are the spokesman for the field. As the spokesman, one of our jobs is to understand what goes on out there with our customers and our support personnel, carry it back to engineering, and help them design a more serviceable product. Say that engineering is inventing a black box and they want that box to do 37 different flavors of functions. We tell them that if they take the box and have it do seven of those functions, but do them really well, they'll do much better in the market. That sounds like marketing, and that is a piece of our organization. But we also look at things from a service standpoint. If you do such-and-such, people who are trying to make it work are going to smash their fingers every time they use it. That's going to make the customers very upset. Don't do it! Or if every time the customer pushes this button the machine doesn't do what it's supposed to do, it's broken. It's broken by design—not because a component failed inside the product. So what we try to do is take the service issues and merge them with the product issues.

Our organization serves a largely adversarial function. Our role is to work with engineering and require that they do certain things with their products to make them better products; and it forces us to work with members of the service organization, requiring them to commit to strategies and spend money and do things they really don't want to do. Often we're described as the classic example of being between a rock and a hard place. It's like sitting at the controls of an atom bomb. We can blow everybody up if they don't do their job. The problem is, the button's on the nose of the atom bomb, so in a sense, we're the most vulnerable. And we recognize that we don't really control most of the organizations we have to deal with. We have to influence them. Our stock in trade is technical knowledge,

knowledge of the marketplace and the service business, service expertise, and most particularly our interpersonal abilities—the ability to sit down with people and get them to buy into an idea.

Right now I'm in the stickiest situation I've been in as a manager. Let me give you some of the background. I have an individual working for me as an engineer. Mac will turn 61 next month. He has a family, he is sick, his son is out of work, and his wife is not in good health. He has been with the company less than five years, which means he's not vested in pension benefits. In fact, his history indicates he probably doesn't have a pension anywhere. His skills are, basically, obsolete, as are his knowledge and his experience. He's a vacuum tube engineer. His engineering knowledge and its application are way behind where the rest of us are. More importantly, his style makes him very difficult to work with. He has, in fact, created such a difficult situation that several of our peer organizations are demanding that I minimize their contact with him. Some of them refuse to attend a meeting at which he is present; if he shows up at a meeting, these people will leave.

As I said before, the position this group plays is an adversarial one. We often find ourselves with the potential of having a real shouting contest. And you have to be able to give in; you have to recognize that you're not going to win a particular point and may need to address it on a different day. You have to be cognizant of what other people are feeling: did they just get out of a budget meeting where they got all hell kicked of them because they're running late? That is certainly not the time to go in and ask for something else. There are things you have to be aware of. Mac's style is to go in and pound the table: "Thou shalt do this." "We demand." He uses that verb an awful lot. "I demand you do this. I demand you do that." In this adversarial relationship, no matter how cooperative everyone is trying to be, the word "demand" gets an instinctive "like hell" reaction. If it does that to me, I can imagine what it does to the engineers. You have to be able to listen without demanding, to share the problem, and to compromise. Mac has a nasty habit of picking nits. There is nothing that can be written so perfectly that he cannot find something wrong. It wouldn't be so bad if the nits were important ones but, by definition, they are very unimportant and generally a waste of time for everybody in the room, which upsets everybody and quickly loses him support. Everybody who agrees with him finds it hard to agree with him once he starts picking nits.

This company is managed by consensus. Many people think we're a true matrix-managed company. That's not true. Just about everybody has a single boss. What is true, though, is that we manage by consensus, which gives the appearance to the outside world that we're matrix managing. Managing by consensus is very difficult when the first word you say gets everybody's hackles up.

Mac also lacks knowledge of our products. When you go into engineering and say "We know we need this tool to support this product," it is implied in that statement that you know the product. If you don't know the product there is an obvious question of "Who the hell do you think you are to tell me what I need when you don't know what it is we're looking at." Mac doesn't have the technical knowledge of our products. His credentials are okay, but his knowledge is obsolete by about nine years. As a result there is an enormous credibility gap.

Unfortunately, when we interviewed Mac we did see value there. In fact, I still see value in him. In the interview process he interviewed quite well. We checked his credentials, we checked with personnel, we checked with his manager. Everybody told us "Hey he's really good. He really does good stuff, he's really positive," and so on. I even checked with some peers of mine who had worked with him and they had nothing bad to say—until three months after I hired him. And then they began saying, "Well I could have told you what kind of person he was."

Within a period of about two months Mac had managed to alienate my entire organization. Within another three months I had a delegation from other organizations telling me he was a nonperson; they could no longer go to his meetings or participate in discussions with him under *any* circumstances. And they said it was our problem to solve, that they wanted to see it solved, but not to ask them to get involved. Let me repeat his major faults: he has no knowledge of service delivery; his interpersonal skills require major development; his technical knowledge base does not exist. The man is being paid to be a leader—not a manager, but a technical leader, like a project manager. He doesn't have people reporting directly to him but he is managing projects that involve other people's activities. And he lacks most, if not all, of the leadership qualities. He doesn't listen. He doesn't think about what other people are doing or feeling. His management style is one way. Professionally he's just truly unqualified, technically as well as interpersonally. He has no common sense and is totally impractical. There is no future career path for him. Making it worse, he is overpaid for his contribution. And there are other minor things.

There is some good stuff. I don't want to paint a totally black picture. The good stuff is that he does have an ability to look at and develop standards. He does have a basic understanding of quality—not what it means but how to test for it, what we call quality control as opposed to quality assurance. He does a decent job at documentation. He's fairly adequate in theory in the areas where he knows what he's talking about. So there's a little bit of good stuff. There could be some value to some organizations in this company.

Why is it ethical? Number one, I have people making a lot less money who started with less knowledge and who are now contributing on the order of two to three times as much value to the organization as he is. They're making $10,000–20,000 less than he is. The problem I'm faced with is that as a manager I'm paid by this company to ensure that all my people contribute in a way that is appropriate to their salary and toward the purposes for which our organization was established. Mac does not do that. Number two, we have to respond to two personnel organizations. The solution of one was to fire the individual. The solution of the other was give him another chance. I have difficulty with the "other chance" theory because this would be his seventh chance within my organization, not his second.

For instance, over the last six months I have met with him once a week for one hour to do nothing but talk about his schedule and progress. I have made a perk chart out of his activities, which I have never done for any employee no matter how junior. I have invested on the order of about 15% of my time over the last six months attempting to make him successful. We hired him in May. By August he was not succeeding in the job we hired him to do. At that point we started September with a new chance. So in September we actually gave him a second chance. His third chance came in August of the following year when he wasn't doing the job that we hired him to do; he said he needed more technical information. We gave him that chance. That was his third chance. As a result I lost a very good manager. Mac alienated everyone else whom he hadn't already alienated and cost me a manager by putting her on the line. But I gave him his fourth chance, what I call a clean sheet, because I didn't know whether it was the manager or him. I wiped the sheet clean and started again. This was his fourth chance. In May (at the end of his second year with the company) he had not met his goals. I delayed his review and gave him a fifth chance. He said he did not meet his goals in May because he was not given clear goals. The fifth chance was clear goals. In August I delayed his review again and did a performance appraisal saying he did not meet the requirements and gave him a sixth and last chance. At that point I did this very discreet and detailed appraisal. I did that instead of terminating his employment because he said he had not had enough management direction to succeed. He has now run out of excuses that I accept. A year ago August I couldn't blame him or his manager; I didn't know who was at fault. In May I knew he was at fault but maybe I hadn't given him clear goals. In August his excuse was I hadn't given him management direction. We are now in March. I have met all the requirements of my ethics. The man will be terminated July 1 if he has not found another job in the company. He doesn't know that exactly. He knows that by July 1 he'd better be performing or have found another job or else. I haven't said explicitly that he will be fired July 1.

Where my ethics comes into this is that I do not want to terminate any employee or tell an employee to look around unless I believe I have done everything I can to help that employee be successful. I have at this point done everything necessary, and the individual has failed. He cannot point to me, my management staff, or my organization. He has now failed miserably on his own record and there are no more excuses. He's run out of chances. Actually he's getting a seventh chance between now and July 1 to do well. If he does that I probably will be able to buy the Brooklyn Bridge as well.

The tough question is, do I terminate the individual? I have all the facts and figures necessary to terminate. I have to watch out for EEO because he is over 60 years old. One personnel organization says to terminate him. The other set of personnel people are telling me that, well, maybe I didn't give him a good enough chance. I want to give the employee a chance, but sooner or later you run out of chances. So I'm also caught in a battle between two personnel organizations, one which says "Fire his ass" and the other which says "Let him work on." Ethical again.

I have fired people. But I believe this individual has value. He has value to contribute to his company in some capacity, in another organization. Of course, every human being has value, but I'm talking about professional value to the corporation. I have identified the capacities and I am pursuing them with him, trying to find a position. My standard of ethics requires that I do that. But I get caught in the ethics bind. What if he doesn't find a job he wants? Do I keep him? I have lost three individuals almost directly as a result of him, and I'm in danger of losing two more. And there is another part of the ethics bind. I know there is little or no chance of him finding a position in another organization because I refuse to lie to a new manager. Mac knows I will give an honest opinion, an honest recommendation. I will refuse to lie. That happened to me; to a certain extent that's why I'm in this position today. Other people weren't honest enough. They were getting rid of a problem, not solving it. I am unwilling to transfer a problem. His new manager, if he has one, will know there is a problem. Mac knows that; personnel knows that. And that's the situation. What is the resolution?

I know I will fire him. And I know a week before I do, I might as well not plan to sleep. I don't fire people easily. That's the price you pay. I think the manager who can just say "You're fired" probably hasn't done his job. But there's also the chance the individual could go away and commit suicide. I'm not placing all the responsibility on myself. I don't want it to haunt me if something should happen. I cannot judge myself by things that other people totally control. But that's going to be hollow if something happens.

The issue I'm struggling with at this point is balancing what's the best thing for the employee and what's best for the organization. I think I have made the decision. What I haven't yet done is manage to live well with it. And that won't happen until I find that he's found another job and he's successful.

One of the things I fear is that I am violating my own intent to be fair. I've been accused of that by one of the personnel reps who says I am judging the individual too harshly. This is the first failure I've had working with an individual and getting him to recognize what he is doing. This company's culture takes people's careers and the commitment to the individual very strongly. And the commitment means making sure I have not only protected the company from EEO but that I have made sure the employee has the opportunity to succeed. You always think: I want to make sure I give this individual everything I would want if anything like this ever happened to me. And the odds are nowadays that it will happen to every manager. Supposedly, part of the career of a manager is that when you're in your early 40s you get terminated and you have to change companies.

Anyway, the guilt trip is over. He performs or he's fired. It's simple. Except it won't be that simple. It's just easy to say.

COMMENTS

Wendell's problem concerns what he should do about Mac, an older, low-performing subordinate who is the victim of a number of personal hardships, and whose on-the-job performance has driven away younger, top-performing employees. If Wendell keeps Mac on he feels he is being unfair to other employees who are better performers, who earn less money, and whose work, we can surmise, will be adversely affected by Mac's negativity. He also feels he is being unfair to the organization whose mission must be carried forth. We can presume he also recognizes that his own neck is on the line. He has already lost a couple of top people because of Mac and another is threatening to leave. Without good people, how can Wendell achieve his group's productivity goals? And what happens to his career if he doesn't? On the positive side, however, if he retains Mac, he will be providing care and income for a man and his family who might otherwise become destitute, and thus is acting according to personally held values. He also will be upholding a pair of deeply held corporate values: (1) firing is a last resort; do everything you can to retain an employee, and (2) employees must have the opportunity to succeed; good managers create the opportunities for their employees to succeed. In other words, a subordinate's success is a manager's responsibility.

If Wendell fires Mac, there's good chance his problems may be solved. That's the positive side. But, on the negative side, there are a number of critical threads waiting to tie him up. By terminating Mac, he will be acting against well-entrenched company values—values of which the firm is very proud and to which it believe all of its managers have made an implicit commitment. (The practice of transferring a problem employee with a glowing reference, as was done with Mac, is a frequent and apparently unchallenged coping mechanism.) So Wendell's career may still be in some jeopardy if he challenges the firm's values, even if the discontinuation of Mac increases group productivity. And if Mac is terminated—and as a result falls on hard times—Wendell feels *he* may be the one responsible for causing harm to the man and his family. He is caught in the middle of competing, legitimate claims: he cannot both retain and fire Mac; he cannot easily retain Mac and support the needs of his other subordinates; he cannot terminate Mac and be true to the company' values. Above all, as is the case in so many ethical dilemmas, Wendell wants very much to do the right thing; he just does not know what that right thing is.

One of the concerns he raises is fairness: What is fair to Mac? What is fair to the other employees? What is fair to the company? But Wendell's concern is not simply "What is fair?" His questions really ask: Will each of these stakeholders see "fair" in the same way I do? Will they see "fair" in the same way as each other? Given the different needs and wants of each of these stakeholders, it is reasonable to assume they would not answer the "What is fair?" question in the same way. So Wendell's concern is not with the principle of fairness so much as it is with value conflicts around what fair is in this situation. Implicit in this dilemma, of course, is the fact that once Wendell makes a decision about what to do (i.e., what is fair), his implementation of that decision will require that he impose his values (his definition of fairness) on someone else, an action with which he is not completely comfortable. This fairness concern, however, is only one piece of the ethical pie for Wendell. Consider next the question of harm. Wendell's immediate focus is the possibility of causing harm to Mac and, by extension,

Mac's family. But the range of possible harm he perceives does not stop there. If Mac is kept on, his coworkers may suffer harm in the form of compromises to their professional growth and ability to be contributing members of their unit and the organization. Similarly, the organization may suffer harm in the financial consequences occurring as a result of this key intermediary group (advocate for the customer) performing its critical role less effectively than it should. So, Wendell faces a dilemma in which he sees the causing of harm as inevitable in one way or another.

Important as well to Wendell is understanding what his responsibility is. Clearly, his role requires that he evaluate his subordinates and take appropriate action based on a "fair" evaluation. Further, his role responsibility requires that he do his work in a way that contributes to the accomplishment of the organization's mission. These role responsibilities, however, are not the cause of his ethical discomfort. The distress lies in an interesting mix of causal (what *he* caused) and capacity (what he can do) responsibility. Remember that this company has an active belief that managers must provide the opportunity for employees to succeed. Wendell appears to have internalized this value to the extent that, despite Mac's failure to make the most of any of six chances, Wendell still questions whether or not he may be at fault in terms of the level of support and assistance he has given Mac. And, if he perceives he is at fault, then he must also believe he has causal responsibility to correct the problem. As well, Wendell recognizes he may be the only one who has the capacity to help Mac, if in no other way than by simply keeping him on the job. Wendell's questions about both his causal and capacity responsibility come poignantly to the fore when he considers the chance that Mac could "go away and commit suicide." He says, "I'm not placing all the responsibility on myself." But it does sound as if he holds himself, at least in part, responsible for what he fears Mac may do. So, Wendell's already complex dilemma is further compounded by the nagging question: "What is my responsibility?"

Wendell's first sense of the problem is not focused on the variety of demands from a number of stakeholders or the complexity of the fairness issue; it is centered on a responsibility/relationship concern that grows out of personal beliefs bolstered by corporate values. Think of Arthur Miller's play *Death of a Salesman*, and the role of Willy Loman. In many ways, Wendell's Mac is Willy— a man who was at one time pretty good at his job, who never was "a great man, never made a lot of money, not the finest character that ever lived. But he's a human being and a terrible thing is happening to him." Unlike the young manager in the play for whom Willy's age and fatigue and inability to get the job done mean the end of the line, Wendell sees those same conditions as triggers to his responsibility; he believes, as Willy's wife puts it, that "attention must be . . . paid to such a person." I cite the play *Death of a Salesman* very specifically because I think it has had a profound and lasting effect on our national culture in that it raised a consciousness of human worth and the responsibilities of all people to recognize that worth. More than that, it looked at a man and his work, and the responsibilities of work organizations to people who have contributed to them. It is this cultural value that is part of the ethical trigger for Wendell. That personal concern is strongly reinforced, however, by the organization's values which carry the potential accusation of dereliction of responsibility for failure to respond to that human need.

In fact, Wendell seems to have become fixated on Mac's condition because of the organizational reinforcement. This fixation by both Wendell and the organization has the potential to turn the dilemma into an "issue" question: Is it right or wrong to terminate an older, needy employee who is no longer performing at an acceptable level? And, as we noted before, an issue focus implies a right answer which can oversimplify the problem, denying many other legitimate concerns related to it, and lead to an ineffective resolution.

JACKSON
TAYLOR

**Vice-President
Fifty years old**

*"Our biggest concern was our customers;
and the issue was our implied commitment,
what we had led them to believe."*

My title is vice-president of Operations. My job is to make sure the company has an operating plan: I manage the process of putting our plan together. Our corporate plan involves the financial plan, the inventory plan, the product plan, everything. Then once we have the plan in place, I have to manage the process of getting the plan accepted. Once it's accepted, then it's put in place and monitored on a month-by-month basis. If it starts to go off the track, we plug the holes and put it together again. So it's a planning role; it's a monitoring role; it's a fix-it role when things start going off the track. I guess one of the things I would say about myself is that I have a fair amount of credibility in the company from being here a long time. Without it, this job couldn't be done.

Right now we are in the process of going through a very interesting situation which has ethical overtones to it. I'd like to describe it. We have a new product that handles the same workload as one of our original switching systems. That line started back in the sixties, and we have continued to build new models of it since then. Obviously, as a result, we have established a customer base that is using that product and has designed a lot of their communications around its structure. Even though the structure is now fairly old, the product still has very powerful characteristics, so there is a very loyal body of customers. We had a new project underway to build a new version of that product. We started that project about three years ago with the idea that by now we would have it available and we would be shipping it to those who wanted to purchase it. A few months ago the project ran into some difficulties, and the difficulties were severe enough that we knew that in order to bring the project to fruition, we would have to spend another three years on it. The problem as we saw it was that, in three years, that product wouldn't be very competitive, and therefore it was questionable as to whether or not very many people would purchase it. The product has, over the last 10 years, fallen out of the mainstream of our design, and our newer lines really have been the focus of our development. Our development is oriented primarily toward a more technologically advanced pattern of switching than our former product can achieve. So with the bulk of our customers we've been stressing the new technology. Our longer-range strategy was to build the capability for connecting the older systems into the more advanced product so that over time our long-term users could interconnect with the newer network.

The question that came upon us when we discovered our new product would be at least three years away was: Should we embark on that project or should we embark on a project which would interconnect all of the old products into a larger system so that they could continue to use what they had for what they are doing, but that their expansion would be using the new product, which will be available in a much shorter time period than three years? The ethical consideration in that whole question was: Are we abandoning that long-standing customer base? Are we following through on the commitments and implied commitments we made over the last 20 years to those customers, that we would make sure what they have would not become obsolete and we would provide them with a continued and embraceable expansion as they needed it? What we chose to do was to discontinue the development of the product and put our development resources into making a faster implementation of the new network so that the users could be interconnected into the rest of our networks and continue to use all the functionality they had used over the years with their older product. We also committed to developing products that would fit with their systems. We thought a long time about this because again the question was: Are we abandoning this set of customers who have grown up with us, and who are now out of the mainstream of our development but who, nonetheless, are an important set of people? Our old switching system business is not more than 3 or 4% of our total revenues, so it's not a big proportion of the business. But nonetheless, it's still an important set of customers.

We announced our intentions a month ago, and we asked those customers to participate with us in helping us to define the projects that we could do which would make this transition an easy transition. We are prepared to throw a fair amount of development dollars into making the transition.

Some of our customers feel we have not acted ethically in this case. Some feel we are abandoning them to some degree. Some think we're just crazy because the older product is so good we ought to perpetuate it forever. Our feeling is that it is not the way of the future.

Q. *Did your customers know you had started working on a new version of that product three years ago?*

We didn't announce it publicly, but we told a lot of our good customers on a confidential basis that we were developing it. And there's no question that the fact that we told them we were doing this development encouraged some of them to do their own new developments on the product because of the expectation that there would be this more powerful unit which would give them an advantage. No question about that. And they feel the older product is so unique that we'll never be able to duplicate it in another guise.

We do really spend a lot of time and effort listening to customers and getting their opinions. We care a lot about our users, and we knew this would be tough. They're feeling angry and abandoned, some of them. But it's all out in the open now; it's all announced. We're doing a lot of surveying and asking questions about what would be most helpful for us to do to make this transition easy for them. We're involving them very much in the process at this point. We're not doing that just as a sop to them. We're doing it because we think we'll get some good ideas from them as to how we should proceed. But it was a very tough ethical question. I think the way we got through it was to say, "We really do honestly believe that communications in the future is going to be different, and the old way of doing it is, over time, not going to be the right way of doing it. We really feel we should be leaders with our users and help lead them into what we feel will be the more effective way of communicating in the future."

Now, clearly the dilemma was brought on by the fact that we failed in developing the new product, and so there's no question that it's tied up with a failure on our part to deliver on our expectations, or their expectations of us. That's what made the decision more difficult. We had clearly failed in following through in delivering around now a product which we had thought we could build in that time frame. We had led them on to believe that this year we would be able to deliver. We honestly thought that's what we were going to be able to do. But our design engineers just didn't succeed. We believe we could do it the next time around, but by then the product would be obsolete.

So what we are now saying is that another course of action looks like it's going to be better for us and for you the customer, in the long run, and what they're questioning is whether or not it really is going to be better for them in the long run. They have only our faith that it is the right thing, and it is our belief that it really is the right thing which brought us through the hassle. We believe we're doing the right thing. We're not doing it to save money because I really think this is going to cost us a lot of money over the next couple of years. A lot of people look on it as "Oh, you're just saving money. You know you stopped this project because you didn't want to put your development dollars into it." Well, that's really not the issue. We'll probably put even more money into the transition.

Of course, some of our customers will be angry enough that they will probably not stay with us. Whether it's wise or not they'll leave because they're so angry with us. And that's painful for a company that prides itself on being an affable company. And it's not because of any of the legal ramifications at all. We never made any legal commitment. It was an ethical situation.

I've been leading the management of this whole process. But really all of our top managers have been involved. I would do a lot of work and then bring it back to them. It was ultimately the top managers as a group who made the decision. I can remember the final meeting where it was decided that all the evidence was weighing up as to how we should proceed. And finally at the last meeting we dealt with this particular issue. It just was so clear that all of us were feeling the same way about what the right thing to do was. So I finally said, "It seems to me we've really made the decision. I mean, everybody is going in the same direction; we're all saying the same thing. Let's just solidify the decision and agree on it." It involved all the top managers right through the chairman. In a decision like this, where a major set of our customers has to have the right kind of support, if there's even one or two senior managers who really think it's not the right thing to do, we try to keep going because if the top five or six people in the company don't believe it, then you know that people who are down in the organization will think it's the wrong decision. And no one will be able to provide the customer support that is essential.

No one thought this dilemma was easy. Everyone approached this question with the idea that it would be a difficult decision. I think the fairest thing to say is that I led us through the process, but I couldn't have done it without the support from my peers. I couldn't do it alone. Nor could the chairman. Nobody could do it alone. It was just too important a decision.

So we're still, as I said, in the middle of it. We're now in the process of going out to our customer base and they're helping us to formulate our new project. It will be about a year before we really know how successful we've been in implementing the decision. We know we've made the decision; we don't know about the implementation and how successful we're going to be at it.

We made the decision one morning, and two o'clock that afternoon the development manager brought all the people who were involved together. Of course, they knew we had been meeting. It was not a secret we were discussing the issue. And he informed them of the decision, and then talked with them on a one-by-one basis to assure them that there would be no negative career consequences for them. There were about 15 people in all, and he worked individually with them to make sure they each made a transition to a new project and to a continued successful career here.

I consider the problem ethical, because it affected our commitments, or our implied commitments, to our customers—not our legal commitments, but our commitments to stick with them and to make sure they had the best systems in the world. That is what we feel we owe to each of our customers with whom we deal. We've always prided ourselves on our relationships with our customers and keeping those relationships open and honest and straightforward. I think it's important. It's not just what we promise legally, it's what we imply that's terribly important to us. In this case the employees were not the primary concern. We didn't feel we had particular ethical considerations there. They clearly failed on the project. We understood that, but we didn't feel their failure meant they had to leave the company; they had just taken on a job that was bigger than they were capable of at that time. But when you fail on a job, you do expect the possibility of cancellation, whatever the cause. So our biggest concern was our customers. And the issue was our implied commitment, what we had led them to believe. That's why it became ethical or moral.

COMMENTS

Jackson Taylor, like others who deal with customers and suppliers, is a boundary spanner—a person who is responsible for creating and maintaining a productive relationship between the organization and the outside world.

Jack's ethical dilemma was triggered by a breakdown of trust and a disconfirmation of the expectations set up by the unspoken rules of the game—the implicit contract between company and customer. Although no public or formal commitment to development of the new version of the communications system had been made, Jack acknowledges that good customers, those with whom there was the deepest bond of trust, were told the new version was in the works. In return for the advance information, the customers were expected to remain loyal to the company by staying with them until the new product was ready. When the company did not come though, the rules were broken.

The most significant reason the game rules were broken is because the company deviated early on from a basic principle. The company—or the managers acting as its agent—decided to make exceptions to the "rules." A basic tenet of customer relationships is equal treatment. We can assume, that, like all the other principles, policies, and so on, that tenet has exceptions. And in this case, that exception was exercised. In Jack's situation, standard operating procedure was to provide the same information on future products to all affected customers (or to provide none to anyone). Jack's dilemma was set in motion by the company's decision to *not* formally announce the development effort and *then* to tell a lot of good customers about it on a confidential basis, presumably to keep them from turning to a competitor. The problem is that once the company made an exception to its own rules vis-à-vis customers, there was no support system of policies, values, or norms to guide them when adverse conditions appeared; the assumed rules of the game no longer held.

Actually, Jack faced a two-part dilemma. The first part was to decide whether or not to invest another three years to produce a promised product at major cost to the company, or to cancel the product and find an alternative and competitively less costly route to make amends. That was the tough part. The second part of the dilemma—how to implement a decision that might be perceived as unethical by some affected parties—was considerably less painful. When decision making was guided by the strong company culture that says, "We care a lot about our users [and] we spend a lot of time and effort listening to customers," implementation by customer participation became the clear route.

What is evident in this case is that dispassionate anticipatory management might have prevented the dilemma point from being reached. Although Jack does not say it explicitly, we can assume that someone was minding the store over the last three years and had become aware, before target time, that the new version was not going to make it. Either earlier withdrawal or informing of the customers of possible problems might have prevented embarrassment and the dilemma. Furthermore, if all customers had been treated the same at the beginning of the project, the dilemma of who and how to notify, and questions about what the obligations were, would not have arisen. That the company failed in its product development is *not* an ethical problem. Companies can have failures, even after good faith efforts. "Promises" for future products or services may have to be broken if the company is unable to perform as predicted. That is not an unethical act. The critical concern is the process by which the relationship is established and maintained through the passing of information in a timely and equal fashion.

In reflecting on how he resolved his dilemma, Jack points to how important it was that others were involved in making the decision. Although Jack was providing the information and the process to the other senior executives, the group decision enabled both company employees and the outside world to see the organization leadership acting as a united front on a difficult and unpopular decision.

It is also important to note the emphasis Jack places on "'protecting" the company, while recognizing the necessity of balancing the needs of the company and those of the customer. "Protecting the company" is a phrase that may draw a negative response from many who believe that business is concerned solely with efforts to increase its own profits to provide greater and greater return to shareholders. But we have to look at Jack's concerns from a broader perspective. The decision to give greater weight to the company than to other stakeholders recognizes the company itself as a representative of many stakeholders. It meant that the company could continue to fulfill its mission in the corporate world, to provide meaningful employment, to offer quality products and services to the public, and, yes, to make money. The important learning from this situation is not that in the end the company comes first. It is, rather, that if the company is a high-priority stakeholder, really protecting it means picking up the clues that something is amiss early on and acting effectively to change direction. Although it is not always possible to detect problems that lie further down the track, in this case it could have been done. And earlier intervention might have prevented the dilemma from arising and maintained the critical trust across the company borders.

RONALD
HARRIS

Manager, Customer Products Division
Forty-three years old

*"These guys steal technology from each
other all the time. Nobody else would have
your concern!"*

L et me talk about the hardest ethical dilemma I've had, personally. It was early in my career. I came to work from a university environment, and prior to that I was in the military service. So, I came here to learn about business; my role was to do factory research. I just really wanted to find out what business was all about. I had expected it to be a two-year stint, and it's twelve years now, so something happened. But, at any rate, after I'd been here about two years, they gave me the responsibility for a test system development project. One of the things included in the development was a memory system involving a core memory. At that time we did not have a core memory manufacturing capability, so we bought our core plans from outside vendors and we built all the electronic circuitry around it. Typically, we were involved intimately in the design since what we bought was a customized product; it was not a generalized product sold to other people. So the design was ours, but a vendor would supply us a core stack that would go in our machine.

A core stack is old technology; it's not used anymore. But the way we remembered pieces of information in the machine was by magnetizing little ferrite beads and then sensing which poll each was magnetized to, to remember a bit of information as being true or false. Nowadays, there are semiconductor devices that do the same thing, but in those days, they made a matrix of cores that were about 20 mil in diameter (very, very small), and they had a little hole and you ran wires through those cores. And when you ran the current through the wires, you magnetized them in one direction or another. And then, when you ran the current through them in the opposite direction, if they've been previously magnetized one way, they put off a disturbance to another wire called the sensor wire that was also run through the core. So you knew whether that core had ever been a 1 or a 0 before. Anyway, that's the basic memory unit core for a computer, and in those days, for 4000 words of information on which there were 24 bits (bits are like characters), it cost about $1200. Then you put maybe $3000 worth of electronics around it to make the memory subsystem of a tester. As I said, the technology's changed a lot, but at that time, it was an important cost element in the machine.

For our security, there were about six vendors, all of whom made core memory systems. There were two elements: one was the design of the core memory in terms of the physical layout so that it had the best properties for reliable signals, and the other element was manufacturing them with high reliability. There were a lot of manufacturing issues and a lot of design issues. In this program we wanted to go with multiple sources for the memory so we wouldn't be exposed. So we turned on four vendors, all of whom were designing their own solutions to our problem based on our specifications. The design would be ours when we were done. We evaluated the four vendors and from the four we selected a primary vendor and turned him on to 70% of our volume and a secondary vendor to 30% so that if the primary vendor stumbled we'd push harder on the secondary vendor. We would also qualify—to be held in the wings, so to speak—a third vendor and decide whether to bring him on or not.

There was a company at the time who had no engineering capability, but they could manufacture memories. You'd give them the design and then they would give you a price on it and manufacture it. And because they had no engineering capability, they had no overhead. Consequently, they had a very low cost structure. The situation I found so tough was that our purchasing agent at that time had identified this vendor, but I didn't know anything about him until late in the program. We selected our two vendors and the third in the wings, and we were ready to go when this manufacturer came in with about a 15% cost savings on the manufacture of this very critical element, an estimate based on a verbal description of what we were looking for. He wanted the core stacks from one of the other vendors to take a look at so they could see if they could really manufacture it. And the problem I struggled with was: the design was *ours*. However, all those other companies put their design effort into trying to get themselves qualified to manufacture our core memory. The qualification was based on the quality of their stack which had two elements—one was manufacturing, but the other was the design characteristics. What I struggled with was, the design was ours, but they invested all this effort. Was it fair to give this manufacturer one of these core stacks and let them look at it to give us an estimate? The property legally was ours. I had immediate reaction that I didn't want to do that because it wasn't fair. And the purchasing agent said, "You ought to think about that. We're out here trying to get the lowest cost of production for the company." That was one of the most agonizing factors. There were other engineering programs in parallel who did that. And that company was qualified to do the work. The reason I agonized over it was because there was a temptation. One of my goals was producing a product at low manufacturing cost, and I struggled with what was the right thing to do.

The fundamental question for me had nothing to do with whether it was legal or not. It was. But the real question was, Is that the relationship I want to have with vendors and the reputation I want to have? I had worked very hard with these other vendors to get them qualified and they put a strong effort into the work, and was it fair to take that effort which they put in and hand the designs that came from them to someone else and let someone else build an absolute copy? I thought, "Let's see, one of the things we could do is let them get a certain amount of volume and at that point say, 'OK, now we're sure you covered your engineering costs, we're going to take this stack and give it to other people and now you're going to have to compete with other manufacturers.'"

But the issue for me was, what was fair? And I just felt I couldn't do that. The criticism I got on the other side was people saying to me "Ron, I think you're crazy. These guys steal technology from each other all the time. There isn't anybody else in the business who would have that kind of concern." They would say "Gee, I really respect you; you stick to your value system. But I don't relate to it. Why do you want to do that kind of thing?" Finally I said, "The decision's clear. We're not going to do it." I then agonized and reevaluated for a long time.

That was probably the toughest one I've run across. And in looking back on it, maybe it was the toughest because there weren't sufficient external extenuating factors to pressure me, so it was all left up to me. There were no external influences strong enough to rationalize the decision. The pressure was self-made. You see, you usually rationalize after. When you have a tough one, cognitive dissonance takes over once you've done it.

The nub of the problem was: Is it right to take the technology of some other company who has worked hard with you in partnership, even though you have rights to it? You know it's legally right, but is it morally right to give that technology to someone else, and let them, through that technology, have an opportunity to be more competitive because they omit one step, the design, from their process? That was really the nub of the problem.

COMMENTS

Ronald Harris begins his tale of fairness to suppliers by stating that the situation was "about the hardest ethical dilemma" he had encountered. His difficulty appears to have had two sources. One was the conflict of obligation to stakeholders. While Ron believed it was his responsibility to the company to produce a product at low manufacturing cost, he also felt an obligation to his vendors to provide what he perceived to be a reasonable return on their investment of time and effort in designing a core system. Also, not inconsequentially, Ron was concerned about compromising his own values of fairness in vendor relationships.

The second source of Ron's difficulty was that he essentially had a choice of action in a situation in which he might have preferred some corporate constraints. His statement that there "weren't sufficient external factors to pressure" him is an interesting twist on the "whose choice is it?" question. In many of the situations in these interviews the pain of value or stakeholder conflicts is exacerbated by the pressures managers feel are applied from above in support of one side of the conflict. The pressures are particularly uncomfortable because of the often implied consequences of failure to act according to those directives.

But here we have a manager saying, in effect, that some support and guidance from the company might have been appreciated because the decision Ron was required to make was not really a single-situation decision. It was, or ought to have been, a policy decision. On the surface, a cynic might conclude that what we have here is a typical "profit versus people" situation—save a dollar for the company as opposed to caring about people with whom one has relationships. But that is not the case. In this situation, the company's task of producing its product requires that two outside services be obtained—the design of a core memory system and its manufacture. The company knows that and the vendors know that. The company also has budget, and cost and pricing structures that determine how development and manufacturing dollars ought to be spent. A policy statement specifying the limits of return on a developer's investment would not only have eased Ron's ethical dilemma by providing appropriate guidelines, it would have provided a measure of fairness in vendor relationships. When there are standard decisions that must be made by managers throughout the company, the lack of a company statement on what constitutes responsible management invites both arbitrary treatment of critical stakeholders (like suppliers) and ethical dilemmas for conscientious managers.

TOM
BENJAMIN

Vice-President, Head of Strategic Planning
Thirty-four years old

"Right from the start I found myself
attracted to her. . . ."

think ethics is the personal decision you make on behalf of someone or something for which you have a responsibility. It forces
you to take more into account than just your own self-interest, to
think about the effect of whatever decision you're making, the
impact of that decision on people, on organizations, or whatever
outside yourself. And it includes a responsibility to be sure that
what you're doing is not being done at the expense of others. One
word that seeped into my mind was conscience. Your conscience
is talking to you while you're making ethical decisions. Ethics
definitely implies going beyond yourself and your own self-interest
and looking at the broader effect of what you're deciding.

Most of the ethical issues I face in the business world have been
personal issues that have happened in the business environment,
as opposed to *business* issues on which I had to take a personal
stand. Let me tell you about one situation that comes to mind. I
was managing the regional office of a West Coast bank in New
York, with 125 people and half a billion dollars in assets. I decided,
and suggested to my manager, that we needed some management
skills training, and then negotiated with the training department
at the bank to send a couple of people out to do that. One of the
training consultants was to handle supervisory-level training; that
was about a dozen people on my staff. The other was to handle
senior-level training; that was six of us. The training for the six
of us was structured so that we met for three consecutive weeks
for a half day session each day. That was a big chunk of our time.
By phone I had planned with the training department exactly what
the content would be, and we really had some clear objectives for
the program. The woman who was doing the training was also
going to serve as a consultant to the six of us during the time she
was there.

Right from the beginning I found myself attracted to the woman
who came to give this training, although the attraction, at first,
was mainly professional. I thought that she was excellent. She
seemed to have the interpersonal skills to pull it off; and it wasn't
an easy group. I had a couple of older managers who were rather
fixed in their ways, and she found a way to play each person. I was
very impressed professionally. But on the third day, I realized this
was a person I'd like to get to know better. And I felt a real dilemma,

which I would dub an ethical dilemma: I had brought this person in for managerial reasons, I had a professional intent, and she was going to be here for three weeks. But I felt a personal draw to her and didn't know how I could deal with the two at the same time.

I have to add a footnote here. I have had problems in my office with managers who have gotten involved with people on the staff. In each case, it was men managers and women staff who worked for them. So I had had a meeting of all the professional staff (about 25 people) and laid out my concerns. So that had occurred a couple of months previously. And now here I was. Let me say what I did. I did two things. Now remember, there was another woman there doing the training for the lower level people. First, and I probably would have done this in any case with people from out of town, I asked them over to my apartment for drinks and for dinner. I asked them both for the same night, which I thought was safe, right? So I had them both come over to my place and we had drinks and then we went out to dinner. I certainly had a personal motive, in addition to responding to them in my role as manager of the office by making them feel more comfortable. My motive was to get to know one woman better. And I probably didn't do a tremendously good job that evening. The woman I was interested in was not staying at the same hotel as the other woman. So all of a sudden it was just the two of us. We sat and we chatted very romantically in front of her hotel just getting to know each other. And at that time, although nothing had been said, we realized there was an attraction there. And I still was facing my dilemma.

The second thing I did was related to a crisis in my office. One of our customers was throwing a fit over a load of historical things that had happened over their five-year relationship with the bank. They were threatening to pull back from us. That was very upsetting. So I brought her in and talked to her about this business issue of how to deal with that problem. I thought my neck might be on the line. So I asked her if she would have a drink with me. She did do that, and then she said she was going to see her brother on the upper west side. We walked around the block and she said, "Listen, I'm obviously attracted to you. I feel you might be to me, but I've got to keep my professional distance." I think in this case there was almost more at stake for her than for me. If it ever got out that there was what people would see as "hanky-panky" between the two of us, it would really hurt her professionally. So we both agreed we would play it as straight as we could on the job. We saw each other a couple of times in the course of those weeks in the evening. Then, when she was done with the three-week assignment, she extended her stay in New York.

One of the dilemmas, though, which I still had was that I had to evaluate her work. She had done an outstanding job. But the way I dealt with that situation was to ask my managers to submit their evaluations. It worked pretty well. This was a situation where I knew I had fallen in love with this women and that I would try to marry her. It was one of those romantic stories. And I knew some day this was all going to come out and I felt I had to do things as above-board and as deliberately as I could. In fact, when I finally told my boss I was engaged, I talked to him about all that had passed before and how I had tried to deal with it. He felt I had handled it properly and there were no questions in his mind. That's the story. That's how I dealt with it. I had strong concerns throughout the three weeks, especially, that intensive period when we were spending all that time together, seeing each other sometimes on the sly, so to speak, at night. But when I look back on it, I don't think I compromised her in any way.

I give her credit for bringing up the situation first, but we both recognized the tension we were feeling because of the personal attraction. It was very important for me to protect her—to protect myself, too, in front of my staff. But I had more concern for her because she had more at stake. One of the concerns I had was that I would let my personal feelings for her get in the way of giving my staff what they deserved in the way of quality training. I wanted to make sure I didn't lose that certain amount of professional detachment necessary to ensure that. That was hard to do, because at that point in time, anything she did was wonderful to me. And again, the way I dealt with that problem was opening the evaluation process to the group; having them describe what was working for them, what was not, and how they wanted to change things. It became a little more democratic than it could have been.

My managers were totally floored when I announced we were engaged. That was a couple of months after these first meetings, and they were just shell-shocked. Their mouths were wide open, just confirming that they didn't know. There had been a certain amount of sexual innuendo that went on. But that is not unusual with a woman and six guys around in a room five days a week, for four hours a day. But there was never any ill feeling on the part of anybody, and nobody ever threw up the problem that we'd had with sexual involvement with our staff members. Nobody ever seemed to link the two.

There was risk. There was professional and personal risk in it. Much more than I would normally enjoy encountering on the job. If I had developed a sexual interest in her and knew at least on the front end that that's what it was and that this woman was returning to the home office, it would have been one thing. But it was the intensity of my feeling and my attraction that really allowed me to overstep my standard. And here's another thing. If she was in New York and I had felt an attraction, I would have waited until the assignment was over, and she was out of the office, and then I would have made an overture. But here I had a one-shot deal. In three weeks she would be going back home; maybe she'd come back in 12 months to do some follow-up work. But that would be it. So I felt I had to play my hand. Does that sound like an ethical decision?

If I go back to the definition I gave you of ethical, I wasn't sure it was a good decision. But it was making choices that had an effect on other people, and I guess I was concerned with that. Let me try to think of anybody or anything that suffered. I don't think anyone or anything did. Part of what helped is that both of us are very serious professionals so we were not willing to compromise what we wanted to achieve professionally. But it was very difficult. From an ethics perspective, it troubles me that I had to hide something. There was another issue. It concerns the perceptions of other people, as to whether they think I am acting in the best professional interest of the organization or letting my personal life get in the way of good professional decision making.

I think the ethical decisions that get in the news are the exceptions. The ones where people decide to extort somebody or to pull money from the till or something like that. To the average guy those alternatives aren't even within the realm of possibility.

Where he or she begins to make compromises, to face conflicts, and to make decisions usually is in dealing with people. Do you want a quick story that comes to mind? We had a woman who worked for us in New York, a very hard working and lovely person. She had to go on jury duty. She was on jury duty two days, but she forged the form that the government gave her to change it to 12. She had been an ideal employee. She was Cambodian and spoke English very poorly. It was a clear case of dismissal; in the banking business people have got to be trustworthy. Her manager told me about it and brought her into my office and talked to her about it. She then said she would like to talk to me alone. She said she felt she was being harassed on the job and that, for instance, when she was going to jury duty her boss ridiculed her because she could hardly speak English. She was feeling such heaviness about the job and being there that she used the excuse of jury duty as a tool to get away. I really felt there was something in that. As a matter of fact, I went after her boss after that too and found there was a lot more to it. I found out there had been some sexual harassment of women on his part—dirty pictures he was showing. Once we began to interview some of his people, we saw problems that he had. I eventually got rid of him.

I still had the dilemma of deciding what to do about this woman being made to feel uncomfortable to the point where she couldn't deal with coming to work versus her forgery. Should I excuse the forgery and allow her to go on? I went back to my human resources manager in the home office and asked his recommendation. His recommendation was along the same lines of what I would have done, which was to let her go. I talked to her a second time and said that if she had come to us with the problem we could have grappled with it, and dealt with it. She was a lovely person and it was so hard to do. But a couple of months earlier I had terminated somebody who had forged a time card. He was a guy who had a disciplinary record and had had some problems, and I was happy to get rid of him; it was almost an excuse. But I couldn't fire him on the ground of forging something and getting paid for extra time and not fire somebody because she is a sweet, hard-working lady. I explained the dilemma to her and that I had to let her go. That was definitely an ethical decision in my mind, and it was a personal decision, too.

You have got to be consistent. You can be the hardest ass in the world, but you've got to be consistent. You have got to be basically fair, too.

COMMENTS

Several years ago, a colleague who was teaching a business policy course asked me if I could give him a list of "guidelines to managing ethically", which he could distribute to his students. I jokingly asked him if he wanted a "Ten Commandments of Ethical Management," to which he replied, "Oh, it needn't be 10; 15 or 20 would be all right, too." Although I could neither come up with such a list, nor direct him to an appropriate source, his request reminded me of how eagerly we all seek some form of absolute answer to— or way to deal with—those problems which have an ethical or moral connotation. If only "do not lie" *really* held in all circumstances. If only one did not feel driven to attach the word "except" to the end of statements of principles or values, particularly when applied to real-life situations. But the pluralistic society in which we live rarely allows us the luxury of a "sure thing" or an absolutely right response. To cope with this ambiguity, substitutes for a universal rule book are frequently sought. And one substitute to which many come is the idea of the consistency, the principle which Tom invoked at the end of his interview.

In both of the situations he described—with the attractive consultant and with the Cambodian woman—Tom faced a dilemma to which recent historical events applied. In the first case, Tom had spoken to his professional staff about "hanky-panky" between male managers and women staff which created "problems in the office." In the second case, an individual had forged a document reporting time at work. With such recent history, consistency seems a useful goal to help Tom, in his perception, be fair to all concerned. Tom mentions consistency only in connection with the second dilemma he recounts, but we can keep the principle in mind while examining the first as well.

In that case, Tom was torn between adhering to his own admonitions to his staff and pursuing a woman to whom he felt a strong attraction and who, if he did nothing, would walk out of his life in three weeks. At the action level, Tom wanted to do exactly what many of his male managers had done. And if he focused on the action level, that is, if he said, "Everyone who engages in that action must be treated the same," his decision would have been pretty clear: stay away! But Tom did not focus on the similarity of the actions. He looked at the dissimilarity of (or lack of consistency in) the thought or the intention. Although he does not say it explicitly, Tom implies the intention of his male managers had been to engage in "hanky-panky." And he further implies that had that been his goal, he should have acted as he wanted his people to act. But, Tom says he knew he loved this woman and wanted to marry her, so that although his behavior might be the same as his managers', the thought behind it was different. Therefore, his response—to continue the relationship—was, for him, acceptable *and* consistent.

In the second situation, we see, again, two similar actions. The former problem employee forged a time document, and so did the "ideal" employee. And here, again, we see two dissimilar thoughts, or intentions, driving the action. From what we can tell, the problem employee forged the time card to get extra pay. The woman forged the jury duty card to get a few additional days free of harassment by her boss. In this case, Tom's desire for consistency focussed on the similarity of action and not the different intentions (i.e., all actions must be treated the same way, regardless of the circumstances). And the firing of an "ideal" employee whose claims of harassment proved to be true, is an unsettling outcome.

It may be tempting to say that the difference between the two situations is that Tom had a personal stake in the first and simply found a way to meet his own need while not compromising his principle of consistency. But, I think the reasons behind the differences are more complicated. The critical question is, at what level are we being consistent?

First, the normal psychological process of seeking internal balance or consonance tends to be subconscious, rather than something done by conscious decision. So it is not clear that Tom—or anyone in his position—intuitively identifies levels of consistency. The instinct is simply to find a way to feel better. Those who find the principle of consistency a comforting substitute for absolutes need to acknowledge the less than absolute nature of consistency notion.

Second, Tom's focus on action in the second case may have been the result of that action being an infraction of explicit company policy. Although we know nothing about the culture of the organization, it is possible that this bank expected and reinforced across-the-board policy compliance. If such were the case, the institution was implicitly limiting the exercise of both managerial and moral judgment in managers like Tom. Point two is supported by the fact that Tom sought counsel from the corporate human resource manager who, knowing nothing firsthand of the situation, spoke solely as the voice of human resource policy.

We might also look briefly at the mechanism of using others to help solve ethical dilemmas. I think Tom would agree that he went to his human resource manager out of a desire to, if not diffuse, at least share the responsibility for a decision which caused him some distress. It is possible that had he chosen to make the decision alone, he would have done a more extensive search of the circumstances surrounding the two instances. On the other hand, Tom's use of his coworkers to evaluate the consultant for whom his feelings were admittedly biased was an effective and responsible action. It *does not* serve to lessen Tom's responsibility in the situation. If anything, it enhances his accountability by, as the saying goes, "keeping him honest."

CAROL
MILLER

Executive Director, Foundation
Forty-five years old

*"He wanted me to give that proposal
special consideration, based on him.
He's going to bad mouth me now."*

My job title is executive director of the corporate foundation. What that essentially means is that I run the day-to-day management and policy management of the foundation. This company has its own incorporated foundation as opposed to a gift-giving committee. It's a separately incorporated entity; it is now endowed. It receives its money each year from the corporation as any operating division would, and it is basically responsible for all or most of the giving made on behalf of the corporation, whether it be in the area of financial grants, product grants, in-kind services, scholarships, matching gifts, and a variety or range of other activities that benefit the corporation, the community, and the public at large. I sometimes think that I'm more of an operating director than I am an executive director because there is a lot of the day-to-day work of reviewing proposals, of making sure they get to the right places, of sitting in on all the meetings that keeps the process working as opposed to just overseeing and running the staff.

There is a staff of three people that work for me. We're all employees of the corporation. Then there are subcommittees that review all proposals after we get an opportunity to look at them among the staff to make sure they fit within the guidelines. There are between 40 and 50 employees that staff these subcommittees. All subcommittees meet monthly, and they break down in program areas. I sit on all those committees and oversee their operations to help them participate; I give them guidance and work on budgets with them.

We have an education committee, a community committee, a cultural committee. Those program areas get the appropriate proposals directed to them. Each committee is made up of members of the corporation from manufacturing, marketing, administration, publicity, and from a range of customer service areas. What it leads to is a fabulous interplay of everything the corporation is made up of, and it allows me as director of the foundation to interact at all levels of the corporation with people who represent where they come from, whether it's research or marketing or sales or manufacturing. In addition to those subcommittees, there is an operating committee of the foundation which I co-chair with the president of the foundation. The president of the foundation is always an officer of the corporation. He and I run monthly meetings of the operating committee. Recommendations from all of the subcommittees come to that operating committee, and the operating committee gives its final blessing on the range of proposals that come through. So essentially you have all the subcommittees meeting monthly with agendas, and you have the operating committee meeting at the end of each month to review what the subcommittees have done. So much of the good, hard, solid work goes on at the subcommittee level, which is what we envisioned. The operating committee has more or less become a policy group. It is very rare that anything a subcommittee will recommend will be voted down. Occasionally it will be sent back for further study, but it's very rarely challenged, and that's not because there is either lethargy or a lack of interest. It really is because we have gotten the power where it belongs, and that is with the people who are sincerely, honestly, and en-ergetically spending their time looking at proposals. They go out and site visit. They call agencies. They invite people in. They talk to each other, and they spend a lot of time on proposals. As executive director it's my job to make sure that keeps humming along and that process stays fairly well honed so that everything is working okay.

Influence and entree, that's what I have. But there are a few things that make that easy. One, there has never been any scandal around the foundation. There has never been any bad press. I remember years ago a vice-president saying to me, "If I read one day that some nonprofit has got three thousand pieces of our equip-ment locked up somewhere and is selling them, you'll pay." And there has been this implicit notion of trust that I have had which I've been able to put out there. So far nobody has taken advantage of it to any great degree. I'm sure there are things that happen along the way I don't know about, but on the whole there's been none of that.

One of the things we insist on at the foundation is that when you come to the table you come as a peer. We rotate subcommittees and operating committees. We had to institute a rotating tenure, which means you serve two years and you can renew for two years. But you can serve no more than a total of four years. And that can be very painful. You get some very, very good people, and you hate to lose them. You build up relationships. I feel like I'm always saying goodbye.

We have really put in place what I believe to be as close to a participatory democratic process as is possible. It doesn't always work so well; you can get stuck in things. Sometime I would like to be able to go out and make some very quick decisions on things I know are going to pass, and I get stuck in a bureaucracy. I always have to fight to make sure we don't get bogged down too long. Here's something else that's interesting: each committee chooses to operate the way it wants to. There's a chairperson of each committee who changes every four years. Each subcommittee works differently. The cultural committee insists that everybody read every proposal that's been sent. So there's a green bag that circulates all month long with proposals. When they come to the table, everybody's read every proposal, so people are reasonably articulate and able to discuss them. It's a lot of reading for people. Some people can't always do it. If you don't do it, you're not in on the conversation. That's one *modus operandi*. The community committee works by handing out proposals so individuals are responsible for proposals and prepare a report on each proposal for the following month. Theirs is a slower process because you have to decide who's going to get what and hand them out. Then they come back the next month. There are a lot of site visits. Now, one of the reasons community is able to do that is because our community grants tend to be within the local area. There's so much need here that we're never going to get out of it. We don't have enough money. We don't move out to other areas. So every program around housing, shelters, criminal justice, human sexuality, mental health, and day care will be looked at by individual members. Then they come back and report on each program they've looked at. It's a tedious, arduous, but very thorough review of programming.

The education committee has worked in a different way. I put the agenda out for education. I read all the education proposals. I do a precis on each of them, and I report on them. Then, individual members argue about the pros and cons. The committee is less informed, more reliant on me, but also very strong in their own ego development. We tend to call on research people. We tend to call on people who have a real interest in education, so there's a lot of room for participation. I think it's probably the committee in which I have the most power because in the end they will say "What do you think?" and I'm the only one who's read all the proposals. Many times what I will do is what I just did with one. I sent it to the chair of the education committee, who is a scientist, because I feel, on this one, although I will review it for the group, his input is very important. The one thing that both troubles me and pleases me is you need a very fair, honest, hard working executive director. If you've got that, it all works. If you get someone in here who wants to abuse the system, the system can be abused. It's a little bit like assassinating the president. If anybody really wants to assassinate the president, the president's going to get assassinated. And, you know, that's how I feel about it. It's both weak and strong, but I will make sure those things get covered.

I really do believe that when you are making a profit, and when you have been lucky enough to be in a position where you have been able to reap the benefits, that what you can turn around and give back into society is very important. It gives me great pleasure to know a lot of my efforts come to fruition around what this company does. It's very hard to represent a corporate foundation and worry about being sued, worry about the IRS coming in and taking away your status, worry about embarrassing the corporation in a scandal. I think my own politics, and my own view of life, is somewhat more radical than the way I am able to carry out my function, so I sometimes find myself not being able to be supportive of programs I feel I really should support. To some extent I always feel I'm selling out a little bit when I do that. I don't know whether I am. You know, when you compromise you really don't want to see that you're compromising, so there are a whole lot of defenses you use. And I know that if I let my credibility go out the window, I won't be able to get anything through. But I think about Helen Caldicott's film, *Eight Minutes to Midnight*. We had an opportunity to fund that. We didn't. And it was a mistake not to. And I should have gone to bat for it. The interesting thing about that is it's so in today. It's so amusing, because it's so in, that anybody who did fund it is golden. But we got hung up on mixed feelings about the issue of nuclear waste and hazardous waste. So there are times like that that I don't feel really good.

What I want to do now is talk about something that has just happened to me. I described for you the process at the foundation, and the way proposals come in and get funneled to subcommittees. Subcommittees look at them and make recommendations, and then they go to the operating committee. Now any proposal that falls generally within our guidelines gets to committee, and I'm diligent about that because there's no way I want to sit here making decisions in an autocratic way. There are many, many I turn down personally because they really fall outside the guidelines. It's very easy for me to figure out what has a chance, what doesn't, what belongs, and so on. So there are some immediate turn-downs. But if there's something at all sensitive, I will make sure there are a number of people who get to look at it.

There is someone whom I work with at the corporate level on a fairly regular basis. I'll call him Dan. We work flexibly together in a whole lot of areas, so there's a kind of good will that we count on. Dan currently is reporting directly to the president and CEO of the company, so he's got his ear. Even with as good a reputation as I have, I wouldn't want to go out and purposefully do something to alienate him if I didn't have to. Dan lives in the suburbs. His youngster goes to a preschool program in the community. It used to be a very well-known model preschool program and demonstration school; it did a lot of the training of teachers. The school, which charges tuition, has been for middle and upper class, mostly white youngsters. They have no low-income youngsters. But it's a fine education model, no doubt. They charge $2200 a year for a preschool program. They are looking to build up a scholarship fund so they submitted a proposal to our foundation for $4000 a year for each of two years: an $8000 commitment. Dan contacts me about it because he cares very strongly about it. It's all on the up-and-up; he's just telling me he cares. Because we're always interested in employees' input, I say, "Dan, send a memo that we can put with the proposal," which he does, supporting it strongly. I then bend over backwards and call him, because I read it, and I know the committee is going to look at this and ask why we would want to fund this? I mean we are a foundation that basically works with the less advantaged. We do some programs of excellence, but this is a preschool program not unlike ten in every suburb you could find. So I say to Dan, "How would you like to come in for 15 minutes when the education committee meets so that you might speak about the proposal?" He comes in. I present the proposal while he's there. He then—and I just corroborated this with a colleague—comes in with a cold, and in the most lackadaisical way, as if he doesn't want to get his hands dirty by being too much of an advocate, speaks about what he feels makes this a special school. He leaves and the conversation gets down to why would we want to support this program? Good for them, it's a wonderful program. Find ten more. Four in one community, five in another, six in yet another town, at $2200 a year, charge $2600 and start a scholarship fund. And it goes down. But it got a fair hearing; we've done everything we can to give that proposal a fair shake.

On my return from lunch today I get in a personal and confidential envelope a note from his man which says, "Carol, I finally heard from the subcommittee chair that the committee decided not to fund the school proposal in spite of the fact that (1) it was for low-income minority education, (2) in the community, and (3) received a request for very serious consideration from an employee. I don't even know if anyone from the committee had visited the school or talked to the school's director. You should know that I never support programs lightly. Somehow I had the illusion that you could influence serious consideration at the foundation. Next time I'll redirect my efforts and send outside parties directly to the committee chairman and members. [Signed,] Dan."

Now it seems to me, that aside from all the other angers that I feel, he really wanted me to act unethically. He wanted me to give that proposal special consideration, based on him. He is going to bad mouth me now. But if I had it to do over again I would do it the same way. In all of my history at the foundation, which is lengthy, I've really never gotten a letter like this. I would say that when a vice-president makes a request, we lean over backwards, and whether that is ethical or not, we tend in the long run to direct some dollars. The officers do it rarely. The president of the corporation, if he does it at all, always gives us money to do it. That's how ethical he is. Our founder, in all the years that I worked with him, maybe did it two or three times. So this fellow now comes out of the woodwork and sends me this kind of letter. What it does is put at risk our working relationship, which I think we both need, but which I certainly don't need to have headaches with. And what I am struck by is what he was implicitly asking me to do.

It's a dilemma, dealing with employee-supported proposals. We tend to do what I did with Dan. We had one guy, who, it was clear, cared very, very strongly about a proposal. It had to do with a youth chorale group going to a small European country, and it seemed to me that it was not going to fly. But I could see he cared deeply, so I asked him if he would like to come in and talk to the group. I told him I was not going to be able to do for him what he wanted done. In fact, he came in and he got a couple of thousand dollars.

So I was furious when I got this note from Dan. I wanted to pick up the phone and tell him what I thought of him, but I knew that once I got into a point-by-point debate, it was all going to get lost. But I did have the immediate response of wanting to say to him "How dare you. This is scandalous." My second response was to send it to the president of the corporation, with a note from me saying that I think this is outrageous, it makes me very uncomfortable, and I think you ought to know about it. But then I think that the president of the corporation needs another headache like he needs. . . . And I will be perceived as a headache carrier. So I think politically it doesn't make any sense for me to do that. The problem is if you don't let people know about it, guys like this get away with it all the time. I always remember the film *Gentlemen's Agreement*. If you don't stand up and say something when people do things that you think are abhorrent to do, it gives them license to continue to do them. So there's a part of me that would like to make public that kind of a statement. I put in a call to one person I wanted to talk with just because I needed a sounding board quickly. There's a part of me that's looking for public exposure. I mean by the weekend I'm hoping that it will go away, and I think it will, because I think it's probably not a wise thing to do. At the operating committee meeting on Monday all of the turn-downs get listed because we want the operating committee to see everything, not only what we're recommending but what we've turned down and why. The fact of the matter is we do bend over backwards to keep everybody as informed as we can. One of the things I was thinking of doing was making copies of this note along with the proposal, and distributing it so the operating committee, when we get to the turn-downs, gets to see this. I would love to do that. I'm not sure even that form isn't too public. What I would like to do is show it to my boss, and tell him what happened, and then let him do whatever he wants to do.

What I'm thinking of doing with Dan is not acknowledging it, which I think will make him crazy, so that he will finally say, "Did you get my note?" I was thinking of being absolutely Machiavellian and saying, "What note?"

It seems to me the ethical dilemma here is it would have been very easy to try and get him a little bit of money. If I got him a little bit, if I said to the group I would go out and site visit, and I came back and I'd said this really is an incredible program, I think if I wanted to work this into the ground, I could have put myself on the line and found a way to do it.

But my ethical dilemma now is: Do I blow his cover? If I don't blow it, am I doing that to save my ass? In other words, the less waves I make with him now, the better off I personally am going to be. The more waves I make, the more difficult the situation's going to be because he will be more vindictive. You say to yourself, "Do I need that?" On the other hand, should somebody be able to get away with something like that?

So I think there were two ethical components for me. One was that the only way I could have come out right in his eyes was to have given him special treatment, and in giving him special treatment, I think I would have been acting unethically. OK, there is that. The second gets back to what we talked about before: Does one have a responsibility to, in some thoughtful way, expose that kind of behavior, after all of the anger and immediacy of the reaction is past? And if one puts it away and doesn't deal with it at all, has one acted unethically in that one allows that person continued license to bully? I think those are the two ethical pieces of the situation.

MARK

HOFFMANN

Manager, Manufacturing
Forty-eight years old

*"I would be intervening in her life and
that bothered the hell out of me."*

There is a development group in this organization that has been in existence for some time, and their charter is to design technology products. The person who runs that group is a woman who has been in this business for many years. Her name is Jane. She has had to struggle with all the typical prejudices and biases men have had and that society has had against women working in science. Jane has a very liberal vocabulary. Her vocabulary is liberally supplied with four-letter words, which she uses regardless of who she's with. If she's in a meeting, she'll say, "Oh, f--- this," you know? Excuse me, but I think it's appropriate for me to. . . .

Part of the process here is that Jane's group does some work, and then they transfer the results of that work to my organization and we proceed to place the result into production. It is very difficult for my organization to do that. There's a long history behind the relationship between the two groups; some of the people in my organization used to work for her, and there is a lot of personal animosity there.

I had hired an engineering manager, Ken, who had been very, very successful in his former job. To use his words, "I took the worst manufacturing area there and converted it into the number one performing area in the course of four years; I'm pretty good at what I do." The first few interactions between Ken and Jane were tentative, to say the least. Ken was just trying to find out who she was; it was pretty obvious because of her vocabulary and how she treated people. She was very possessive about her own group, and very antagonistic toward all the other groups. It is difficult, to say the least, to deal with a person like that. But dealing with Jane's group is key to our organizational effectiveness, so we tried to be very low key in working with them. We hadn't been getting into arguments; we were trying not to be critical about anything that they did. I'm not sure I know the specific event that caused Jane to take the following action, what motivated her, but she walked into the cafeteria one day after Ken had been with the company for about two months, and said to two of Ken's employees, "Your boss is a f------ a------." She's in the middle of the cafeteria, in front of 200 people.

For me that situation presented the biggest dilemma in the world. First of all, the words she had said got to Ken, and Ken said, "I don't care what happens, but that has got to stop. You've got to do something about it. I've been trying to work with her for the two months I've been here; I don't think anything has happened, and her action was just absolutely uncalled for." So I thought about it. This kind of behavior probably has been tolerated in the past. She'd been known to do things like that, although nothing quite as blatant. So I said to myself, "OK, you've got to do something. You've got to go fix this damn problem. Here's a woman with years of experience, who's well thought of in the company in terms of her technical ability and the amount of information she has, but who is recognized as kind of obnoxious or ill-mannered. You have got to do something about her."

It was clearly hard for me to take action because it might do damage to her career or to her own self-image. I would be intervening in her life, and that bothered the hell out of me, even though it was important for me to do something because one of my people had been damaged by her behavior. But it was a hard decision for me to make. The question was: Do I take this responsibility for correcting a situation that occurred between two people—or didn't even occur between the two people directly? If Jane had said directly to Ken, "I think you're a f----- a------," I think that would have been Ken's problem to manage. But when she said it to some of Ken's people, it somehow became my problem and not Ken's. I felt my values say to me that it was my problem to face.

She's a tough lady. I didn't want to go talk to her. I was convinced that some peer or someone not directly in control of her future telling her she behaved badly would be ineffective in altering her behavior. That was probably some rationalization on my part. Also, I was probably scared to go over and have her tell me that *I* was a f----- a------. This whole thing was probably the hardest thing I've had to deal with in 20 years of working.

The question was: What was my role, what was my responsibility to my employees and to the well-being of this company? I guess I got the answer for myself: I would have to do something; this kind of behavior was destructive. I hadn't liked it in the past, although I hadn't done anything about it, and it was personally objectionable to me to have a person behave that way. I'm not sure if it was my ethics that drove me or my belief that Jane's behavior, as a manager in this organization, was unethical. I think it was the organizational link that I was making; that a senior manager in this organization should not behave that way to other employees. I felt the company was suffering. The company has values and positions it takes about how we treat people. I believe behavior of this kind is counter to that set of values, so it became an ethical situation for me. I also thought about my own self-image, about my responsibility as a manager in this organization, and how my behavior conforms to what the company wants itself to be.

Another thing that made it hard for me was that I could not understand why that situation had been permitted to exist. Clearly there are a lot of things that are hard to deal with—there are technical problems, resource shortages, and so on. But to do something about a person—to intervene in a person's life—I think that is tough.

It would have been easy to cop out and not do anything. It probably would have been easier for me to provide Ken with enough data about her behavior and tell him, "Forget it. She does that kind of crap all the time. Let's just accept it." It would have been easier to try to deal with the problem by making Ken feel better about the situation, than by trying to do something about it. But there was my loyalty to the company and my own personal sense of responsibility to my employees. There was also some anxiety on my part that Ken might not want to stay.

I wanted to keep Ken. That was important. But I had always disapproved of behavior like Jane's. I just had no direct mechanism for getting involved. I guess sometimes we all feel things are not right in a lot of places, but unless there's an entry vehicle we don't do anything about it. I have this fear of getting into the Don Quixote syndrome of jousting at windmills. You can pick up a cause any place you look if you'd like to, but that just doesn't seem necessary. It's interesting to think about why I would do something now and probably would not have done it 10 or 20 years ago. I think it probably took till I was in my middle forties to get up the courage to take on this kind of problem. My boss believes you are almost incapable of being an insightful, high-integrity manager until you get to be 40. I do think you are always pursuing something, whether it's just the poking around in the corners of your life that you do in your twenties, or the dedication to family and career that you go through in your thirties. You somehow gather enough information and you turn that corner in your forties to someplace that says, "Hey, this is what it's all about." You finally believe that you're going to continue breathing, and that you'll always be able to find something to eat, and that there's water to drink and that you're going to survive. You're secure, so you can take some risks and do some other things.

COMMENTS

The Carol Miller and Mark Hoffmann interviews differ from many that have preceded them in that in each it is difficult to identify the ethical concern. Both interviewees are saying they dislike a coworker's behavior and are not sure how to deal with it because (1) they have had no formal authority over the coworker, and (2) they need the cooperation of the person to continue to be productive in their own jobs. But neither is saying that the dilemma of having to chastise a coworker while maintaining a good working relationship is an ethical dilemma.

Carol indicates that her situation had an ethical component because her coworker, Dan, had wanted her to act "unethically" by giving special support to his proposal. For Mark, his evidence of an ethical problem is his belief that if he demanded a change in coworker Jane's behavior, he would be "intervening" in her life. The most striking feature of both interviews, however, is the anger the individuals feel about being put in a situation in which their integrity could be compromised. Reflection on the two problems suggests that the intensity of Carol's and Mark's feelings may have resulted from the awareness that they set the conditions that allowed Dan and Jane to act as they did.

In Carol's description of proposal evaluation, she tells us that each subcommittee designs its own process. The education committee to which Dan submitted his proposal is, by Carol's description, the least participatory of the subcommittees, with Carol taking the lead in setting the agenda, reading, and writing presentations on all the proposals, and reporting on them. Because the committee is "less informed, more reliant on" her, it is the committee in which, she says, "I have the most power because in the end they will say, 'What do you think?' and I'm the only one who has read all the proposals." Since the subcommittees are composed of employees throughout the organization, it is likely that the processes of each are generally known. This situation creates a setting in which the Dan incident can easily occur. If it is known that Carol has the power she acknowledges having on the education committee, it is not unlikely that coworkers, particularly people like Dan with whom she has been closely associated, would assume that if Carol sees the merit in a proposal, she will recommend and secure the funding. This is not to say she does exercise her power for preferred proposals, but that the structure of the committee encourages people to believe that could be the case. It is also not to say that Dan's note is not brash and inappropriate. But what the note does is make explicit an implicit belief about the education committee's selection process. The public statement (Dan's letter) of a condition which might pave the way for an inequitable process is what raised an ethical red flag for Carol.

Mark did not as much create the environment for the Jane incident to occur as he simply allowed it to develop. By Mark's own account, Jane had been behaving in an "obnoxious" fashion for years with no sanction by him or anyone else. Her public attack on Ken to his two subordinates seems to be the "kind of crap she does all the time." So the question is: Why does this become an ethical situation all of a sudden? It is evident that Mark's anger at Jane is for acting in a way that threatens him (Mark) with the loss of a valuable employee (Ken). It is only when he begins thinking of appropriate sanctioning measures that the ethical components entered his mind: What is my role; what is my responsibility? Am I intervening in her life? And these concerns are exacerbated, like Carol's, by his lack of previous response to similar behavior and, therefore, his contribution to allowing the situation to occur.

Mark's dilemma raises another interesting point. Although he does not say it, it appears that at least part of what made the problem ethical—and tough—was that his antagonist was a woman. One can only wonder (1) if Ken would have been as upset if the name-caller had been a man; (2) if Ken would have been less inclined to have his boss, Mark, handle the situation and would simply have addressed it himself, had the name-caller been male; (3) if Mark would have felt the discomfort confronting the name-caller—and thus the concern about intervening—if it had meant going one-on-one with a man. The point is not that men and women should be evaluated or treated differently for similar behavior, but that the values that Mark and Ken may have about appropriate ways of dealing with offensive aggressiveness may conflict with their values about correct behavior toward women.

* * * * *

Until this section, the interviews have dealt with ethical dilemmas created, at least in part, by organizational stumbling blocks. These three interviews—Tom Benjamin, Carol Miller, and Mark Hoffmann—reemphasize how organizational conditions can produce ethical dilemmas for managers, but they also demonstrate how this can occur even in situations where the managers themselves have created, or "are," the particular part of the organization in which they find themselves caught. These three interviews' special value is in diminishing the notion that organizations and individuals are natural antagonists in the ethical arena. Of course, they can be, but they can also be unaware collaborators—a condition that is addressed in subsequent sections.

EVELYN GRANT

Personnel Manager
Fifty-six years old

"If I did nothing, the only persons possibly hurt were the ones who 'failed' the tests. To report my findings, on the other hand, could hurt several people, possibly myself."

My title is personnel manager. My responsibilities include employment and placement, benefits, equal opportunity, training, the keeping of the records, and the maintenance of privacy and security of those records. I've been in personnel for most of my 22 years in this company, with the exception of about a year and a half when I worked in the shop as a first-line supervisor.

There are a lot of changes occurring in this company and in the way we do things. There is less tolerance for things that go wrong, for a product that may not be shipped on time, or for poor quality. Now there is a greater emphasis on doing it right the first time, on satisfying the customer, and on getting and keeping all the business we can. It's a different environment. I'm not saying it's bad. As a matter of fact, I find it very stimulating and interesting. In the past there was never that sense of urgency there is now. But some people find it difficult. They are not able to adjust to the new environment.

Formerly, things ran on a pretty even keel. If business increased we would hire people and promote people. When times were tough and there was a cut in orders, we would lay off people. We always had these ups and downs. We used to provide whatever training was needed: the shop would ask for a certain training program and we would provide it. Now, we are looking ahead; we are doing better planning. I am not too sure we are forecasting any better, but we are trying to see what is down the road in terms of our manpower needs, and trying to anticipate those needs so that we can plan for those ups and downs. We are looking at what our new products will be so that we can provide the training now, rather than waiting until the product is on the shop floor. There is also a great emphasis on getting our shop floor inventory down. We have had consultants come in; we've dedicated seminars to the management of resources; we've involved purchasing to make sure that what we purchase from outside suppliers meets our quality standards. All management is getting involved in these activities. I ask myself, "Why should I go to this or that meeting, since I'm in personnel?" But I am involved, too. I go. I am responsible for providing training to our people. Also, we are looking to do other sorts of training for management, for example, "How do you motivate employees?" "How do you develop and maintain trust?"

Basically the big difference between then and now is that we are involved in training our employees—both management as well as the rank-and-file—to develop different attitudes about quality work and good performance. That is the major thrust. We also are trying to develop an environment that will make people want to come to work. We're also moving in the direction of worker involvement.

Another thing that's changed is our performance appraisal program. We now follow a program to make sure we are doing things on time, we are documenting everything, we are consistent, we talk to employees, and make sure that they are informed during the year about how they are performing.

We always did have a yearly performance appraisal. In the past, 20% of the population could be rated outstanding or very good, usually, 5% outstanding, 15% very good, and then 80% were good. Occasionally there were some unsatisfactories. All the manager had to do was keep within those percentages. He could put anybody he wanted in any category without any documentation, without any kind of formal assessment. In 1979 we developed a definite performance appraisal program in which the supervisor met with the employee to outline the responsibilities, what was expected on the job, and how those expectations were going to be measured. They both would sign that agreement, and the boss's boss would sign it as well. We did that for a while, but we didn't continue. Now, we're doing everything. There is still the 5%, the 15%, and the 80%, but now we've got the full documentation. We move slowly.

What I like best about my job is the people. I like working with people. Actually I enjoyed my shop job. In terms of personal satisfaction, it was probably the best job I ever had. I was a first-level supervisor and I worked directly with people. Contrary to what a lot of supervisors told me before I went on the job, I found those folks to be very honest, hardworking, eager to do a good job—just salt-of-the-earth-type people. I could relate to that. I still see some of them. They call me up. They come in to see me. I like that.

I'm comfortable with my position now, but at the time I was promoted and moved into a management role I did not know what my position was with my peers nor with the people with whom I associated before my promotion. I never really felt comfortable.

For instance, I would go into a meeting with all men. I would sit down and sometimes nobody sat next to me. "Well, gee," I'd think, "What am I supposed to do now?" It gave me a feeling that I was not really wanted. But now I think they were not anymore comfortable than I, and simply didn't know how to relate to me. I had an experience once where I was at a meeting off-site with some men who were co-workers. When the meeting was over, it was lunchtime and they talked about going to a restaurant near the plant. I naturally assumed we were all going, but no. They actually left me off at the plant and went off to lunch. They thought nothing of that. A lot of the barriers are down. It is easier now, definitely easier. I think women are more accepted; and men feel more comfortable with women, too. So I think things have come a long way.

What I like least about my job is that there are so many things that are beyond the control of the job, yet the solution is still expected. Sometimes there is no acceptable solution. But you get— I don't want to use the word blame, but there is an awful lot of that going on. I don't know if it's like that in other companies, but it seems like there is more here now than there used to be. Everyone is looking to make sure he or she is not going to end up in a situation where somebody could point a finger at him or her and say "You didn't do a good job." I don't like that kind of atmosphere.

I have always had a good feeling about being part of this organization. I've had few negative feelings; I've always felt very proud to tell people I work here. This particular location has a very good reputation. Whenever we are hiring we never have a lack of applicants. As a matter of fact, that has been a problem. People who are working at other companies—even good companies—will come here to apply for work. So I think we've got a good reputation in the community. I feel I have been treated very well here; I've been given very challenging assignments. For the most part, I have been treated fairly. The company has been very sensitive to its employees' needs. In fact, even retired employees are treated with respect. We have a good product. It's nice to be involved in a product that is a benefit to mankind. It does good for mankind. It isn't something that can cause cancer later on, or blow up somebody. Even the manufacturing processes are clean.

I would call the company "caring" and "tolerant." It is also a little slow to change, and, right now, maybe a little defensive. But there is also an eagerness to get on with the job, a lot of self-confidence. This is an able company; it's a smart company. The "slow-to-change" is changing, too. We know that some of our products are being made better and cheaper by our competitors. And we know we will lose some markets if we can't get our costs down and our product quality up. We see a big challenge there.

I remember when I first came here everyone said this company was like a big dinosaur; you kick it in the tail and two years later it feels it in the head, or something like that. That was probably true then.

Q. *Where does "ethics" come up in this company?*

I have not really heard it come up. I think it's because we never really were involved in "business ethics"—that's not the right way of putting that. Our company has a certain way of doing things which I believe to be ethically and morally correct. Thus, ethics was never an issue. There have been cases where people will do something wrong because they think they have no choice. Their boss tells them to do it and so they do it, knowing it's wrong. They don't realize there are ways around the boss, and that they are not going to get fired, and are not going to get in any trouble. In fact, they are going to get into trouble if they do what their boss tells them. They think that because an authority has told them something, they have to do it.

Everyone has a sense of right and wrong; at least I think they do. There probably is agreement on the basic values, like honesty versus dishonesty, the clear black-and-white ones. On some other points, some personal feelings of my own, I'm not sure that other people feel the way I do; I don't expect them to have the same feeling I do.

Most of my ethical problems deal with people. They don't deal with the company. They deal with the company only because they happen here and they wouldn't have happened if I weren't working here. But I think they could have happened in any company.

One experience that comes to mind goes back to when I first became an employee of the company. I came to work for the company with the idea of getting into psychological testing. I have a background in psychology and statistics. I wanted to do some test validation and research. I was hired at a fairly low level. I think they wanted to see what I could do before they made a real commitment. The company at that time was depending on tests as a hiring tool to predict performance. One of the tests was a finger dexterity test. I tried to validate it and it was not significant. It seemed everyone passed the test; the only people who didn't pass it were those who had very short fingernails. They were told to go home, let their fingernails grow, and come back. That test was eventually discarded.

Part of my job was to administer a battery of tests to employees who had been recommended for supervisory positions. The tests were supposed to predict those who would most likely be successful as first-line supervisors. It took two straight days of testing to administer the entire battery to a group of 10 or 12 people. I also had available the statistical analysis of the test research that had been done by the corporate psychologist. When I went over his data and analysis, I found errors both in assumptions regarding the data, as well as actual errors of computation. This surprised me— and it bothered me. I reviewed some of the other statistical research the psychologist had done on other tests we were using. I found computational errors in some of them as well. A problem for me was "Gee, I'm a newcomer; the new kid on the block."

I had two choices: I could do nothing, or I could report my concerns to my supervisor. If I did nothing, the only persons possibly hurt were the ones who "failed" the tests. To report my findings, on the other hand, could hurt several people, possibly myself. The ethical problem I felt could be stated something like this: Was I willing to take a risk that I might not be believed or, perhaps, ignored when I present my findings versus the more likely possibility that I could come out of it looking like a competent professional at the expense of the chief psychologist, who could be damaged professionally. I rationalized a great deal before deciding to tell my boss. As it turned out, the chief psychologist did not attend the meeting that was arranged to discuss the discrepancies, and the entire issue evaporated, along with the test battery. I felt good about the outcome. No one really got hurt. The chief psychologist continued his job as though nothing had happened, and was eventually promoted to another job.

In thinking back, I guess the first question I asked myself was: Am I right in what I suspect? Do I know everything about statistics? Answer: No—I don't know everything about statistics, so maybe I am wrong, and if I'm wrong, it will make me look incompetent. That also was in the back of my mind: If I challenge him could he say that in this particular situation, or with this particular kind of variable, you can do that? I just didn't know. So that was the first question. The second one was: Who do I tell? Actually I don't think the questions came one, two, three. The thoughts just came rushing. And it was the consequences that really concerned me. If I don't tell, what does that mean? If I do, what does that mean? There was concern for the people who were being tested; there was concern for the person or persons who did the original research— what does that do to their jobs? There was concern for myself— what risk is there? Being new, maybe I felt I did not have much to lose. Basically, my concern was simply that the test criteria were not correct. I came out of school striving for objectivity. After being indoctrinated that way I could not continue to do the opposite, knowingly.

It surprised me that a person with that much power to implement this kind of testing, which was very costly, could have done it without there being some way people would know whether it was right or wrong. It seemed odd to me that some person at a very low level could be the one who could determine that the research was wrong. It seemed like I was indicting a whole system. That somebody could do some research—or anything, say, implement a policy—that was wrong, morally wrong really, and there was no watchdog who could evaluate objectively what was being done, was startling to me. It seemed like somebody else should have done that, not me. Of course, I could have come out a hero; it certainly didn't hurt me. It sort of gave me a reputation of knowing what I was talking about.

Let me talk now about a more recent ethical concern. One of the problems with our performance appraisal system is that it is too static. That is, rankings vary very little from year to year. A person's relative position in the ranking remains essentially the same one year to next. One person will rarely be moved above another person unless there is critical reason for the manager to do so. I have a department head, Fred, who was rated "Outstanding" many years ago. In about 1973 or 1974 (I'm not positive here, because I was not an assistant manager at the time, I was a department head like he was, so I would not be really privileged to what I am telling you—it's more from what I understand from talking to him), he suffered a loss in performance rating that was a result of two things: one, Fred had a very serious personality conflict with his boss which resulted in his asking to be transferred. The manager transferred him to the shop where he again suffered a loss in performance stature because of an experiment in a new style of management that he was conducting in the shop at the direction of his new manager. For one reason or another, the company felt the experiment did not work, and held him responsible. Now that's debatable—whether it worked or didn't work. The people who were involved said it worked, but they had no measurement to arrive at any conclusions. People were being transferred in and out of the department, and with the change in personnel, it was hard to get any stable measurement. So it was deemed unsuccessful, and Fred was moved laterally into personnel. During this period of time, and for the next three years, his performance appraisal remained low.

In 1977, Fred was in an accident, and he was out for almost a year. During that time, while he was on disability, I was promoted to assistant manager—the position to which he would report when he returned. When he came back to work, we had a talk to bring him up to date and to discuss the salary increase he was entitled to. The increase was small, and I informed him that the raise reflected his performance prior to his disability. I also told him that I had not participated in his performance appraisal, but that his former boss had. We talked about his performance standing, and Fred felt the low rating was unjustified, but that there was nothing he could do about it since it was the result of the previous shop experience. I told Fred, "I'm willing to give you all the help I can to move you up into a better position if I am convinced your performance warrants it." I didn't know him very well, and I didn't know what kind of work he could do. I really believed he was a bottom-of-the-barrel guy. One thing that really upset me was that during the year he was sick, after I was promoted, he was supposed to keep me informed of his progress, but he did not do that. He had an unlisted phone and nobody knew his phone number, so I couldn't reach him. He was also spending his time at his summer home, where there was no telephone. Now, here was a fellow who had worked in the benefit organization at one time, so he knew what he was supposed to do. When he came back I told him I didn't feel badly about giving him so small a raise because he should have known that he should have kept me informed regarding his progress. He acknowledged that. So you can see already I was a little bit down on him.

But here is the other part of the story. Fred turned out to be the best department head I have ever had. Now, granted, I was new on the job. I've been at these things for only a few years. OK, maybe I have not had many department heads; I've had three on that job. Fred was fourth. So I've had experience working with four department heads. But I've worked with a lot of first-level supervisors. Fred is one fellow who, if I ask him to do something, no matter what it is—difficult, on short notice, responding to a panicky female, whatever—he is responsive, he doesn't give me a hard time, he does a good job, he does everything I want. If I had had my choice, Fred would have been number one department head. Now here is where the ethical issue comes in. I couldn't do that because if I put him in as my number one, then anyone in the organization who was rated below him would be pulled down with him in the final rating which is done by higher management. Where he went in the previous year was going to be where he went in again, because you can't drastically change position.

We have four department heads in the personnel organization. Two report to me and two report to Carl, the other personnel assistant manager. My opinion was that Fred was number one. Now Carl didn't share that view. But I did have two department heads so I always could have rated Fred above the other one. Right? And if

I believed he was number one, he certainly should have been above the one who is my number two. But Fred has this reputation that no matter where I put him, he was going to be at the bottom. The process is that this list of four goes to my boss who melds them in with the rest of the universe in the organization. If we said, "These are our four guys and Fred is number one," then my boss would have said, "Since we 'know' Fred is the bottom of the department head universe, if you say he is your best department head, then these other three fellows have got to be pretty bad." So, do you take the risk of tearing down the other three people to get Fred moved up?

It's a selling job I have had to do since I have been on this job. In November of last year, for the first time we were able to move him. I had all the assistant managers (many of whom were new to the position) together and I went through the whole litany of how Fred got to where he was, and how I now viewed his performance citing specific examples. I got support from Carl, not to say that Fred was number one, but to say Fred was better than his ranking. Then I got support from a couple of the assistant managers' subordinates who dealt directly with him. It took me five years to do it, but I finally got Fred off the bottom. That was, to me, a real ethical problem I did not know how to resolve. I talked with him and he understood it. I wouldn't say it didn't bother him; he saw the unfairness of it. But it hasn't affected his performance. It could have. But it hasn't. He knows the system. He never complained about anything. He finally got a good raise this time because he moved up in performance ranking.

The ethical issue I saw was that I placed a lesser performing department head, my other department head, above him. Had I rated them as I saw them, it still might not have enhanced Fred's position, but it could have hurt the other fellow. Or if the positions were reversed at a higher management level, I could have been viewed as incompetent to rank my own department heads. The question is, do you take the risk? Can you change your mind if it doesn't work out? I talked with my manager. He understood and he agreed that the ordering was wrong, that it was based strictly on reputation, a reputation that was not even deserved. I don't like this feeling of playing with people's lives, and that's what we are doing. I've had three other department heads on this job. None of them had personnel backgrounds, and none of them was totally effective by the time they left the job because it takes a long time to learn. There's so much to learn in personnel. It keeps changing. So maybe in time they would have been higher, in my estimation, than they were. They were all competent people. But the fact is, at that time they were not as high as their performance appraisal would indicate. The first one was transferred from another location. He was on a fast track; they only wanted him here for about a year so he could get a little experience in personnel and in the manufacturing organization. And that's exactly what happened. That fellow went through a swinging door. They had him rated high potential. Maybe he was, but he wasn't on my job.

What troubles me in this situation is that, in my opinion, I was being dishonest in ranking the lower performer above the higher performer. It bothered me to do that. It still bothers me to do that. I had always had the ability to give Fred a little bit more money. But last year was the first time I was able to move Fred from the bottom into the middle.

I really feel personally very good now. Fred doesn't know all this. I would have liked to have shared it with him but it would have sounded like I was asking for some sort of gratitude. I really was very pleased, very, very happy, that I was able to get him from the bottom to the middle. To have gotten him up only one step would have been great, but I moved him into the middle. I don't know whether I overwhelmed them or what, but he got there, and we were able to maintain the relative ranking of the other department heads.

Because I knew what was right to do, I really felt I was impotent, that I couldn't do anything, that I didn't have the power. I was stymied by the system, so the only thing I could do was to work through time within that system, and get him into a position where people saw him from a different perspective. I was very thankful we turned the corner. I'm not saying he'll every be viewed as an outstanding performer again. I don't think he will.

I am not sure that for me the ethical part of a problem comes up first. I think I deal with a situation from an action perspective. I start thinking about how to implement a solution and I might start feeling uncomfortable. Then I start analyzing: "Why is this bothering me?" And then I say, "If I do this, then that is going to happen, or this could happen, and if that happens, maybe it's not right." I analyze the ethical issue, but I don't think it is the first part, unless it is terribly obvious.

There are some general types of situations that raise ethical dilemmas for me. There are times when I'll say something, or take a position, or give a direction that turns out to be wrong or a mistake. If it's with subordinates, they are not going to challenge or bring it up to me. But it bothers me if I do not tell that person what I said or did was wrong, and let him know I recognize that it was wrong. I don't want that person to think I still believe what I had said was right, when he knows I wasn't right. It goes back to that feeling of being truthful. I seem to think of that all the time. How does that person view what I have said in terms of being open and sincere? In a position like mine, you say things to other employees, and sometimes you say things that are incorrect. I always feel compelled to go back to that person and say, "Hey, I goofed." I want them to know that I know it. I don't know whether that's ethical or not. It would be easy not to say anything since I am the boss and it is embarrassing to have to go back. It's saying to somebody, "Hey, I may be assistant manager here, but I don't always have the right answers."

COMMENTS

With Evelyn Grant, we begin those interviews in which the protagonists deal with personal ethical conflicts within an organizational context. In these situations, the organization is either neutral in relation to the manager's concern or else provides the support and resources to allow the manager to implement a painful decision. At this midpoint, we will recall the factors that affect the emergence and management of ethical dilemmas at work by looking at Evelyn's two situations from the perspective of key organizational and individual factors.

Evelyn's first dilemma, the testing situation, is particularly interesting because it is an example of an ethical concern frequently discussed in business situations: whistle-blowing. The accomplishment of effective whistle-blowing depends on an intertwining of organizational and individual factors. An organization must provide a receptive environment, with appropriate mechanisms and safe-guards, that encourages healthy questioning but not irresponsible finger pointing. An individual must have certain values, needs, and skills to question thoughtfully and respectfully.

Organizational Factors

Four organizational factors seem to have provided an appropriate environment in which Evelyn was able to question the validity of the assessment tests. The organization was caring, it was tolerant, it valued research and inquiry, and it admired demonstrable technical expertise. The first two characteristics, if not real, were perceived so by Evelyn, and made it easier for her to voice her concerns. The second two values enabled Evelyn to challenge the testing materials and to draw on the support of her manager to find a way through the ethical dilemma and to protect herself from unpleasant personal fallout. We can assume her manager was comfortable in asking the challenging questions because he, as well, believed the company's values would support his doing so. Of course, the "don't rock the boat—maintain the status quo" aspect of the firm might be thought antithetical to a challenge to ongoing procedure; had the challenge been drawn more dramatically than it was, the outcome might not have been as positive. But it appears that both Evelyn and her manager recognized the need to move slowly and cautiously, to question rather than challenge, and to engage only those people (themselves and the psychologist) directly involved in the situation. Of course, the outcome was not dramatic either. The psychologist was not publicly castigated nor did he suffer any personal consequences. But the unethical practice was stopped, meeting Evelyn's ethical concerns.

Evelyn's second dilemma concerned performance evaluation. Until a changing, competitive environment resulted in increased attention to quality and productivity, Evelyn's company managed effectively with a simple performance evaluation system. A result of that system was the development of a norm, or implicit value, of performance ranking. Everyone "knew" where each employee "fit" in the performance structure; no one questioned or challenged it, because to do so would have been contrary to the culture of the institution. However, when new competition hit, the company was forced to find a way of responding. Hence, a performance appraisal system, requiring full documentation, was put in place to develop and reward excellent performance and to treat employees in a fair manner. In Fred's case, however, the intended outcome was elusive, resulting in Evelyn's ethical dilemma.

The dilemma is not a result of the new system. Rather, it is due to the incompatibility of the formal procedure with the decades-old norm of performance ranking. I am in no way suggesting that the formal procedure was "bad." It was not; in fact, if implemented properly it should have prevented what actually happened. But the imposition of a procedural change into a well-established belief system created an arena for ethically questionable situations.

Because the culture of the organization had so forcefully shaped the situation, Evelyn had to find a way of managing the dilemma that would respond to the demands of the present value system while trying to change it. Had she simply blustered through, demanding Fred be ranked higher than others presently above him, she would have triggered another ethical problem. Although Fred would have been treated in a just fashion, others would have suffered, and the system itself would have remained firmly in place.

Evelyn describes a feeling common among managers trying to deal with ethical dilemmas. She says she felt "impotent"; she "knew what was right to do," but she was "stymied by the system." The mechanism she chose to correct the problem was to document all of Fred's activities and to build a network of support within the relevant parts of the company. This mechanism, as we will discuss below, depended primarily on her own skills and relationships. And, contrary to her situation 20 years earlier, her commitment to the company and its culture guided her actions to rectify an unethical situation.

Individual Factors

One of the striking things about both of Evelyn's situations is that she was able to draw on her perception of her position, her skills, and her relationships with others to work within an organizational system and responsibly handle an ethical concern. When Evelyn found herself with the task of administering tests that seemed to be of questionable reliability and validity, several aspects of her situation enabled her to blow the whistle. First, she held a loosely defined formal role. The formal task required that she administer and score a series of tests to determine supervisory potential, provide "win or lose" feedback to the candidates, and make recommendations based solely on scores to the personnel department. Her description of the job suggests that she was given testing materials and formal instructions on how to administer and score; then she was left on her own to implement the task at one company location. The designer of the tests was not on site, so there was no "expert" checking on her work. Her interview suggests that her boss was her superior administratively, but had no expertise or experience in the work she was doing. Hence, her formal task was an independent activity with considerable freedom in its conduct.

Evelyn's freedom in the job was enhanced by her perception that she had been hired with few preconceptions as to what she would and could do. One view could suggest that this situation was ripe for all kinds of conflicting role expectations—with Evelyn, her boss, and the psychologist expecting different things. But the genuine flexibility allowed her to perceive and enact her role as she wished; she could expand her task requirements to include "checking" the reliability and validity of the tests she was to administer, as well as challenging those tests when they did not measure up.

Role flexibility alone, however, did not enable Evelyn to take action in this situation. Two other factors were critical. First, as a recipient of a masters' degree in psychology, Evelyn had a strong interest in and enjoyed statistical work. She seems to have been experiencing a new sense of intellectual prowess and was eager to put it to the test. Of possibly greater importance, Evelyn felt she had little to risk. She was new to the job, and her career plans were formulated only casually. Thus, neither job nor organization, at this point, formed part of a grand scheme of things for her. The stakes were not high; whatever the outcome of her questioning, she did not feel she had a lot to lose. Because she had no longstanding relationships in the company, no established reputation to uphold, and no future career plans dependent on successful management of this job—and because she believed she was sufficiently knowledgeable to back up her claims with data, not emotion—Evelyn was able to manage an ethical dilemma to what she felt was a successful outcome.

Evelyn comments that she was surprised there was no "watchdog" to evaluate the psychological testing, and that a newcomer (herself) could pick up something no one else in the organization had noticed. In all likelihood, her newcomer status is the key factor. She had not been around long enough to take for granted the values and norms—"the way we do things around here" feeling—that other members of the company did. Her lack of acculturation enabled her to see the problem.

It is also worth noting that Evelyn chose a method of questioning that allowed the institution to correct the problem and everyone to save face. Her decision to work through the company hierarchy by going to her boss, and her decision to ask questions rather than hurl challenges facilitated the achievement of her ends. Obviously these decisions were largely the result of personal style and skill. But it would be a mistake to attribute success solely to individual personality. The confluence of organizational factors which provided a receptive environment with the individual factors of role flexibility, high interest, and low perceived personal risk was key to the effective management of this dilemma.

Evelyn's management of the performance evaluation situation offers an interesting contrast. First, Evelyn's role in relation to the dilemma is clear. Evaluating performance is a task requirement. Implicit in that requirement is an assumption that the evaluation be done *fairly*. The purist might argue that there may have been different implicit role expectations for "fair evaluation"—and such may be true. But essentially there was little flexibility, confusion, or conflict around what her role was. Second, Evelyn was no longer a newcomer to the organization. This time she had a greater stake in the outcome of the situation: She had recently been promoted and she had a reputation to uphold (although it was a reputation that did give her credibility to act). Similar to her earlier experience, Evelyn was working in an area in which she felt skilled and in which she was interested. Recall that the critical organizational factors were the new formal performance appraisal procedures and the old, implicit ranking system which sat in conflict with each other, the company's basic responsiveness to employees' ethical concerns, and a resistance to change.

Evelyn's management of the dilemma was an action shaped by individual and organizational factors. She moved slowly; precipitous action would have increased potential personal consequences (no time to pull back should anything go wrong), and would have been out of sync with organizational style. She documented everything, using the formal procedure to chip away at the traditional belief. She built a network of agreement among members of the organization who were responsive to her input. And she did all of these things within the formal guidelines of her position, thereby limiting challenges to her right or authority to so act. Once again, a successful outcome was achieved by managing within congruent and supportive organizational and individual factors.

RONALD
HARRIS

Manager, Custom Products Division
Forty-three years old

"It might be tough to rationalize
that in terms of the public good,
but I didn't have a problem with it."

I am manager of custom products division, which is the group that supplies equipment to add to our standard offerings to solve a customer's problem. Our group has the special engineering to solve the problems the customer can't solve with standard equipment. We have a family of specialty products, for example, that came about because customers have unique problems and, since the market for these products is relatively small, they are not the kind of thing our company can invest in. So our customers fund the development. We often see a family of requests for the same product. In the case where we see a trend, we may internally fund and develop that product and supply it to the customer. You could really say we have three kinds of products. We have a product that is totally specified by the customer: he says what he wants, we sit down with him and write the specifications, we provide a quotation, and we sell it to him. Another kind of product we have is a form of standard product, where we hear a trend of requests from customers, and we see that there's a hole in our standard product line. Then we also have the combined case where we essentially go into a joint venture with the customer. In this case the customer funds a part of the engineering costs to develop the product. Since we develop products which our customers specify, our goal is to be very responsive to the customer and fulfill his needs. In essence our organization responds opportunistically, but within a general strategy of responding only to needs which have volume potential.

We're a very engineering-oriented organization in that everything we do is engineering intensive. We have engineers, but we also have marketing and presales people who support us, and postsales people who support the services end. We're probably the most complete division in the sense of having all the functional areas contained within us. Most of the other divisions in the company are marketing entities and draw on central engineering resources and corporate manufacturing. The reason we have self-contained resources is so we can be responsive opportunistically to customer needs.

I'd like to talk about a situation I was involved in when I was down in our southern region business unit. Our group was an active bidder on a municipal procurement for which there were six competitors. Usually a municipal government contract is awarded on a lowest cost basis, and we don't want to get involved if that's the way it's going to be awarded because I just guarantee you we won't be the lowest bidder. The person we were dealing with assured us that, first of all, he wanted us to bid because we were good, and second they would not necessarily award to the lowest bidder. So, we did a factual review of the terms and we shipped the contract off to Legal. We needed business badly as our shop was only booked three months out. I said to Legal, "We've got to agree which of those terms are business issues and which are legal problems for us. Let's break it apart."

So we went through the contract and there were half a dozen legal things that we had trouble with and ten or 15 things that were all business or financial problems. Then there were some issues that were gray, like consequential damages. We just don't accept a clause that says a customer can sue us for damages that are of consequential nature, which occur because we fail to perform. For example, say we were unable to deliver a test system on time, and the company had taken out their existing system so they weren't able to do testing; if they think that the impact on the organization was that they lost 40 employees and it cost them $10 million, they could sue us for $10 million in damages. We just don't accept those terms because they tend to be unbounded, that is, a combination financial-legal issue, and the only way it can become acceptable is if it is bounded financially.

The best way to describe the situation in this particular case is that there were a number of these kinds of terms, so we went back to the customer and said, "We aren't going to bid. We can't." He said, "We'll fix it." And I said, "How are you going to fix it?" And he said, "Let's put a limit on this. For example, I'm going to put a ceiling on damages, we'll limit them to the value of your system." So I called our legal guy and said, "Does that work?" He says, "Oh sure." So we chalk that up as OK.

As we worked our way through our concerns we just kept getting roped in deeper and deeper. We wanted the business badly, and our customer kept knocking down all our issues. We were crossing the Rubicon, inch by inch, in terms of getting committed. Each time you go through one of those tough little things, a little cognitive dissonance comes up, and when you get through it, it's harder to go back. You keep building up a commitment and eventually you find you're sunk in and all of a sudden you lose sight of your objectives.

Finally, we got to a point where I was ready to turn in the bid, and I said, "I told you we weren't going to be the lowest bidder. What are your selection criteria?" And he said, "You don't need to know the selection criteria," and he handed me a sheet of paper with the bids of our competitors. We knew what the other guys were going to come in at. Now I had a tough decision. The decision was: Do I bid? Do I report this individual because he's clearly breaking the law? His motivation was, as far as I could tell, not corrupt in the sense of increasing his own pocket. He simply wanted our equipment. That was very clear. He was going to solve his problem; he was going to get our equipment for the contract. So the decision was a tough one of (a) do I, on one extreme, make a big deal about it—let it become a public incident and get this guy run out of town on a rail?—that's probably what should happen to him; (b) do I take the information and put in a bid $1.50 less? or (c) do we withdraw? So that was the situation.

It was clear we had to disqualify ourselves. We had soaked a lot into this bid attempt, but to go forward, even if we made it public and got it all squared away just would not work. So we immediately withdrew and said, "We're sorry, we can't bid. You just made it possible for us to pursue the bid at this point." That was the easy decision—now for the hard one.

I went to my boss for help. "OK, we've got two alternatives, either to withdraw in silence or to get this guy out in the open." We agonized over it a lot; I got a lot of help from the top, and we decided that we would walk away quietly.

The reason we decided to walk away quietly is that we tried very hard to construct whether or not we thought the guy was operating from some situation that we didn't know about, or whether in fact he was just driven to get the best technical solution. We did a lot of work on that, without complete data, and concluded that he was going for his technical solution, and that's all he was doing. And on that basis we just withdrew and decided it was hopeless at that point because it would never get handled the way we wanted it to. We were the ones who came out worst.

The hardest issue in that one was whether or not to expose this individual. There was no easy recourse at the top level, because this person tied right into the top level of the municipality and it wouldn't pay. It would be impossible to take it the next level up because that level was political.

The guy was very heated about it, angry, upset. He tried to restructure his bid proposal and start over and get us to bid. We just wouldn't talk to him and eventually he lost his job because he never closed the deal, never got the bid. In other words, what he had shown us was what these people were intending to bid, but he withdrew the document so everybody went into wait mode. Then he tried to maneuver around. It ran into delays and when he was ready to come back again, they had lost patience with him.

I don't know what he was saying to the rest of the industry. It was just one of those things where to this day I'm still not sure we did the right thing by not exposing him and getting it out in the open. The real issue was how do we get this guy exposed on the one hand and on the other, protect the company?

When it happened, I was angry on the spot. The reason I was angry was because we poured a lot of effort into this thing and I just knew instantly that everything was gone. There was no way we could have just lost the bid, so I was angry not only from being challenged personally that way but because I had dumped so much effort into this thing. I was also angry at myself because the legal guy was really warning me all along. He said, "You can't meet that contract." In this case, the only reason I got sucked along was that our customer said he's be willing to work the issues.

Everything seemed straightforward and harmless until he came down with the memorandum and said this is the number you have to bid. His words were "Pick what you would take out in order to make the contract meet that number. I'm not asking you to cut your bid to this, because you said you can't come in the lowest. Just take something out. Tell us you're going to do that and we'll make sure you're happy."

There are probably some people who would accept that, but to me that's just wrong. But the hard part was knowing what to do next, now that you know this guy's behaving totally irresponsibly. To this day I still have a problem. I don't have any trouble rationalizing it because he never even awarded the contract. He disappeared and never came back. The contract was awarded but under a different management structure, and to this day I don't know if there was some other form of corruption occurring. The dilemma was "Do we expose him?"

I'm sure 99% of our people would have broken off the discussion, but I don't know how many of them would make sure that it got exposed. Most probably wouldn't. It was a hard decision to make in terms of what to do about this individual, but it was made easier for me because I got help.

The major influence was the legal fellow. He did a very good job in constructing a decision process. In fact I learned something about decision processes to which I can apply all my life problems. He said, "Here are the alternatives. Let's play through all the scenarios before we do anything." And he said it's a morality issue: ratting on a bad guy versus having a tough situation in the company. We decided the losses would be too great.

It might be tough to rationalize that in terms of the public good, but I didn't have a problem with it. I didn't feel we were being particularly selfish. One of the scenarios was that we'd back away and then the story would come out through another vendor and we would get accused of being culpable anyway. There was a point there where we almost thought we should expose the rat because of fear it would come out anyway.

We wrote a formal letter of withdrawal, with notification to the entire program, which is unusual. I'm sure the competitors must have been wondering why we were doing this. It worked out fine, but it could have been a real nasty one. Careers can be broken over things like that. I took some heat about my judgment when the issue became obvious.

The question was: Should we have done this from the start? My perception is that I didn't get hurt the way I could have really been hurt. And in looking back on it, I think if one of my managers ran into that problem I would probably have given him some feedback that we got too close. We should have been aware of the tip-offs that this could be a compromising situation.

If I had backed out early on, it wouldn't have been a question of ethics. I would have done it on the business consideration which was: Is it smart to spend company resources chasing after that bid?

Of course, there was pressure from the sales organization; it was looking for an order. But I don't believe there would have been pressure from the top, and the reason is that in the scheme of things this wasn't that significant. They knew I was looking for business. They knew I was bidding on this thing. It wasn't as though I was working on my own. It never became a moral issue until the end. In retracing everything up to that point, there wasn't any signal that it would become a moral problem. We first saw the great creativity which this guy went along happily helping us to be a successful bidder, which we felt was great. It was just a question of what we should do. " We obviously will win this bid if we overcome the obstacles, and this guy's working his heart out to help us overcome them." Now that series of events happens all the time, it really does. It just never comes to—well, I shouldn't say never—it probably also often comes to the point where you get some hints. The issue here was that it was blatant, but I wonder how many situations there are where salespeople say, "I'm going to need a price tag on it. I'm telling you, you're going to really have trouble with us if it's $125,285." And you know that's somebody's last bid. I'm sure it happens all the time and salespeople deal with it everyday. I almost dread to see how it gets handled. I bet it's highly variable and I bet we probably make mistakes all the time. And sometimes it's appropriate. Because it's said in the context of "that's all I've got to spend."

Where's the point where it becomes ethical? In this case it was just too blatant. The other thing was that I'm not sure we would have reacted with quite the same emotion and vigor if it were a private bid as opposed to a municipal bid. A municipal bid, the practices and the policies and the mechanics, are enacted by law. In a private bid, the purchasing behavior of a company may be highly variable. In some cases we have open competition. I have been to a bid meeting where the purchasing manager sat down and there was three of us—Company X, ourselves, and Company Y sitting there—and he said, "Now Company X bid this. And Company Y did this. And Company Z (us) did this. And the problem I have Z's bid is this; the problem I have with Y's bid is this; and the problem I have with this guy's bid is this. And I want you guys to come back with your offer." And I guess that's a reasonable practice if the purchasing department runs it that way. In that case I guess there's equity because you call all the competitors. But the point is, it's so variable.

COMMENTS

The case of Ronald Harris and the municipal contractor is, in many ways, an analogue to the situation recounted by Jackson Taylor. Taylor, whose company defaulted on a new version of an earlier switching system, faced a dilemma largely because the company had neglected to act anticipatorily on information it should have known. In Ron's case, it was not the company, but Ron, himself, who should have attended to early warning signals and anticipated the outcome of continuing down a potentially thorny path.

Ron's dilemma was triggered by his decision to make an exception to his own standards about the submission of bids. Because his shop needed business badly, Ron disregarded an early gnawing in his stomach, which suggested to him that the negotiations with the municipal contractor might lead to a compromising situation. Ron's standard practice was to prepare a bid for a customer according to specs and his own best judgment about what was required to provide the product. Only in exceptional cases did the customer feed back suggestions to allow Ron and his group to tailor the proposal to win the bid. So at the very beginning, Ron laid the groundwork for a potential ethical dilemma. And he is well aware of this when he alludes to "crossing the Rubicon," and getting himself further and further committed.

Once the contractor showed Ron the other bids, Ron was faced with two problems. The first was relatively easy to handle; the second much more difficult. The first concern was: Should he cut off the relationship with the contractor? For Ron, this concern was not a dilemma; it was a relatively simple matter of right and wrong. He had been asked by the contractor to break a legal contract and to behave in a dishonest fashion. Despite the need for business, and pressure from the sales department, Ron *did not* feel pulled in several directions. The issue was straightforward: Do you look at others' bids in a blind process? His answer was "no."

The subsequent concern, however, posed a difficult dilemma: Should he "rat on a bad guy" at the risk of the company suffering reputational consequences (e.g., "who wants to do business with a whistle-blower"), or should he just keep quiet and allow the fellow to go his way, possibly masking other corruption and/or allowing the contractor to engage in corrupt activities elsewhere, so that the company could be protected? The dilemma was further compounded by the concern that if the contractor were not exposed but the story eventually came out, would the company not look even worse?

For Ron, the personal standard about blowing the whistle was nowhere near as clear and answerable as were the personal standards about honesty and law-abidingness. In the latter case, he did not agonize over that problem; where to draw the line was not in question. So, the dilemma nature of most ethical concerns in business notwithstanding, it appears there is a time when competing claims no longer exercise control over decision makers, and this is characteristic of ethical dilemmas in general. There is a bottom line of personal principles that will *not* be compromised. The fact that blowing the whistle was above that bottom line when juxtaposed with potential company harm was a different circumstance. In the first case Ron acted with the belief that the company would stand behind what, for him, was an act of conscience. In the second situation, Ron, himself, is less clear on what his own values would dictate, and, thus, in less comfortable imposing them on the company. Once comfortable that his own principles could accept a decision either way on exposing the contractor, Ron moved to resolve his dilemma by turning to others in the organization.

FRANK
McGRAW

Manager, Purchasing
Fifty-seven years old

"This is the kind of ethical thing
you get into. It's not black; it's not white.
You're not responsible legally;
but you are responsible. The question is,
what are you responsible for?"

In many purchasing situations, the major concern is fairness. How do you determine being fair? It's a matter of your ethics, your beliefs, your guidelines, the way you do your work, the way you live. The word "fair" has to have the same meaning to every one of my buyers. "Are you being fair?" Now, that same question may not mean the same thing to everyone. Am I right? For example, I talked to one group this morning and I said, "Joe, you've changed since you came out here from L.A." He said, "What do you mean?" I said, "Well, you remember when you were out in L.A. the world used to be real big? You bought all over the place, right? Now that you're buying here at this location, what did you tell me yesterday? That you only deal with your local suppliers? How come? How come you changed and you only deal with your local suppliers? What happened to the big world out there—competitors, L.A., San Francisco, what happened to all that? You've changed."

Now when I talk about being fair, I'm not sure being fair means the same thing to Joe as it does to Frank McGraw. He said, "Well, I really don't want to go out of this area because I've got to have my guys close by in case I need them for this and that." But, he may be able to get a better price if he goes down to New York or somewhere where it's more competitive. The whole thing was just an exercise. I thought I'd ask, because that's not the same way I think. Is that ethical? That's what I ask myself. I'm saying to Joe, "Is that ethical?" And he's saying, "Yeah, sure, that's ethical. I've condensed my world to this." And I said, "My world is out there." We're not always on the same wave length. What is best for the company? What is best for you? What is best for him? What is best for the supplier?

I've got a situation now that I haven't resolved yet. A product that we have been making here at the plant has been canceled out; we no longer are going to make it. I have open orders with an existing supplier, Supplier X, and the value of the open orders is roughly $475,000. He has cancellation charges in there for around $300,000. Now, in addition to that, he's got another $300,000 worth of material to build a product that he thought I might be planning to order. Is that an ethical problem? Well, I'll tell you—we haven't gotten into the negotiations yet, but this is one. He says, "Frank,

*cancel your own
order 300,000*

I know that legally you're not compelled to accept the other $300,000, but I went ahead on my own to satisfy your short interval needs. I wanted to have the material there to support you, so over time, I've built up over a quarter of a million dollars worth of raw material components in various stages. For you." The first $300,000 that he talks about is the cancellation charge for the $475,000 open order. We can go through that exercise pretty easily to make the determination that we will concede those dollars. But now you get into the area that I would call gray. My company would take the position that they are not responsible for that second $300,000. You've got to remember when I submit cancellation charges to the company, they will say they are responsible for the first $300,000 and not the second. Therefore, it's your problem, Frank McGraw. So that's the dilemma I'm involved in today. I haven't gotten into negotiations yet, but I will have to. Somehow I will have to assume some responsibility for part of the second $300,000. I have to share some of that with the supplier, and as of this moment I don't know how I'm going to do that. No question about it. A lot of the business that I placed on him was short interval. He needs X amount of time to get the raw material and to make these particular types of components, so his raw material lead time is quite long. He has to have enough raw material on hand so that when I say I need something next week, he can respond to me. Legally there's nothing compelling him to have that material on hand. But he's had a business with us that's been going on and on and on. Now all of a sudden the bottom falls out, and the bottom falls out very quickly. So before he can cancel what he's got open, the material is in there.

Some of that is part of the risk of doing business, there's no question about that. I don't precisely know what's there and why it is there at this stage of the game. All I know is he's got another $300,000 for which he says, "I'm in trouble and I need help." There is no question there's a risk in doing business, and he has to assume some of that risk. So, there is no question—I'm not going to pick up $300,00, but I may share in some of it.

The company relies on my judgment. They won't like to pay more than what they're obligated to, but they do know the product and the difficulty in trying to forecast it. This is the kind of ethical thing you get into. It's not black; it's not white; you're not responsible legally, but you are responsible. The question is: What are you responsible for?

Let me tell you a little bit more. This guy happens to be a one-of-a-kind supplier. He's the only supplier I have had for these parts. I don't have an alternate source of supply. It makes it even that much more binding. He is really part of our family. He knows that. He's like a supplier that's a partner to the company; that makes a difference. We didn't have anybody else to go to, since no one else can make what he makes. Now he's going through a real retracting period, laying off people and shrinking his work force, and he's got all this capital involved in materials. Now he's in a declining industry. Unfortunately he was picked up by another company, and that company was picked up by another company, so now he's part of a conglomerate. But if you look at his business as a whole, we are probably 70% of his division's business. One of our policies is that you should never have a supplier become overly dependent upon you, and you should never become more than 25% of a guy's business. But this supplier is a division of a large company, and that division lives on the business from us. That is a current problem I have, and I'm not sure how I'll deal with it yet.

Why should I not pay the $300,000? I feel there's a share in the risk. This is not something that you go through every day. Each situation is different. I have another situation that I'm involved in, the same kind of thing, the same product line. This supplier is looking for $2.5 million cancellation insurance; he wants me to pay for everything but the kitchen sink. But in this case, what he wants is lost revenue, lost anticipated revenue. There is no risk on the part of the supplier. It's a completely different perspective. The first situation that I just talked about is like a relationship, a friendship. In the second situation, it is again a captive supplier, part of a conglomerate. Maybe they've got 20% of their business with other customers. But 80% of it is with us. We have a dollar obligation of about $4.6 million as far as open orders are concerned, and they want about $2.7. They're starting to bring in a lot of legal involvements. Naturally I took their data and sent it down to our legal people and asked them to look it over. The simple answer I got back from our legal people is: everything is up to negotiation.

I believe they're trying to capture their total profit for the units that have been completed. It's a situation in which we do have a very strong obligation, maybe for $1.5 million. We took them up to making 55 of these units a week and each unit is worth $4,000 apiece. All of a sudden we dropped them down to here—there was no slope at all. Just like that, and we said, "Stop." And of course they laid off all their people. They've got all those layoff charges which they want us to pay. I don't know. It's a whole new experience for me to get into, for my people to get into. It's a big, a very huge, messy problem.

The first company I have more of a feel for. I've known them for a long time. People that I have working for me developed them and made them a supplier of ours. We created them; we brought this company on-stream; we worked with them and developed their engineering, their purchasing. We worked with them and developed them and, finally, we made them into the company that we wanted them to be. They really didn't know they had the capability. But they developed the capability. So we really created them.

With the second company, we were looking for a device to do a certain job. They took a commercial device they had, they modified it, and that device turned out to be what we wanted to buy. They already made this product on a very small-scale basis. But when you start making 55 of these a week at the price of $4000 apiece, that's big dollars. So before you know it, we're doing millions of dollars worth of business with them, which is what we did last year and the year before. We went there and got them to get their volume up to the level we wanted. They were a very cooperative supplier, very good supplier. We felt the price was fair and, again, they were the single source of supply. But, there hasn't been that long-lasting relationship we've had with the other supplier with whom we've been doing business for 20 years. We've been doing business with the second supplier for maybe now five years and we didn't develop him. He was just a guy that had something on his shelf that might do the job; and we picked it out. Whatever helped them, we have done it. The gray area you get into is the money and how they want to settle the money. One of the things you learn to believe in in our end of the business is fairness. When you negotiate, you want to be fair. You don't want to be taken, but you want to be fair. I guess that's a very, very difficult area to measure, and being fair may not mean the same thing to everyone. What's fair to me is not necessarily going to be fair to the supplier. I'm sure that the $2.7 million the second supplier is asking for includes everything but the kitchen sink. If I can settle for maybe $2 million or $1.5 million or $1 million, I'll be happy. There is no question—I'm sure I have a $1 million obligation. The plant knows that. I've already let them know that this is the biggest cancellation we've every had. But, it puts you right on the defensive. You immediately say, "Oh, boy, they're out to really hold me up." I don't feel that way about the other $300,000. He's saying, "Help me. Help me wherever you can." And I'm going to help him where I think I'm obligated to. But do you see what I mean when I talk about being fair? You see how those things tie together? I think they are similar cases, but yet they have different cross currents. The first case will probably be something I can handle; there's no problem involved in it. The second case, I'm not sure who will get involved in it: my boss, or his boss, or my legal people, or whoever. But it's not something I really know the answer to.

See, I live by honesty, fairness, integrity. You don't even really have to talk about it. It's just understood. Ethics is very hard to define. It's not easy, you know. You don't know the answers in many cases.

COMMENTS

The relationship between an organization and its suppliers is highly interdependent. The organization is dependent upon the supplier to provide necessary resources in a timely and efficient manner. The supplier depends on the capability and honor of the organization to deal fairly in the exchange of goods and services and to carry through on promises that have been made. These interdependencies work not only because of trust and commitment between specific parties, but because of a general cultural agreement defined by laws, contracts, and by acknowledged "rules of the game."

The individual manager who deals most frequently across the company boundaries with suppliers is the purchasing agent. As Frank McGraw's interview suggests, purchasing agents and suppliers see themselves as collaborating coworkers. This fact is important because despite the concerns with fairness—which is what Frank wishes to achieve—the dominant ethical element in his tale of two suppliers is *relationship*. In reality, the situations he faces with the two suppliers affected by the product discontinuation are virtually identical. This fact would suggest, therefore, that the two suppliers receive identical treatment (e.g., nothing above the cancellation fee or else some percentage of each company's investment costs). For Frank, however, the ethical concern is triggered by his different relationship with each of these companies, and his belief that the type of relationship is the basis for differential treatment. Although he argues that the first company (with the 20-year relationship) is trying to get some money for parts it held in inventory to meet Frank's short interval needs, whereas the second company is trying to pick up lost revenues on forecasted sales, Frank's *real* point is that Company One was invested for him while Company Two was invested for itself. However, while there is a difference between the two types of financial commitment, the implicit contract driving both is similar, and, thus, deserves similar response.

Most purchasing departments, and Frank's is no exception, have stringent guidelines that control the level of "relationship" that can develop between purchaser and supplier. Unfortunately, guidelines cannot prevent the sense of collaboration that a successful buyer/seller team can develop over time. So Frank's dilemma may not be the result of overly casual corporate regulations or laxness on the part of the purchasing department, but rather the uncomfortable outcome of a well-intentioned and productive partnership.

PETER
LATHEN

Manager, Manufacturing
Fifty-one years old

*"There is no danger to anyone, but people
are putting up their dough, and they're not
going to get the results they want every
time."*

T he standard interview question is: "What do you want to do?" I would answer, "When I grow up? When I retire? Next year?" How the hell do I know what I want to do? I want to contribute; I want to have some responsibility. I guess the bottom line is that I would like to be able to achieve some of the goals I have set out. I may not have everything written down, but in my mind I know the things that have to occur to get there. The company wouldn't be paying me what they're paying me unless they recognized that doing those things is hard and requires management of a lot of resources and using a lot of my intelligence to get them done. It's not easy; you have to overcome obstacles. I think the thrill of overcoming problems is most exciting. I get a big kick out of being a hero. But I also get a big kick out of seeing a team that I've pulled together accomplish something. That I like. That's what I like to do during the day. I've found out there are a lot of glamour guys who walk around with presentations all day long. That works up to a point, but there are a lot of us who have walked hard roads, and if you make things happen, it doesn't take long before the people who ultimately judge your fate in the corporation recognize this. You just don't fool people for long.

Our success depends on products. Our inventiveness is what's kept us alive. In no way could we compete in manufacturing capability or capital with any of the big firms. What has kept us on top has been our inventiveness; and that means new products and a lot of them. Anybody who has ever been in this kind of industry understands what bringing new products in means. It's a pit. You climb out of the pit to go on to the next one. It's a very tough job. You are competing against yourself time and time again.

From a quality perspective, there are all kinds of ethical problems. What is good for the customer? What's good in an image? God knows what's good in an image. Is it good color? Is it good sharpness? Is it how long it will last? All those things are good. But what does the customer really want? We do an awful lot of field testing because we are continually trying to figure out what the customer wants. In a field test we send out a system. People take images and the images come back with 1, 2, 3, 4, 5 ratings, category 1 being the best, 5 being no good. In one test that came back there were some images for which the system had been used in the shade. This was before we had the system to handle that situation; shade images in the late day were a very difficult process to handle. These damn pictures—which were images of ducks—were almost completely underexposed. You know, the person had ranked them as number one, an outstanding image, liked it! I thought they were awful. Well it turned out that these were the last pictures of her two ducks before a dog killed them. And that's why she liked them.

Then there's also the problem of time. I find that if you are not responsible for making a shipping date, your requirements somehow get a little more demanding. But under the pressure of time and the inability to meet all those requirements, you often rationalize. For instance, with one of our products we designed a unit with four structural pieces, all of which had to match in a specific manner. We got so damn fouled up in our underwear trying to get matching sets of everything. And, we were trying to make thousands of them a day. We needed not only the pieces, but they had to match perfectly. We kept coming out with the match below standard. There was nothing wrong; just a slightly different color. We finally got some corporate officers to come and look at these products. We made the combinations up with a range of up to the biggest contrasts we could find and we got the officers in the room. We said, "You make the decision now. What's good?" "But," I said, "before you make the decision, you have got to understand that there is no way that we can meet our shipping schedules if you want this stuff to match closer than one level apart." And immediately the responses came: "Doesn't that contrast look good?" Now was that good or bad? I don't know. I think the customer really didn't give a damn about it.

In quality considerations, you go from that kind of thing to a situation in which you are shipping product where you know that out of every 500 cycles, 10 will fail. Is it right to ship that to a customer? Those are the tough ones, the functional ones where the customer will not get an image. Those really bother me. If I am responsible for quality, those bother me because although I am working for the company, I feel I have some obligations to our customers. And I feel the company will have to understand that somebody has to represent the customers in the product line we ship. You understand that people buy the system, and they expect that over the weekend they will take some pictures. It is the only chance they have to take that picture, and if it doesn't work, they'll never have that picture again. That's kind of tough.

One quality manager I know of used to hold a meeting every six months with all the officers. We had a manager who ran the consumer complaint group at that time. This manager would get all the consumer complaint calls or letters. And he was really something. He was brilliant; and boy, could he set a stage. Part of the presentation of this quality manager was to have this consumer complaint manager read some of these letters that came in. I'll never forget one that came from a 76-year-old grandmother in Minnesota. I mean this consumer complaint manager gave it everything—the sun going down, tears, you could practically hear the music in the background. The grandmother had had a Thanksgiving dinner and her grandchildren were there. It would be the last time she would ever see them because she was very sick. So she took one of our systems and she tried to take some images. The system didn't work. How do you make up for that? How do you make things right?

But that's not the real decision we deal with. If we could design and manufacture a perfect system, we could not afford to make it because it would cost too much. We would have to shut down and put all our people out on the streets. So obviously we have to come up with a compromise. And strangely, the market has a way of pointing to where the compromise is, because if you make the wrong decision either way, you don't get sales. You don't get sales because it's too bad or because you try to make it too good and it's too expensive. The problem is to predict ahead of time. To run right down the middle; that's where the judgment comes in. We always try to shade toward giving the best we can, but it's tough. Decisions that are clearly based on laws and rules are easy, as long as the manufacturing process for producing a product also adheres to those rules and laws. But when the process doesn't hold to the rules, that's where the rubber hits the road.

It's interesting, different perspectives on right and wrong. Take technical people, say design engineers. They work on their one program, their one thing, for maybe two or three years. If they are wrong, it's goddamned devastating; in their peer society, it's devastating. Then you bump into the manufacturing guy, and he says, "Forty right, 20 wrong in one day—it's been a good day!"

Bringing in new systems and getting them into the marketplace raises some real ethical concerns. By bringing them in I mean you bring them from a drawing stage through a model prototype, pre-production pilot, and finally into production. As I said before, the only way we can compete is to be inventive. And the next result of being inventive is that you get a lot of new ideas and a lot of new products, and if they are going to pay off, you have to turn those around and get them into the market very quickly. There's always a problem in that the people who invent and develop the products can put them together themselves; they know the innards and they put them together in a controlled way with a few pieces from a specific vendor. When you try and make thousands of units a day, where you've got a lot of vendors and a lot of people that probably are not as skilled in this field as the inventors, it becomes a big problem, a hard job. To my way of thinking, to take a very demanding state-of-the-art unit which has many new inventions in it, and bring that into production, is as much a technological breakthrough as the invention itself. It's a very hard thing to do. Look at the VY-8 system. We must have had eight different state-of-the-art inventions in that. It was a very difficult product to bring in. We work for a corporation where the potential for the invention is really great. And we get mesmerized by that; it's beautiful. Now you've got some poor guy outside who's going to buy the product, and all he wants is images, he doesn't give a damn how it works. He doesn't really care that much that all these break-throughs have taken place. He just wants a nice image. And he wants the system to work. But we take this invention and we keep slipping dates because we can't get the same results in produc-tion as the developer saw in his few samples put together by his own hands.

That's really oversimplifying an extremely complex situation with a lot of different factions interacting. And I mean factions: engineering, manufacturing, quality, marketing. Often, much of the problem is people, not the product. What you find is that as you get into problems, trying to get the product up and going, and as the pressure rises, the people get bitchier and bitchier and tougher and tougher. All our bad characteristics come out—our trying to protect our rear ends, our trying to make somebody else look bad, our getting a promotion over somebody else's body—they all come out on the table. It's almost a self-perpetuating mess until you finally get some people that understand what's going on and say, "Hey, look at what we're doing. Let's calm down and set some realistic goals; not the ones everybody wants to hear, but the ones we think we can do. Let's get the pressure off people who can't handle it." So in the VY-8 systems program that's what we eventually did.

But we still had some real problems getting into production. We kicked around for about six months and we never made a thing we could ship. Those of us who were responsible for the system introduction finally decided we would take everything else we were doing and all the other products we were working on, and forget them. We lived with the product, we worked 14, 15 hours a day for a long time to get that thing going. Now all of this creates pressure. There's a great need to get the thing out the door because you're spending big bucks. Now I happened to be in the evaluation end, so I had to look at what we were shipping. You start with, "You wanted to do this." Then you find that you can only do "that." Then you say, "Well is 'that' good enough?" So then you go out and take a sample to find out how the customers feel about it. The sample comes back and it isn't quite clear. So you interpret it. You get into this rationalization type of thing where your original quality goals are no longer attainable. You know that you, yourself, are not a perfect indicator of what everybody else wants. So you don't really know if you should ship the thing or not. If you measure it against the specifications and requirements you wrote up some time ago, it's clear it doesn't make it. You shouldn't ship the product. But if you recognize that you're losing millions of dollars and you also recognize that maybe the customer would like it and could use it, you've got a push to ship it.

Now the hell of it is, if you're the responsible manager, you sit there and you know all this. Now if you can find a way—it becomes a game—if you can find a way to get enough data to justify shipping it, everybody loves you. If you take the position that you can't get the data, and say it doesn't meet spec and can't be shipped, everybody hates you. And they probably should because they know you know the spec came from people's minds and doesn't necessarily reflect what the customer needs. Normally, in this corporation, if you've got a good reason and you've got data beyond a set spec, then they'll respect that and work with you. The pressure is still there, though. It's big bucks. It's a big decision to make. And it isn't as if this happened yesterday and we've only worked one day; we've been on this a year. And everybody is sick and tired of looking at it. "Just ship it, don't talk about it," is what they'd like to say. That's what I'd like to say if I were them. Although I was a couple of levels down from the executive office and they should have been involved, by that time they sure as hell didn't want to be involved either. And I knew that too. So I was stuck with the problem. In those days I held the position that we shouldn't ship for quite a while. Then finally in the end I said we could ship. Now I think I wasn't convinced that we should even then. But I had gotten to the point where I didn't see much else. I didn't see where else we could improve the situation. And we had brought the product a long way from where it had been.

It's an interesting problem. There is absolutely no danger to anyone, but people are putting up their dough, and they're not going to get the results they want ever time. And maybe over a period of six months, in one out of every 30 cases, the system is not going to work. Now it is not a health matter, and it isn't killing someone, so that justifies to some degree the decision, because it's a matter of economics. But you keep doing it and don't improve the product, then eventually you go out of business because nobody believes you. So you get your just due somewhere along the line. But it is tough. You get many situations where people get one chance to take an image. It means a lot to them. And the system doesn't work.

So, I guess the decision I had was: Is it correct to sell? If I line 30 people up and I give them 30 systems, I know from the data I've got that I've given a dud to one of those people. I don't know which one it is, but I know I've given someone a dud. And it's my position to say we should or shouldn't do that. If I say we should, I'm being very unfair to one of those people. That's a very bothersome thing.

I grew up a Catholic and had a strong religious education. As a result I believe in a pretty rigid set of rules of morality. I don't always live up to them, and I recognize that. But I guess what ethics and morality mean to me is acting in ways that will make me feel proud of myself. You really can't kid yourself. You can kid yourself if you talk a lot, and if you drink a lot, and if you stay with a lot of people. But when you go home at night and look in the mirror and ask yourself whether the decisions you made that day were right or wrong, it's pretty tough to lie to yourself. You kind of hope that when you ask that question to your mirror you get the right answer, and if you don't you feel pretty bad. You try and do better. I don't always live up to my goals. I don't always do what I think is right. I wish I did.

COMMENTS

There is a similarity between customers and subordinates in their relationships to managers: both are highly dependent upon the managers, and both are vulnerable to inappropriate intervention by them. Customers may be better able to mitigate their dependency by the potential economic sanctions they have. But they are still, like subordinates, dependent upon the integrity of the managers in the organizations with whom they deal. And the recognition of that dependency is, for Peter Lathen, the ethical trigger to a variety of product quality concerns. He sees this relationship to the customer as the bond between customer and company. He also sees the relationship as holding a set of obligations which he feels bound to fulfill. He says, "I feel the company will have to understand that somebody has to represent the customers in the product line we ship." Peter is that somebody. And his self-assignment as customer "representative" develops in him a sense of capacity responsibility, which says, essentially, "If I don't, who will?" So, for Peter, many product quality problems hold an ethical component based on relationship/responsibility factors. Peter also raises a critical value concern around product quality. In discussing what he is responsible to the customer for, he talks about three different concepts of harm: (1) harm as the compromise of style, for example, parts that don't match; (2) harm as the psychological distress caused by the failure of the product to function, as in the case of the Minnesota grandmother; and (3) harm as danger to health or physical well-being, which is not a concern with his product. For Peter, as representative of the customer, it has become necessary to decide for himself what constitutes harm with his product. He recognizes immediately that physical danger is not a concern. So if he chose to, he could let himself off the "do no harm" hook by focusing on the fact that he deals in a safe product. But he doesn't do that. On the other side, he feels considerable ambivalence about whether or not a compromise in styling elegance constitutes something harmful to the customer, and seems to come out saying, "I'm not going to worry too much about it." Peter recognizes, however, the psychological commitment made by a manufacturer of imaging equipment to its customers and, therefore, acknowledges that, for him, the nonfulfillment of the customers' expectations that the product will function correctly does constitute a harm which the company has an obligation to try to prevent.

The factor that comes to the fore as challenging the company's ability to prevent harm is the competing claim of the company's need to control costs and to price products at a level the market will accept. If Peter's company could spend as much as it wanted to develop and manufacture its product, harm would not be an issue. They could make a failure-proof system. However, if the system were priced reasonably, the company could not sustain the tremendous cost and continue to operate. If the system were priced to reflect the cost, few people would purchase it. So Peter could pose for himself a most disturbing dilemma: either I prevent harm and bankrupt the company, or I support the business at the expense of human well-being. But instead, Peter redefines the problem so that he is not seeking to prevent all harm (he cannot). But his question now is, "How do I decide on an acceptable level of harm to be responsive to all the claims that are made on me?" Peter's redefinition of the problem responds to the characteristics of ethical dilemmas that have emerged in this study. Because of the needs and values of many stakeholders, there is no simple "right answer" to his problem. We will discuss this kind of problem redefinition in the final section of the book.

WILLIAM
ROBERTSON

Vice-President
Fifty-nine years old

*"To me it's immoral, but that doesn't mean
it's immoral in terms of what
big business does."*

My own ethics are the result of a Catholic upbringing in a suburban neighborhood. I was not exposed to some of the things that occur in the business world. Politics came into play in the business world, and that's why I think there is a difference between what I do as a businessman and what I would do as an individual. My upbringing was very straight. I didn't look for white lies or for things that would let me attempt to rationalize something that my stomach was telling me was wrong. When I got into the business world I found that those things do occur. At home, when I have a decision to make, it's based strictly on what's right and wrong as far as I'm concerned. Sometimes my definition of right may not be right, but it's what I believe, and I have no qualms about going by what my stomach tells me I should or shouldn't do. When I'm at work I get the same feeling in my stomach, but I also have to remind myself of the fact that this is a business decision and maybe I have to go along with what "they" are saying or what I know is a practicality of the situation.

I have a man working for me right now with whom I'm going through a bit of a trauma. This man is an officer and he has emphysema, which is a deteriorating illness. I feel we should let him keep working for as long as he wants to continue working, even though he is physically unable to give a full day's work, for the next eight or nine years he has until he retires. He's got 30 years in this bank. However, I can't go just by what I think I should do for this man. I have to consider the effect on the bank. And the effect on the bank is that we're not getting adequate work out of him. If I did not have to think of the bank, I probably would go along with his doing whatever he was capable of doing—like come in a couple of days a week—and keep paying him because the guy still has expenses. But I can't go that route. I'm trying to work out the best way I can to get him the most money for the longest time the bank will go along with. The only thing I can work out under that premise is to put him on disability. He *is* disabled, and yet if I were making the decision outside of business, my decision would be to do whatever is best for him as an individual psychologically. Under the premise I have right now, I'm saying I can't do that because business says you have to get productive work out of a person *all* the time. If you don't, then you ought to be cutting down what you're paying for him. I realize the practicality of this, and I know I'm not really going to hurt this individual tremendously. I am hurting him a little psychologically because he'll have to make a decision that he doesn't really want to make, namely to stop working. In terms of legality, there's nothing illegal about it. To *me* it's immoral, but that doesn't mean it's immoral in terms of what big business does. Big business has to go on the premise that they should get a dollar's work out of a dollar's worth of pay. This man no longer is producing. And yet 30 years of this man's life was given to the bank. My values are different than the business values in this case. I have a tendency to believe we have to look towards the individual first and the company second. But when it comes to this decision, I have to look towards the company first and the individual second. I wonder if I am calling this an ethical decision as a way of letting out my unhappiness at the fact I cannot do what I think is right.

It bothers me. Let me tell you a secret. After 30 years of running a human relations area, I still get into discussions as to why I think the bank should do something, "humanly" versus practically. I run a big organization. I'm involved in the mechanics of it. But the majority of what I would call ethical decisions I face have had to do with my dealings with people, rather than what I have to do to get my job done. I assume there have been times when the bank has, in effect, asked me to do something that if I were outside I might refuse to do. But those times thankfully have been few and far between. I think that as far as the bank is concerned, I haven't run into too many situations where I've been asked to do something that was against my will or against my grain. I have to say, though, that in the last 20 years, when it came to dealing with people, there have been vast differences of opinion between what they have set as corporate policy and what I try to do in a lot of cases.

Because of the length of time I've been here, I've been "brainwashed" so that I know I don't go to the bank with this fellow's case saying, "Damn it, you're wrong. We ought to do this another way." I start with the premise that this is what the bank says is good and this is what it says is right. Yet if I took myself out of the shoes of vice-president in this bank, I would say, "Gee, we ought to do more." So the bank doesn't get into a real ethical problem with me. I have been trained now. At least I've been trained long enough so that I don't come to confrontations anymore. I think ten or 15 years ago I would have come storming downstairs to the personnel department, and I did in many instances saying, "It isn't right!" Now it's more something inside of me saying it's wrong. But at the same time I have enough knowledge and experience so that what could have been black and white is now gray. Years ago, the bank would have been the black, and I would have been the white. Now I've shifted into a gray position in terms of how I make decisions about what is right and wrong. I think that's a result of living in a practical world and having to bend. I'd love to be able to get outside myself and critique what I do. But now it's to the point where I think I understand, and I play politics; that's what has to be done.

This situation with the fellow with emphysema is the third such case in my 30 years here. But this is the first one completely under my domain. In the other two cases I was on the fringes; I felt more strongly on those two because I wasn't the one who was making the total decision. This one is all in my ball park. The fact is this guy should have gone out about six or eight months ago. I have used all the manipulations I can to get him up to this point. He and I talked last October about the fact that we were going to have to face this situation soon. Now it's to the point where in the next month or two we are putting in a whole new system and his job is affected by it. So I've come to the point where I think I've stretched it as long as I can. I am going to try to get him another month or two, but as for trying to make the bank do what I think is right in this case, I don't think I will go that far, partly because I don't have enough examples of situations of this sort that could be used as precedent.

There have been some good changes in relation to minorities and females in this bank, some of which I think the bank did too slowly. In those cases I did go to the forefront and try to speed up the process. I think that if I feel strongly enough about a situation I will go and try to change the decision factors that are there. In the disability case, I don't . . . I keep coming back to it because it's on my mind. I spent a very tough two hours with this guy yesterday, and I'm still thinking about how I can help him and not hurt the

hire college intern

bank. When we talk about the changes in regard to women and minorities, I feel I can fight for those, because I see that the bank is doing, or not doing, something I think I have enough power to influence. In that case, the power comes not only from my own position, but also from outside influences I know will help me. In other words, if I ever told the bank they were not treating a particular woman well, I feel I could put enough pressure on them to change, partly because I am not alone in this. All I have to do is say, "Gee, I'm going to go to the *Tribune* and tell them what you're doing with this woman," and the bank is practical enough to react. So on some things where the bank and I differ, I would attack. But again, I would attack because I know I've got enough to win. The ones where I know I may not win, I don't know how strongly I would go after them.

The bank does offer disability. Most big businesses have what is called short-term disability. So, for six months this fellow will get his pay, but he will not be working, or he will be working very little. It requires that a doctor say he's not capable of working. At the end of the six months he will go on long-term disability. Long-term disability varies with different companies. In our case it means that 60% of his salary will be covered by an insurance company until he's 65 years old, at which time he will start getting his pension. This fellow is 56, 57 years old, so we're talking about a seven- or eight-year time frame. But the bank ought to have some other way of giving him full pay or even putting him on a schedule that allows him to work X number of days and gives him 80 or 90% of his present salary. Part of the problem in this case is that I know too much about the individual. I know his home circumstances; I know his family. His wife used to work for me. So there's a whole array of things. If this were a common occurrence in the bank then I would attack it. But I'm so personally involved, and know so much about what's going on with this individual, that I don't know if I could find other cases that would fit these circumstances.

Maybe in this situation, because I'm so personally involved, I should not make a case. But I could use it for background. There are other types of medical conditions that should be considered. Maybe we should take another look at the medical side of all these things and not be so business-practical. After all, this bank, and most big businesses, like to be considered humane. I think that is something I may look into. Not the individual case, but the question of what the bank's practice is going to be in terms of illnesses where there is some productivity, although less than 100%. That's a cause I might be able to get into, because I'm not afraid to attack decisions of the bank, as long as I can convince myself I have some solid arguments and an opportunity to have some effect.

COMMENTS

Bill Robertson believes that some attention is owed to an individual who has given more than half his life to an organization. In fact, Bill's words could have come from Arthur Miller's pen: "Big business has got to (get) . . . a dollar's work out of a dollar's worth of pay. This man no longer is producing. And yet, 30 years of this man's life was given to the bank." Although Bill's concern seems to be compounded by the close personal relationship he has had for 30 years with this employee, his perception of a difference in values about human welfare between himself and his organization is what makes the situation ethical for him. Bill *is* offered a mechanism for aiding an ill and no longer productive employee: the company does, in fact, have a clear, implementable policy to provide the care and prevention of harm that Bill seeks. His bank is stepping in not only to alleviate the concern Bill feels, but to actively provide a responsible mechanism to relieve it.

And yet, carrying out the disability policy still leaves him with a nagging ethical concern. It does not enable him to respond to the psychological needs of his employee—the need to work—which the two-thirds-salary disability payment does not address. This concern is triggered by a personal belief, which Bill holds, that despite his obvious loyalty to and pride in his organization, big business (of which his organization is part) must, because of economic demands, hold a set of values that are more limited in their scope of human care than those held by an individual. For Bill, values about care engendered by relationship are deeply held. In portions of the interview not included here, he talked about very special care given him as a child that has clearly shaped his values. And he does recognize, without extreme discomfort, that the organization's position may be wholly appropriate given the other demands upon it. But, in many situations with human welfare at stake, it is likely that Bill's ethical sense will be triggered by conflict between personal and organizational values.

Bill's situation raises an interesting question: how do people assess the significance of value differences they feel with their organizations? How can they separate the tolerable from the intolerable, the conditions that may cause some personal sadness from those demanding some form of action? Although Bill says his ability to have an effect is a determining factor in whether or not he decides to confront a situation, I suspect that in this case he recognizes the organizational measure of a generous disability policy, even it it does not fully meet what he wishes, is different from an attempt on the part of the organization to either disregard human need or to drag its heels as Bill feels it did with some of its affirmative action programs.

ROBERT

McDONALD

Director of Manufacturing
Fifty years old

"The 'anonymous letter' bothers the hell
out of me because I don't really like
to lie."

I look back at my early career as a supervisor, in the early sixties, when the whole society was different. I think of things, like the way we viewed women. We had a quote merit unquote system for paying people. And it was not uncommon to talk openly among ourselves and our bosses about bypassing Alice because she was a secondary wage earner and her husband had a good job with Smith and Jones, or wherever he was working. And it was not uncommon to bypass people because of their race. Less openly discussed, but nonetheless really there. When I think back about how I felt about and dealt with those things, they didn't offend me. Faced with the same situations today I would be incensed. But I was part of that. And in most of the cases, I didn't even view it as very important, just, Alice doesn't need the 25 bucks, but Joe Blow certainly needs it. And part of it was that we really didn't think Alice should have that job anyway. There was certainly a strong feeling about the role of the male as the primary wage earner. The female's place was in the home, preferably barefoot, I guess. It clearly was an ethical situation that I put no ethical thought into. But I have changed—hopefully for the better. It clearly was terrible behavior, I think now. And I marvel that I didn't raise a concern about it. In some of the instances it was because it didn't make much difference. In reality, it didn't make much difference because the merit system I mentioned was such a farce. It was really a rotational system. It was not merit. Maybe six months or a year from now we'll think differently about Alice. We've punished her enough. She didn't get a merit increase for a year now, so we'll give her something. The rationale that went into it amazes me now. But some of it was serious business. The way we thought about minorities and females was very important. And it wasn't an ethical choice at that time. My system of beliefs was that you folks [women] were all inferior in some way or other. It certainly wasn't a dilemma. I don't think anybody ever thought of promoting a female in those days. And other minorities were identified on placement lists as being a minority. There were codes next to peoples' names on the consideration lists, and a certain code meant "minority." As a supervisor you understood what that meant. It was pretty clear, by setting them off separately, that something was supposed to be done, or preferably, nothing was supposed to be done. And that shouldn't bother you a great deal. But that bothers me a great deal now.

My perception at that time, because of my lack of dealings with blacks, was that they were bad people. I come from a family of cops in a big city, and the only exposure I had to black people was through my relatives who were cops. The only black people they dealt with were bad black people. They had no good black people to deal with, so all I heard about was the bad black people. I can recall when I was a little kid about nine years old, I was listening to the radio and there was a report of a fire. The address clearly indicated that it was a black neighborhood, and the report said that everybody perished in the fire—13 people. And I can recall sitting there and saying, "Good. They're all dead. That's what they deserve." My father scolded me for it, and I couldn't understand why he was scolding me because it seemed that that's what you were supposed to want. But apparently not. I've thought about that so often, I'll probably have to go to a shrink some day and get myself straightened out about it. God, I thought about that so often. I can imagine what would happen if one of my kids made a comment like that. I don't think they would, they've grown up in a different world. So that was the beginning, when I was nine years old, of somebody telling me that maybe they're not all bad and they shouldn't all be punished.

I guess over these many years my whole view of the world has changed, my understanding that women don't have to be at home barefoot and pregnant. And I've come to know that there are some very smart, very competent women and very smart and very competent blacks who have been pushed to the side over these many years. I can have some appreciation of how pissed off they probably are at the traditional establishment or the people who run it. I have trouble picturing that situation today. We have gone from a position where you don't promote anybody, you don't give anyone a raise, except a certain color or sex, to a point now where we seek people out because of their color and sex. We're anxious to promote them. But lurking behind it all are still some very, very questionable motives. The motive often is that it's a good thing to do because somebody thinks it's a good thing to do. I came close to it this week in a discussion with my peers. Some people in some other factories who are dealing with some sophisticated processes are saying things like, "We need some relaxation of EEO rules because of this new competitive environment we're getting into. You just can't have all these dummies walking in off the street." And I really applaud those words; you just can't have dummies walking in off the street running an expensive process. But what got me were the guy's words, that "we need some relaxation of the EEO rules so we don't have these dummies walking in off the streets." We had a big, long debate about that, just talking about ideas, not talking about any specific corporate action. I'm not sure how to describe this, but when I look back I see that the object back then was not to have any minorities and women in important positions. The object now is to have them in those positions. I suspect the motives back then were wrong, and I suspect the motives are still wrong. A lot of us put a lot of nice words around it, but I think the motives are still wrong.

A good friend of mine who's a female manager in another company was recently promoted. She's a very, very, very competent person, the kind of person I suspect anybody would like to have head their business—smart, hard working, all kinds of things. She goes for an interview for a promotion, and one of the first questions out of the boss's mouth is, "Are you married? Do you expect to be raising a baby?" She said to me, "I bit my tongue. I really wanted the job. It seemed like a good job, so I didn't say anything, I just said to him, 'No, I'm not going to.' And that seemed to satisfy him." She subsequently got the job. She told me, "I really bit my tongue because I wanted that job I got. But I wanted to say, 'You've got one hell of a nerve asking me about those things. It's none of your business.'" And this guy, according to her, is a fairly sensible, understanding guy. She doesn't perceive him as being any kind of a bigot, but that's just what he is. I don't know what his motives were. I just have that little vignette that she told me. But clearly there are a lot of folks who go ahead and say, "I've got to achieve this good objective and get more minorities and females in important jobs," with the full belief that those people aren't qualified, whether they are or not. I guess the sad part for me is that things have ostensibly changed, but I think the concern's kind of shallow.

I have some real strong feelings about our selection process. Like most companies, it is crappy. I mean it is crappy. I got selected to be the boss, and one of the reasons I'm successful is because the guy who selected me was successful. Very slowly that is changing, I mean, very, very slowly changing, but it's still the great expectation, self-fulfilling prophecy. I think we have a need to be much more scrupulous about selection of females and minorities because I think we need to have successes. We had an opening for a manager here a few years ago and I spent months searching through the whole corporation. Fortunately, I got a good woman and it worked out very well. She was a very, very good model for other aspiring women. There are too many women selected because they're available and convenient. But often they are not ready.

I guess one of the big problems is that I'm as prejudiced as anybody else, probably a hell of a lot more so, but as long as I know what I'm doing, as long as if I say something offensive to you I may not be smart enough to apologize for it, but at least if I can understand I did something offensive I can do something about helping myself in the future. I do real stupid things, too. We've had a lot of women in management over the years. You know, maybe not managers but in management—secretaries like Janice, who is a supersmart person, supersmart. My assumptions about secretaries have always been crazy. As long as she knows how to get the coffee that's all we care about. It's come to the point now where I can't even ask Janice to get the coffee. If I have a visitor she'll do it because she figures I need to stay with the visitor, but if there's no visitor all the managers are expected to get their own coffee, which is the way it should be. I understand I've got to make her feel she's one of the people who work here, like I am.

I've met some women I've gotten to know fairly well, and they've told me about some of their experiences. Their experiences shocked me. I had no idea. Talk about stupid. And I consider myself a smart person. I've got peers and bosses who don't understand what females manage to put up with. They don't understand how they feel when they walk in and the prospective boss says, "Say, are you planning on raising a family?" I can't imagine somebody asking me. I've been fortunate in the degree to which I've made any improvement.

I think it's been because of some females I know in the company who I think are smart people and who I hold in high regard. But also I have three daughters, and I've seen the changes that they've gone through. I've got one daughter who's in engineering school. She's very clever; she can make things out of staples and paper clips, anything. She's interested in art and design. Maybe four years ago she said, "What's the difference between a designer and an engineer?" I tried to describe the work. She said, "Could I be an engineer?" I said, "Yes." She said, "The counselors at school are trying to get me to go to a design school but I think that what engineers do is what I really want to do." So she's at engineering school. I think you can learn a little bit from what your kids do, and what you see happening to them. She's a young kid, in her early twenties. Twenty years ago people would have told her, "Better stick to those dolls; better take your shoes off. You've got to be barefoot one of these days, too."

I think I've got some real convictions that allow me to question a whole bunch of things I do and which other people do. Some managers say, "What do you want me to do?" I say, "You're the spokesman for your company's affirmative action plan." I tell them I know they may feel differently personally; I know how they feel. All I can say is that as long as you're wearing a uniform, that is, as long as you are acting as a supervisor, in this place, in a local bar, any place, I don't care what you believe, but there are ways you have to act. I can't change the ways people believe. And I say, "If you want to go down to your basement and scream and rant and rave and say, 'I wish we never hired a black or Hispanic or female in that goddammed place, they're ruining it,' go ahead, go do it. Then you've got to go put on your ethical clothes and come to work." All I can be concerned about is behavior. Because if the behavior is wrong, I'm going to do something bad to them. If behavior is good, I'll give them rewards. You'd like to change everybody's mind, because you think you know more than anybody else. I guess that harks back to my situation when I was a kid where the only reports I had about black people were from relatives who were cops who were arresting blacks. Now, they arrested white people too but they also knew some good white ones. I had a terrible, imbalanced view of the world. I'll never forget my father telling me, "You're terrible for thinking about those black people that way." He was, to his dying day, the biggest bigot in the world. And he knew so. But that had a lasting impression on me. I'm not ready to say I'm not filled up with all kinds of prejudices; I don't mean that at all. But I take that part of this job very, very seriously. Everybody knows it.

Most of the kinds of ethical situations you face have to do with the kind of manager you are. If you are a manager who sits in the office, like some managers do, and says, "Well, here I am. Somebody's going to walk in here and ask me to make a decision," I guess somebody will walk in and say, "You've got a choice of A, B, or C. What should I do?" Then you can go through all the financial analysis and come up with the best solution. But if your style is to manage by walking around, you find out a lot of things. Sometimes you find out things that are super important that should be dealt with. Sometimes you find out about them in a way that precludes your telling people. Therein lies the most serious problem I've dealt with. I was working at a location and somebody got seriously injured. It could have ended up being a deadly situation, but fortunately it wasn't. In my perambulations, I find out that the reason the guy got hurt was that he had worked two full shifts, 16 hours, and was into his nineteenth or twentieth hour of work. It was the third straight shift he had worked, without any time off. The machine he was working on was one of those baling machines with moving parts that can pull a guy in. The machine had caught part of his clothing and he almost was strangled. It was clear to anybody who heard the story that there was probably a reason it happened. Now the shop floor management had a labor report to make to explain what did happen. The report asks, "Was there anything unusual about this case?" And shop management said, "No." Apparently the management knew the situation and were providing their own stonewall. It was a serious matter. You are responsible for the people who work here. If somebody came to me and said, "We're in a jam, this guy worked so many hours, he shouldn't have done it but that's what happened; he finally got fatigued. What can I do?" I'd give him a kick in the ass and say, "That was a case of lousy judgment on your part or on the part of whoever let him get away with that. I'm not going to forget that that's lousy judgment on your part, but just don't do it again and thank your lucky stars that the guy didn't get killed." But the report came in saying that the guy was careless.

In a place like this, with 4000 people, accidents happen all the time. People get broken feet, things fall on their feet, this and that. You're a busy person. You can't go and investigate all these things, so you've got all these managers to report to you what happened. Chances are if you're like most of us you get the input and you say, "That's the case," and maybe you question the kid's merits. But what happens when you find out what you've been told is not the true situation? They didn't say specifically, "Did not work any overtime." What they did say was, "No unusual circumstances." But in walking around, I found out the truth. But the person who told me about it says, "Don't use my name. I don't want to get involved in this mess because they're trying to cover this whole thing up." In my observation, there's kind of a penchant for covering things up and keeping upper management in the dark. In this case I used a device that probably others have used. I called the shop manager in one day and I said, "Here I am with a piece of paper. I've got an anonymous letter that says maybe this case wasn't what it was reported to have been." What a terrible way to have to do it. But I got down to the brass tacks with this guy. An important point was that fortunately the worker hadn't died. So that whole issue was out of the way. The issue was the willingness of people to surface unpleasant information.

Now in that particular organization everything was handled closely. Few people knew about anything. So how well can you manage in a place like that? It's beyond me. So I guess I started my perambulations because I have to have a way of finding out what's going on. If we can give our people some feeling that we're there to help them, say, if somebody's holding a dike they don't have enough fingers to plug, they've got to be able to come and say, "Listen, we've got a whole bunch of problems, will you help us?" I view that as a serious ethical problem, when people say things like "Here's a problem but don't tell anybody I told you. I don't want to get in trouble." The dilemma is letting the person get in trouble to serve the good that can be gained by surfacing some issue and letting it see the light of day, versus protecting the person and letting the bad situation persist. It's a dilemma. If you present yourself to people as someone they can talk to and tell anything, you don't want to inhibit that by betraying a trust. But by the same token, some of those things are so significant that there's an absolute need to have them surface, like the issue of having people working 20 hours in a row. You couldn't have that continue or else you'd have people being killed all over the joint. I suspect that was an unusual occurrence. I know it was. So it was not a matter of people covering up a system of wrongdoing. It was covering an individual isolated mistake that most of us dummies could make, and that most of us dummies would understand you could make. For me, what made it ethical was that management was covering a serious situation and presenting a view of it as being black. And another view was brought surreptitiously saying, "Hey, it's not black, it's white, but don't tell anybody that I told you it's white—leave me out of this." So how do I protect that person, who, I suspect, would have suffered slings and arrows forever if he were exposed as the one who told me that something was awry.

As it turned out, some good came as a result of the whole thing. As I said, that was an organization that tended to keep things close to the vest, and anybody who let any of those secrets out of the closet got punished. But I think that as a result of this episode becoming common knowledge, a few people realized it's OK to make a mistake. They still have some problems, but things are much better than they were. The ethical issue of how you protect people is a serious one. I suspect it's much more widespread than I think it is. I can't believe it's just me, that everybody wants to whisper in my ear. Although I must admit that if you can get around enough, you're more inclined to get people to whisper in your ear. But it's typical of people in a big organization to say things like, "I don't want to rock the boat." The difficult part for me is to find a reasonable way to know something. The "anonymous letter" bothers the hell out of me because I really don't like to lie. I don't like to fabricate those "letters." But "don't tell anybody" is the prevalent issue. Sometimes I get so frustrated that if somebody happens to come in and say, "Don't tell anybody I told you but," I say, "Don't tell me about it unless you want me to do something about it."

We're all constantly making judgments about what's going on. If I start off being suspicious about someone, like the manager who sent the labor report to me (and I was in this case), and if I happen to trust the person who whispers in my ear, based on whatever experiences I have with him or her, somebody who I have a track record with, I have some reason to say, "I've got to do something about this." In terms of how I viewed my responsibilities, if my perception of the situation was right, a whole bunch of people in that place knew what went on, and they knew it was being swept under the rug, and I think that if it had been left to go that way, it could have been a cancer. And I don't think we can afford that. I think it was the perception on the part of the people who work there that the management wasn't being honest about the whole thing. That's a feeling I have, so I felt it was important that some sunshine come upon the scene so that the people there would know that senior management would not have some little subculture run the place the way they felt it should be run. I thought it was a big issue, not something to be trifled with. I also had a real appreciation that the person who told me about it really felt threatened. He had a real dilemma because he also thought it was very important. So I thought about it and decided I had to find some way to present my awareness to the management without saying how I came to know this. Actually, it happens a lot, but usually it's of such a nature that either it wouldn't be clearly understood who the informant was or it wouldn't make any difference. And hopefully we spend enough time roaming around the place that people understand that if you roam around enough you find out almost everything, so what the hell's the sense of keeping secrets. I think that's what happens if you do roam around enough.

Sometimes there's facts around. Hopefully there's a few facts around. Often it's a matter of judgment. You have to have a pretty firm conviction that something is a lie before you jump in and do something. But it's hard for a couple of reasons. One, I'd like to believe my subordinates are telling the truth. When I find out they're not, it disheartens me, makes me think poorly about them, and makes me think poorly about me. A lot of negatives. Am I contributing to this mess? And it's hard because as important as the facts turn out to be, you feel it's important to protect your people from disclosure. Then you go through all these charades so you can find some reasonable way to say you found out about the thing. It seems dishonest, and I find that hard to do. I find it hard to be dishonest in any service. I'm uncomfortable with it; I feel sullied. Not that I'm a picture of honesty, but I think basically I tend to be honest; it's easier to be honest. I'm not smart enough to be devious; I can't remember a bunch of mistakes. There are so many negatives involved. It seems like everything's negative about it and nothing is positive. The whole scene is negative except if there's a light in the window, and people say "They're not going to let that clown get away with that kind of stuff." In my view a lot of good was achieved. People felt that the management wasn't going to allow it to get swept away.

Old routine things tend to be "thing" things: numbers, machines, money, time. The difficult things to deal with tend to be the people things. All those thing things stand still. The machine, the damn thing is going to stand there until you decide what to do. You know the clock is going to move at a second per second; money is going to be a buck, increased by some inflation over time. But people, one day they're this and next day they're that. One day they're mad at something, the next day, they've forgotten about it, it wasn't important. The mind is a difficult thing to deal with. We could stamp out those people and replace them with machines; you know where machines are all the time. God forbid. All the pain you have comes from people, but all the enjoyment does too. I can't sit around here and look at the tube and look at results and have some intellectual thrill. It just doesn't do anything for me. But when I see a person who is making progress and doing something good, it lights up my day. You don't have many days like that, but some, and they make up for a lot of difficult times. I can't have any feeling for a number. When I retire a piece of equipment, I know it's going to scrap iron heaven and it's going to become another machine, another thing. I would say that all the decisions about people have ethical components. I don't have many ethical dilemmas dealing with machines, but I certainly do with people. I often think to myself, Volkswagen had a good thing. They plugged that little analyzer into the Volkswagen and it told you all the things you needed. We need something like that, a thing that plugs into your belly button that tells you this person's good, this person's bad, this person's smart, this person is a good boss or a bad boss. But until that comes, we're going to have to spend a lot of time on this stuff. But I tell you, when I first heard about that Volkswagen plug, the first thing I thought was "What a wonderful way to appraise people."

I believe being a boss, no matter what level of boss you are, is a very, very important job. I spend a lot of time at it. That's why my day is very long. But it's an awful lot of fun. One of the things you've got to do is to keep finding out from the people, "What do you think about this?" We get a very strange view of our world in this office. You've got to find people to tell you some of the bad things.

I'm concerned about the impact that I have. I know that sometimes I've become part of the problem. If somebody does something terribly wrong, and I bring him in here and we talk about it, and I rant and rave and throw the eraser at the wall, and say "Go out and do better," I worry about it. I think that they'll think I'll do this to them every time. There's an art to being a boss, as opposed to a science. The science—everybody's got a B.S. in something. But the art part of it, that's the challenge. I often think that one of our problems is that so many of our bosses have never worked anyplace else. They don't know how to do anything else. This is the world to them, and they don't understand people coming from other places. So many of our bosses have never gotten laid off. They don't know what it's like to have the boss say "Listen, son, we're going to lay you off. If we need your help, we'll call you back, and if we don't, adios, amigo." They treat everybody like they're just numbers. They don't have any feelings about them. They don't understand.

COMMENTS

When told about Bob McDonald's "anonymous letter" solution to his dilemma, a young manager responded, "It doesn't matter what good was achieved. Lying is wrong. And once you've told a little lie, it becomes easier and easier to lie again and again. He should not have done it." When asked how he would have dealt with the dangerous practice and its cover-up while protecting the informant, the young manager answered, "I don't know. I hate situations like that; they always paralyze me. I guess I would have done nothing." "And," one had to ask, "would doing nothing have been an ethical way of handling the situation?" "No," he replied, "but, at least, I would not have lied."

Bob McDonald, and, hypothetically, the young manager, faced a prototypical ethical dilemma. As Bob put it, "The dilemma is letting a person get in trouble to serve the (greater) good . . . versus protecting the person and letting the bad persist." For the young manager the decision was to do nothing, which would have had the result of "letting the bad persist." But for Bob that was not an acceptable outcome. Identifying the situation as "a big issue, not something to be trifled with," he refocused the problem away from an "either/or" situation and set himself the task of doing both, that is, "find[ing] some way to present my awareness to the [shop floor] management without saying how I came to know this." What Bob did, essentially, is weight, or rank, the claims that were being made on him. He determined that protecting his informant was his weightiest concern so that whatever action he took, the informant's identity had to be protected. Bob's discussion suggests he reviewed a number of alternatives before latching on to the "anonymous letter" device. And he admits he was being dishonest, which troubles him. However, he also says he found no other way to get the "good" achieved (protect other workers from harm, change a subculture norm of cover-up, and protect an informant) at so little cost (lying—which he doesn't like to do, but which, in this case, he sees as causing no harm and being productive).

Reactions to Bob McDonald's action will range from reproach for lying to applause for creative problem solving. On the whole, I lean toward the latter evaluation. Bob got the job done, albeit at the personal cost of compromising his own principle. But the process he moved through raises a couple of concerns. First of all, was it really necessary to commit the blatant lie? Bob quotes himself as saying, "Here I am with a piece of paper. I've got an anonymous letter that says maybe this case wasn't what it was reported to have been." The lie is the "anonymous letter," since he truthfully has information that the case wasn't what it was reported to have been. Could not Bob have said to his shop manager, "I've got information that says, . . . ," or even waved a paper before the fellow, saying "Here I am with a piece of paper. I've got information, ... " An outside observer would suggest that either of these alternatives would be as effective a response as the anonymous letter, while avoiding the blatant lie which so concerned the young manager. Bob McDonald would probably counter that he needed the "letter" as a diversionary tactic to insure the protection of his source's identity. We will not come up with a definitive answer, but we can speculate that Bob's top-priority commitment to his informant not to betray a trust, pushed him the extra step to an explicit, rather than implicit, diversion.

The second concern raised by this event is that the "anonymous letter" seems to have become a standard solution to the apparently increasing problem of a "don't tell anybody I told you" means of communication. My concern is not so much that the letter is a lie or that it will lose its effectiveness if used too often, but that it may become a pat solution, easily plucked from a grab bag of guidelines and standard operating procedures that will have two unproductive outcomes. First, as a readily available solution it will cut short the appropriate analysis of the situation and the search for other ways of resolving a particular problem. Second, it will perpetuate and reinforce a developing company norm of communication by secret informant.

In regard to his responsibility, both in this specific situation and generally in the plant, Bob is very clear. He contrasts two kinds of management, sitting in the office versus walking around. If, he says, you sit in your office, you find out what others want you to find out—and that's what you deal with. If you manage by walking around—and if you're good at your job—you find out what's going on. And, if you find out what's going on, you are responsible for dealing with it. Bob clearly believes he should know whatever is going on in his plant, and that having that knowledge puts him in a position of responsibility. In the case of the worker injured during his third straight shift, Bob states his feeling succinctly: "I felt that some sunshine should come upon the scene." And by role and by capability, Bob felt he was the one to bring it.

JAMES
GORDON

**Manager, Corporate Administration
Thirty-nine years old**

*"The company, because of the lack
of structure, ends up chewing up
a lot of people."*

I am corporate administration manager, although I'm an engineer by background and have only been in the administrative world for three years. The responsibility of our group is to come up with a set of procedures and systems support for our function. Basically, we develop the systems to improve productivity and quality of the personnel work. We train 150 people out in our facilities who are the main interface with employees on administrative issues.

Part of the strength of this company is that it isn't really a company in a sense. It's very decentralized, very fragmented; I believe individuals can use that fragmentation to build for themselves the environment they want. So if you're really looking for a lot of structure, you can find it here. There are some organizations, a finance organization for one, that is very structured. There's no two ways to add numbers together; you do it a certain way. You can also find yourself in a complete lack of structure. I positioned myself in a place where our organization is typically unstructured, although my job has structure to it and I can use both pieces to satisfy myself. And I can be an entrepreneur. I've got a million-dollar budget here. I can run that pretty much the way I want.

The company is many things to many people, so a lot of people feel satisfied with it. I just saw the results of the survey that was done in one of the company's groups. Ninety-five percent of the people that work in that group said they would recommend this place to a friend as a good place to work. I think that pretty much wraps it up. I enjoy our success, I enjoy being part of the company. I enjoyed it even before we became well known, but I'm convinced that in 10 years we'll be as well known as the biggest in the business right now. There's an ego thing for me when I tell people I work here. I feel like I'm part of a winner.

When I joined the company, they handed me the company's philosophy. It was the first time that I said to myself, "I think they're serious." With every other company in which I've worked, they said, "Here are the golden rules for the company." Then when I would begin working for that company, I would realize it was all bullshit, that the profit motive was probably the thing that drove most people, and that individuals would get chewed up because it was best for the system. Our philosophy here says that it's not enough to tell customers the truth; it's your responsibility to make sure that whomever you're talking to understands the truth. And that was written at a time when we had problems with customers because we couldn't deliver enough product; demand was so high. But it was the first time I'd ever seen that articulated in such a way. I sit on a policy committee for the company, and time and time again I've seen things that looked like they would be terrific for the company voted down because they would be bad for the individual. I have seen people being taken care of by the company, far beyond anything that was the law or that the company's policy would dictate, because of a feeling about the individual. I have seen individuals in the company who don't have any formal power change the company because they had the right ideas. I think that's all on purpose and by design.

On the other side of that coin, there are things that happen that are not on purpose and aren't by design, which are as nasty as things that go on in other organizations. But they happen for a different reason. I see them happening in other organizations because an individual decides, "I'm going to get that bastard," and the structure allows it to happen. In this company, because we're so unstructured, because we're so decentralized, and because we are typically comprised of very bright, very strong people, there are no support structures for those individuals who are hired in and need the support. If you're sensing some confusion where people are concerned, you're right. This company, because of the lack of structure, ends up chewing up a lot of people. But it is not by design. It's a function of the culture, and any attempts to try to create structure are going to be countercultural and will destroy a lot of things I like about the place.

What I am trying to do is balance the part that says "This is the best place I've ever worked for, they care about the individual and they really are committed to that," against the fact that if you went out and took some measurements, you'd find some individuals who were in pain, who don't know who the hell their boss is or how to do their jobs or what their goals are. For people who care about what they're doing, that's going to be painful. In other organizations, you see people in pain and it's controllable by one or two individuals who are causing that pain. In this company, I see people in pain but it's a result of the fact that the system is not structured in a way to help the individual. So an employee in trouble may not have anywhere to go other than to work the system. And some people don't do that very well. We don't do a very good job of telling people that, either. We just sort of assume everybody knows.

When I think about ethics, I think there are certain things that somehow get programmed into us early on in life around what's good and bad. And goodness for me, in that context, without intellectualizing at all, is just a gut feeling. Goodness for me is helping your fellow man, and not doing anything to damage others, and spending extra time helping people that are in trouble, and so on. Bad is doing anything that would harm other people. Somewhere in the back of my mind there's a tape that plays that. Intellectually, that's different for me than what's right and wrong. A lot of what's the right thing to do and what's the wrong thing to do, I think is, for me, situational. But there's the whole piece around what's good and bad that has to do with basic values. I think of all of this as a matrix that looks like this:

	VALUES	
SITUATIONAL ACTION	Good	Bad
Right		
Wrong		

Let me give you some examples. The good thing to do and the organizationally right thing to do is fair and equal treatment for folks. The good thing to do but the wrong thing to do in an organizational setting is being too honest, thereby undermining organizational effectiveness. So, for example, good things say you'll always tell the truth and you're always straightforward with people, but organizationally that can get you into a whole bunch of hot water and undermine your effectiveness. So from an organizational point of view, that's often the wrong thing to do. A bad thing to do is to tell white lies; goodness says you never lie. But sometimes that is the right thing to do, for instance, to help someone save face. That's doing bad for the right reason. And bad and wrong is, say, deliberately causing personal pain. This matrix sort of puts things in perspective for me in terms of being able to articulate that constant tugging inside me. I spent eight years in a Catholic grammar school, four years in a Catholic youth organization as an officer, four years in a Catholic fraternity in college. I've had that whole Judeo-Christian good-bad stuff drummed into my head. And yet I know damn well that I operate oftentimes in this matrix.

I have been in organizations where the right thing to do from the organization's perspective felt awful to me, and the reason it did is because I think I felt it was not only the wrong thing to do, but that my definition of goodness and badness was so strong around the issue that I said, "Not only is that bad, that's also wrong." And so even though I've been in some situations where I've been able to say the bad thing to do was really the right thing to do, I've also been in situations in other organizations where the bad thing to do has also been what I thought was the wrong thing to do. And then I've been faced with a dilemma around the organization telling me "You gotta do it," and I believe it was bad and it was wrong. That's when dilemmas have really felt awful to me. The interesting thing about this company is that there are very few organizational imperatives around what to do. So I feel much freer to be consistent with this matrix. Generally speaking, when I do the bad thing, it's for the right reason organizationally, and it feels good in here [points to his stomach], yeah. I have not been put into a position in the three years I've been with the company where I've ever had to do what I consider to be the bad and the wrong thing. I've had to do the bad and right, but that bad, as I said, is not an intellectual bad for me, it's a gut-feel value programmed in very early on by a bunch of nuns and a bunch of other folks, my parents and whomever, who probably didn't always live by those either.

Here is an interesting example. We've got a woman who works in our department, Mary, and she has had virtually every disaster that can happen to a person happen during the past two years: death of both parents, major physical problems, incredible personal problems with a sibling and other relatives. She got very sick. OK. The good thing to do is to take care of your fellow man. There is some question in my mind about whether the company policies would say what I did was right or wrong, from an organizational point of view. I chose to do what I think our chairman would agree was the right thing.

A little bit of background on this woman: she's a local person; she grew up in the community in which we are headquartered, went to high school there, and has always dreamed of working for this company. There's a whole piece around community relations that subtly entered my head around her and I said, "Part of me wants to treat her well because she's a local person working for us." The other thing I noticed was that she works in a place where you start at eight, you take your coffee break, you take your lunch break, and you take your coffee break in the afternoon, and the rest of the time you're just out straight; you get driven by the phones. Two women, Mary and Sue, handle on the order of 3500 phone calls a month. And they love it. When we were getting ready to move over here, Sue came in to me and she said, "Mary and I have talked, and we're not going to be able to pack those files for the move and answer the phones at the same time. Would you mind if we came in on Saturday? We don't care about the pay, but would you care if we did that?" I'm saying, "Holy . . . !" I mean, where do you find these people? Well, that's what Mary is all about, too. She is really dedicated. So I say, "The hell with the company policy. I'm going to treat her well." So, essentially, I paid her for a lot of the time she was out. I didn't want to take away all of her sick time. She was beginning to chew into her vacation time. There she was, someone whose life involves getting up in the morning, taking care of her relatives, working here, going home, taking care of her relatives, and also going to school. She was going to community college to pick up some credits. And I'm saying, "I'm not going to pile any more crap on that lady." Now, I don't know if that's the right or the wrong thing to do from the company's point of view, but I think our chairman would probably support the concept of disregarding sick time, short-term disability, and long-term disability. That, to me, was a fairly easy dilemma to work myself out of. It certainly was the good thing to do. There was a little bit of question about the right thing to do from an organizational point of view, but again, this company has convinced me that the right thing in that case was to disregard company policy and to use my own judgment around what I did with her.

Actually, the only dilemma piece was that the company policy states she should have used up her sick time, vacation time, and then gone on short-term disability. So I said, "I'm probably taking a risk here." The other nice thing was, I went in to my boss and said, "Look, I've got a person in my group . . . ," and I told him her background, and I said, "I'm not asking for you to do anything other than to understand that I'm going to treat her well, because I think she deserves it. She's given loyalty and hard work and dedication to this department and to the company; she's a local person; I just think there's a whole bunch of things that we need to do for her."

Q. *What was the risk?*

Part of the risk was other people in the department knowing that I'd done it, and saying, "Hey, you did it for her. I want to take next week off, because I think I just need some R&R time." Another part of the risk was somebody poking around and finding out I was paying her as if she were here when she wasn't. But I really feel as if no one in the company would challenge what I did because it was the right thing to do. When I say I feel that, I feel that *now*. But when I was going through the decision making on it, I still had some question as to whether somebody would force the company policy on me (which in itself is fairly liberal, it treats people fairly well).

But this company, quite frankly, does treat people differently, depending on their situation, and in spite of all company policy. And I see the only risk being one of doing it in some kind of discriminatory fashion, where you're doing it just for white males, for example. Then I think you're really opening yourself up for a risk. But as I've said before, the company has really made me feel like I'm owning my own business here; I'm an entrepreneur. And if I owned my own business and could afford it, I probably would've done exactly the same thing. So there was a piece of me that said, "Look, I'm running a business here, and what I want to do is to treat that person well, because her loyalty has been such, and the amount of work she's put in is such that I don't think the policy applies to her." If it ever ended up in a one-on-one conversation between the chairman and me, which it never would, I've got a feeling he'd probably support me. I think the nice part about being here is I don't have a whole lot of dilemmas that are placed on me by the organization because I think, first of all, it is very moral and ethical in the way it positions itself, and second of all, it's so decentralized that there isn't that kind of pressure that says "The right thing for the company to do, you jerk, is this. Now you go off and do it."

So the ethical question was: here is a person who I would like to be able to help during a very trying part of her life, but I know that some of the things I'm doing are against company policy and procedure, which, by the way, I helped write. Is that really the right thing to do? Should I really be going that extra mile, or should I say to myself, "Policy was written because we know some people are going to get themselves sick and need time off. She'll get 80% of her salary for a while and then two-thirds of her salary. Sorry, that's just the way life is sometimes." So I went through that whole thought process of "Do I really want to go against company policy around how I treat people? What if everybody did that? Then the policy would be worth garbage, and the company would be spending all kinds of money." So I put all that stuff aside and I said, "Well, let me look at her as an individual. I can't justify not helping her out." Now, she is out on short-term disability. There came a point when we had to say, "OK, we've done everything we know how, and now we're going to try to preserve her vacation time for her, which we did. But I probably gave her seven or eight days that should have been vacation or sick time or something. So I'm not talking about huge amounts of money. But there came a point at which I said, "OK, she is going to be out for an extended period of time. [She had an operation.] Now it's time for short-term disability to come into play."

It sent a message to the other people in the department. I've heard a little bit of feedback that said people really appreciated what I did for her. The message says (a) Jim's a humane manager, and (b) he must work for a fairly humane company to allow him to get away with that. I think most people know it wasn't something I hid, and I didn't have to get devious to make that happen. I just made a decision that that's the way it should be. So there were all kinds of payoffs to the company, because there are 16 other people out there who all say this really is a neat place to work—look what they did for Mary. And they don't even try to personalize it and say, "Son of a bitch, what are they going to do for me now?" or "Why would they do that for her and not for me?" They all understand she's a unique case. In fact, we had one individual who has been out. She went through a real attitudinal thing for whatever reason, things going on at home. Then she hurt her back. She wanted to take some extra time around a funeral, and from everything I could tell, it really wasn't a close relative. And she was told "No, you've been out X number of days." I have two people between myself and that individual, and they came to me and said "We're going to get tough with Ellen about coming in. We just want you to know we're doing it. We think it's the proper thing to do." And I supported it. And never once did she come back and say—that's where the danger was—"Well, look what you've done for Mary and you're not willing to give me. . . . " I believe she knew there was a difference between just being in a lousy mood and being in bed.

Look at the matrix. When I'm in the bad and the right box, the thought process I find myself using is sort of incremental rationalization which means that each step makes sense within the context of doing the right thing from a situational point of view. And I'm fairly comfortable about overriding the bads as long as I can incrementally justify each step as being the right thing to do. Now it feels different when I do it in the Mary case. In the case where it's good but it may be wrong, my decisions tend to be binary. Then tend to be: that's what I'm going to do. I mean, I'll do some talking about it ahead of time, but there's very little rationalizing. With Mary I made a decision that I was going to do something and I didn't have to incrementally rationalize it, I just said, "BOOM. I believe that this is the right thing to do. I know I'm taking some risk personally here, but screw it. BOOM! I'm going to do it." Combined with the piece that said if she had been another employee who gives me 40 hours and goes home and does not have her dedication to the company and dedication to the job, then I could very easily say, "It's a situation defined by the policy and what I can do for you is this. Thank you very much." So there was a rightness that had to do with the quality of the person. It was an organizational rightness, I felt, that had some fringes that were kind of frayed because the policy kept nipping away at me and I had to sort of balance that stuff. But it wasn't incremental for me. It was "Consider all that stuff and then BOOM."

The hardest box in the matrix to be in is the bad-wrong. It's a bad thing to do, and I think it's the wrong thing to do organizationally, and somebody says you have to do it. And I've been in those situations a couple of times. That's a tough one for me to deal with because I generally end up folding and doing it because you can't win. I guess you do have a choice. The choice is to leave. Or to start laying the groundwork for leaving the organization. You can't do too many of those. By the way, lest you get the wrong idea, the matrix came directly as a result of your asking me to think about ethics. One of the things you should know about me is that I don't generally have a very structured way of sitting down and processing my own feelings and thoughts. The matrix came out of my attempt to sit down and take a generic question around ethical dilemmas. I started just playing around with "Well, what is ethics?" And that's how it came up. What I was trying to structure was situations where a dilemma occurs for me. I have a friend who did his divorce that way. It was mind-boggling. He did pros and cons and guess what? He had two pros and 57 cons and said, "It's time to leave." This guy's an MIT grad and very bright. The thing to know about me is I don't have the structure I probably should have around some of these questions. I tend to go with my gut more often than not.

When there are competing claims, what I think happens is that somehow I process all of those claims, give a certain weight to each, and then end up in one of these boxes, saying, "Yeah, overall, after I weigh everything together, the right thing to do is going to mean taking a couple of bad steps or whatever. Understanding that some people are going to be hurt by that, and some people are going to benefit by that, but the overall right thing to do is this." Then the question is, is the right really my new set of values? Is that my real set of values or is the good and the bad my real set of values? It's hard; I haven't thought about it a lot. And it's hard because you can probably argue that my real set of values is the right and wrong, and that the good and bad are just sort of childhood underpinnings, sort of a base which I don't subscribe to all that strongly. Sometimes it feels that a lot of things I was taught were bad, I find myself being able to rationalize in terms of what's right. I mean, if I went out and told the truth to everyone in my department, there would be very few people standing up. And I'm sure they could do the same to me. So I guess my values really are that the right thing to do is to protect that shell, and organizations tend to encourage that. This company less than others. We tend to encourage people to be honest about what they're thinking. The first couple of times I made presentations here, I said, "I'm either failing or I'm doing real good. I can't figure out which." Oh, the stuff that gets stirred up: "I don't agree with that." "That's bullshit." And I found that people are doing that because they were really wired into what you were saying, instead of sort of sitting there. It takes some time to get used to that.

There's a tremendous amount of consistency between the way I view myself as an individual and the way I feel the company views itself and wants me to act. And so I've yet to really confront an issue and have to worry about inconsistency between what I believe is right to do and what the company believes is the right thing to do. And they don't define "right" all that well. They say, "You're sitting closest to it, you do the right thing." "Right" means not doing a dumb thing just because the policy book says to do it that way, or because you've got a memo saying to do it that way. So I guess I'm very fortunate to feel that consistency, that congruency, and it's nice because it's congruent with the rest of my life. I don't have to set up one set of behaviors and values here, and silence all the ethical questions, and just go out and do what's best for the organization. And I don't have to do that at home. I don't have to make decisions at home that are in conflict with what the company wants. It's a nice balance for me.

Postscript

One year after I interviewed James Gordon, he had to make the difficult decision to fire Mary. He had continued to bend the rules for her until it came to a point where, for a number of personal reasons on her part, she was unable to fulfill the requirements of her job. He explains the decision in terms of incrementally doing the "right" thing until it gets to a point where the next step no longer is justifiable from a "good" or a "right" perspective.

COMMENTS

In Jim Gordon's matrix, we see reflected a theme relevant to most of the dilemmas discussed in these pages: How do I balance basic beliefs and values with being effective and responsible in a complex and ambiguous world. We need to recognize that for all the pain represented by his model, Jim, in his present organization, has it easier than some. The reason is that the matrix is based on the assumption that Jim—or whoever is using it—*can* act as he chooses and is not subject to a "do it" command from above. Jim mentions that when he says the "awful" situation to find yourself in is to be in the bad/wrong box on an action which your superior insists you do.

As Jim talks about his dilemma with Mary, it is clear he felt *he* could decide what to do and his decision either would be supported by the company or, if not, would not involve great personal risk for him. According to his matrix, Jim was in the good/wrong box— it is good to help a person in need, but it is wrong to compromise an organizational policy. Jim says that in a good/wrong situation he just does what he feels is right, BOOM, regardless of the risks or other circumstances. Certainly that seems to be the case in the Mary situation.

Jim believed he *could* get the job done, but there was an organizational value system in place as well. Jim felt he could adjust the disability policy because (1) the company does believe in treating people differently, in spite of policy, as long as the different treatment is not discriminatory, (2) the role of policy in the company is not clear, and (3) if he went one-on-one with the chairman, Jim believed the chairman would back him up.

The supportive corporate environment allowed Jim to resolve his dilemma with some useful devices. First, he was able to focus almost solely on a single stakeholder, Mary; so the key question became "What is best for her?" With the company behind him, he did not feel pulled in too many directions at once. Second, he did not have to hide his action or engage in other covert activities. He told his boss and allowed his decision to become public knowledge in the company, which mitigated any sense of "wrong" and reinforced for him the doing of good.

Jim's situation raises a critical concern about the role of policy in organizations. Policy is written to express corporate values in a particular area and to set the guidelines for actions relating to that area. But the general nature of a policy cannot take into account all of the possible configurations of events—the exceptions—that must occur in any organization. The question is: How do you deal with the exceptions? Rigid policy that demands absolute adherence can be dysfunctional and even ethically harmful to a company by compromising both the integrity and competence of managers within it. On the other hand, policy that can be ignored or distorted or interpreted in a variety of ways can lead to similar outcomes by creating a too anarchic environment. In Jim's and his company's case, the line between blind compliance to, and manipulation of a policy was trod with finesse. The outcome supported Mary, the company, the other employees, and Jim. As Jim points out, however, his actions might have set a precedent which could have eroded the respect for policies, rules, and procedures in the organization.

HAROLD

LIGHTNER

Director, Manufacturing Personnel
Fifty-three years old

"There are a lot of crazies in this world
and they may not be out there.
They may be calling from inside
the plant to get out of work."

everal years ago there were a number of bomb threats. You may recall that schools were evacuated. It turned out to be similar in this company. We began receiving bomb threats. Initially, when we received a bomb threat at a particular site, we would immediately evacuate all the buildings. You didn't even think twice about it. The call came in, you evacuated the buildings. You didn't make too many judgments about whether it was real or not, you just evacuated the buildings. That happened two or three times. But after a while it got to be "Now wait a minute here, we're shutting down the operations. Thank goodness nothing is happening, but it's disruptive and it's costing us a lot of money. Maybe we ought to be doing something differently." So what we did was decide that we were not just going to evacuate buildings if we received a bomb threat. What we were going to do was be very careful about the call and try to engage the person making the call to get as many of the specifics as we could. And unless there was a whole lot of good substantive data, we were probably not going to evacuate. It just didn't make sense for us to continue to close our operations. I think we went from being fail-safe, to being rather conservative. What kind of a call came in? What was the voice like? Was it somebody that had called before? Were they specific about the building and the floor? What time did they say this thing was going to go off? And if the information was vague, or if the time was uncertain, we probably would not evacuate. What we would do was to conduct a good inspection, call the fire department and the police to alert them that we had received a threat, and maybe selectively inform some supervisors out on the floor so that they knew what was going on and would be able to explain if a question was asked.

Of course, what that did was raise the question of "Hey, who makes the decision for me around here?" When we went back and reflected on that, it became evident that we could make judgments, and we were in a position to assimilate the data, analyze it, and make a determination about whether company-wide, or plant-wide, we were going to evacuate, but we could not decide for others whether or not they should stay. We decided what we would do was inform the population at large, give them all the facts that we had, tell them we were not going to evacuate, and why we were not going to evacuate. But then we would tell them that as individuals they had a right to leave if they wanted to, and that it would be OK; there would be no penalty. It was interesting that we went from, "My gosh, we're not going to take any chances, everyone out," to, "Wait a minute, what's going on here, we're going to make the judgment for everyone because we know better, we have all the information," to one where we would provide a broad overview that said, in essence, "This is what we think, but you as an individual now can make your own personal decision about what's in your best interest."

What we did eventually was to set up a committee of three or four. The committee included the corporate security officer, who was in the best position to have all of the data that were going around, not only all through the company, but also in the community. He was very helpful by being able to piece the information we were receiving together with what was happening at large. It's difficult to sit there, especially in a situation like this where there's the possibility of harm or injury and say, "Okay, this is what I would do." I might be the type who says "The last thing I'm going to do is give in on this thing, because if you give in once they'll keep calling all the time." The person next to me may not feel that way. The person next to me may have a different set of standards. And I'm not sure that in a situation like this it's right for me to impose how I would do things on someone else, and be offended if that person takes a slightly different point of view. So there was help from the corporate security officer and there were corporate officers involved, and eventually we went from a rather nebulous situation where if I received a call I handled it and I had to render my own judgment and make the decision right there, to a situation in which there were some guidelines so that I could operate within those guidelines. And if I had any question at all, I could contact the experts. Most important though is that we didn't keep the data from individuals.

The first time you don't even consider the financial aspects. It was "Please let's get everyone out, let's not take any chances," and "If I could only get my hands on that SOB that's calling, that would be the last time he would call." But finally, you recognize that "Wait a minute here. There are a lot of crazies in this world, and they may not be out there. They may be inside the plant calling to get out of work. You just can't keep going on like this each time you receive a call; you're going to disrupt the operation." That didn't make a whole lot of sense.

There are a number of situations like this one. Using hazardous chemicals, for example. At what point do you feel the protection that's built in is safe enough, or the cost, on the other end, is justified? Those are difficult decisions, and the more knowledgeable we become, the less for granted we can take things. In the past we've taken a number of things for granted because we didn't have all of the information that's available to us today. It's a struggle; it's an everyday struggle; it really is. We went through a situation here just recently where we were required to use a chemical that had some hazard associated with it. Well we just don't arbitrarily use something hazardous in a process, we find if there are some alternatives to it. In the short run, in this case, there were not. It was a matter of either using this chemical, or stopping production. So the next thing we did was try to minimize the use of the chemical and try to build in every conceivable safety factor to satisfy all of the regulations (and believe me there are a number of regulations, including your own operational criteria). So somehow you have to perform two things: one is to meet regulation because you are required to, and the other is to meet the company standards. And thank God, we have high standards.

But it still comes down, at some point, to a question of "OK, do you produce half as much as you otherwise would have, or do you introduce something that has a certain degree of hazard associated with it?" And can you ever be certain that you are 100% safe? I would submit no. You absolutely have to minimize the risk. I wasn't specifically involved in this case, although as a corporate conscience I suppose I could have always raised my hand and said, "What the hell is going on here?" I see managers struggling with things like that every day. They don't take it lightly, thank goodness. I don't see anybody being casual about those kinds of responsibilities.

The bomb scare thing never really played itself completely out. There were individuals who decided to leave, while many stayed, and we lived with that situation. It would have been interesting, however, if these things had continued, and as time went on, more and more individuals decided to leave. I'm not sure at what point you say "Wait a minute here, let's stop and think about this some more." I'm not suggesting that we would have, but I can envision, if you will, management feeling, "My God, 50% of the people shouldn't be walking out. We could understand 10%, but we don't know why 50%—what the hell is going on here?" We took the responsibility for letting them know when it was clear. Sure, there was concern on the part of those that stayed. I think people left for a couple of reasons. Some legitimate. Those people just absolutely couldn't stand the environment under those conditions, and they had great personal discomfort. And for those, I think most people would say, "Yeah, that doesn't surprise me, I know so-and-so, and I can live with that situation." But there were others, there are always a couple, who felt, "Hey, I want the hour off, see you later." And most of us know them, and, yeah, that's tough. You make a mental note of that and you say, "OK, that's an indication of something else going on." But eventually that gets resolved.

Personally, I absolutely refuse to be intimidated. My inclination would be to gut it out. On the other hand, to consider that that's the way everyone else feels is unreasonable. That's the way I feel, that's the way I want to operate. That's fine. But given a situation like this, where there's a possibility of harm and injury, then it isn't fair for everyone else to gut it out like Hal. I have to be willing to say, "Look, these are the facts. You and I have the same facts. This is what I'm going to do, and this is the reason that I'm going to do it. Now you have to make your decision, and I'll not be offended by your decision if it happens to differ from mine, because you may approach these things a little bit differently than I do."

Decision making is interesting. Unless you are in a position of absolute authority and power, your decisions are going to have to meet the test: do the majority of people believe and agree? To me that's a kind of ethical test. If they don't, then you're in trouble; you're going to get resistance, and it just isn't going to work. I have my set of values and standards, and others may have theirs. I'm not sure we ever test to see how compatible they are. It's an intriguing question; it really is. If everything I did, including my thoughts, was openly communicated to everyone, if all of my actions and all of my thoughts were on a billboard out there, and everyone had an opportunity to take a look at that billboard and make a judgment about the good and bad, that, to me, would be a kind of ethical test. Ethics is the opening up of your thoughts and your actions so that everyone can take a look at them, judge them, and place some value on their appropriateness. If I'm making a decision, my ethical responsibility is to make sure I have a good understanding of all of the vested interests and their positions so that when I can make my decision it's within the context of that understanding. I'm willing to share my beliefs and have them tested against others; I think it's important to test them. And I'm willing to debate my beliefs with someone who doesn't particularly agree with them. Sure. And hopefully, if the weight of the evidence is that my beliefs should change, I'm objective enough to change.

COMMENTS

Hal's problem initially was simple, straightforward, and not a dilemma. A phone caller stated that a bomb would go off in the plant. Hal's responsibility was to protect his employees. He evacuated the plant. But the continued threats, with no evidence of actual danger, pushed Hal into rethinking what his responsibility to his subordinates was. These are the steps Hal describes.

1. With the first threats, Hal's sole concern as plant manager was the safety of all plant employees. Because of a clear and present danger, Hal never questioned the appropriateness of his deciding the safest course of action for everyone.

2. As time went on, and no real harm occurred, Hal found himself thinking not only of employee safety but also of the cost of frequent plant evacuations. He then decided that management was in the best position to judge whether or not a real danger existed and would, therefore, decide whether or not to evacuate the facility.

3. At this point, Hal recalls, the critical question of "who decides what I will do?" was raised. Interestingly, the focus does not seem to have been on management's responsibilities to those who are dependent upon it, or on those subordinates' need for autonomy. The question took a much more pragmatic shape:

what do we have the authority to realistically enforce? And the answer seems to have been: we can't make them stay.

4. At this point management moved to the responsible position of saying, in essence, "We will provide you, the employees, with all the information we have to help you make an informed choice about what you will do. We will also tell you what we as management will do. Then the choice of action is yours, with no penalty if you should decide to leave the plant." In the process of resolving the dilemma Hal turned the question away from an either/or dilemma (safety versus cost) to focus on balancing the commitment to both goals by finding a way for employees to make an informed choice about their own safety and their own commitment to the organization.

Hal was helped in resolving his dilemma by the appointment of a committee, which provided expertise, a variety of viewpoints, and shared responsibility. It strikes me that in this situation, committee decision making and shared responsibility are extremely valuable. The burden of responsibility for the lives of a plant full of people could be a burden too heavy to allow sound decision making by an individual. And, of course, the concern that group decision making might minimize the accountability of any one individual was mitigated by the fact that the committee members were on-site and, so, directly affected by the consequences of their decisions.

The question of which is more effective—group or individual decision making—is certainly not new to the study of management and managerial decision making. Issues of participative management are fraught with managerial and ethical implications that continue to be explored and debated. Most research in the area of individual versus group decision making looks at "effectiveness" as the key criterion. But when we talk about ethical decision making, we must include another criterion—accountability—as either another measurable outcome or as part of what we call "effectiveness."

When asked why a decision about an ethical dilemma was easier if shared, almost everyone who answered said that by sharing the decision making they felt relieved of full responsibility and accountability for the outcome. In other words, they felt that if someone were to challenge the ethics of the decision, or if the results of implementing it were unsuccessful or simply disliked, neither accusing fingers nor pricks of conscience would so readily find them. In addition, several managers said they often felt paralyzed by ethical dilemmas and that sharing the struggle for an answer and the burden of responsibility enabled them to act.

These concerns support the idea of collaborative decision making in situations which managers feel have ethical overtones; however, they also raise some serious questions. Most critical is that question of responsibility. In matters of ethics, it is not clear that shared responsibility and accountability are the way to the most effective, ethical response. Perhaps in decisions around ethical concerns it is critical that someone own the decision and be personally invested in the outcome of its implementation. The dilemma, of course, is how to support individual responsibility and accountability, and avoid dangerous buck-passing, while also preventing scapegoating, which is what many managers fear may happen to them as the sole decision maker in a situation with many values and many stakeholders.

THE "PUBLIC" MANAGER AND THE PRIVATE PERSON

U p to this point, we have looked at and listened to the managers in this book from one perspective—that of the individual at work. We have noted the characteristics of organizations that contribute, often unintentionally, to the development of ethical dilemmas; we have considered organizational factors that affect managers' capacity to handle such dilemmas. We have discussed the characteristics of ethical problems as seen by managers and how those dilemmas differ from the formulation of ethical issues on which policies, codes, and guidelines are based. And we have looked at the managers themselves in their relationship to their jobs, their professional colleagues both within and outside the organization, and in the ways they tackle and resolve the ethical dilemmas they face in their jobs. We also, on occasion, have heard about people and events outside the work environment who affect or are touched by the managers' professional lives, for example Bob McDonald's daughters and Jeffrey Lovett's family. But, basically, the manager has been the manager, not a human being with a family history, social experiences, and personal beliefs, values, and traits that he or she carries into the work role and the work place.

Many people would claim that that is how it should be: that individuals do and must separate their work (or public) lives, and the ethics of those lives, from their personal (or private) lives, and the ethics in that sphere. Robert Bellah and associates writing in *Habits of the Heart* (1985) states that "the manager also has another life, divided among spouse, children, friends, community, and religious and other nonoccupational involvements. Here, in contrast to the manipulative, achievement-oriented practices of the work place, another kind of personality is actualized, often within a social pattern that shows recognizable continuity with earlier American forms of family and community. But it is an outstanding feature of industrial life that these sectors have become radically discontinuous in the . . . moral understandings that guide individuals within them. 'Public' and 'private' roles often contrast sharply. . . . "

The view put forth by Bellah and associates certainly is not new. Since Adam Smith first laid down the rules of the free enterprise game, both critics and admirers have pointed out that the processes prescribed and the very language used to describe them—self-reliant, market-driven, competitive, self-interested—are incompatible with, or simply do not allow for, the values promulgated by the Judeo-Christian tradition—sincerity, compassion, concern for community—on which the American family has been built. Although Adam Smith wrote at the end of the eighteenth century—at the time, presumably, when the families and communities to which Bellah refers were flourishing—it was the burgeoning of the Industrial Revolution in North America in the mid-nineteenth century that brought the free enterprise system into prominence.

By the early twentieth century we began to see the American corporate manager portrayed as a self-interested, power- and money-hungry, achievement-driven creature, corrupted by the demands of the corporate environment and the commercial marketplace. The promotional blurb on the back cover of a slim volume entitled *Three Plays About Business in America* (1964) puts forth the views on business of the first half of this century:

> Here are three plays written between 1923 and 1947. . . . Each play takes as its theme some aspect of the corrosive influence of business on the development of the human spirit. . . .
>
> *The Adding Machine* (by Elmer Rice)—a merciless satire on the white collar drudge, slave to his job and victim of the very system he champions.
>
> *Beggar on Horseback* (by George Kaufman and Marc Connelly)—a courageous attack on the crushing effects of the business mentality on artistic creation.
>
> *All My Sons* (by Arthur Miller)—a deeply moving play with a strong moral sense about the businessman who places his personal aggrandizement above the responsibility to the rest of mankind.

These three plays, covering a 25-year period, delineate a change in public perception of the corporate manager. The early image drew no distinctions between the public and the private person, that is, corporate man was evil man in all spheres of his life. But there gradually emerged the picture, captured by Bellah, of the decent fellow who leaves his decency at his family's doorstep to don the mask of aggressive self-interest in the marketplace. And often, as in *All My Sons*, retribution for the public evil is served up in the sphere of the private life. Joe Keller, Miller's factory owner who ships cracked aircraft engine heads to the military, resulting in the death of 21 young men and the suicide of his older son when he learns what his father has done, cries out to his younger son Chris:

> You're a boy, what could I do! I'm in business, a man is in business. A hundred and twenty cracked, you're out of business; you got a process, the process don't work, you're out of business; . . . they close you up, they tear up your contracts, what the hell's it to them? You lay forty years into a business and they knock you out in five minutes, what could I do, let them take forty years, let them take my life away? I never thought they'd install them. . . . I thought they'd stop'em before anybody took off. . . . Chris . . . Chris, I did it for you, it was a chance and I took it for you. I'm sixty-one years old, when would I have another chance to make something for you? . . . For you, a business for you!

Joe Keller is the decent man, the caring father, corrupted by the demands of the corporate world.

The critical assumption underlying this two-sided view of the corporate manager is, as Bellah points out, that the manager has broken with the traditions of the past and has discarded or disregarded family history, parental beliefs and attitudes, education, religion, friends, spouse, and children. This assumption must then lead to the conclusion that all managers, in their work setting, are alike in their beliefs, attitudes, and the actions they take; that the socialization that occurs in the workplace drives out not only the values with which these managers were raised, but, in fact, the ability to assess a situation and make value-driven choices.

If this assumption is true, it has an important implication for an individual's capacity to manage ethically. The theme of this book is that both organizations and their members are responsible for creating the conditions within which ethical behavior can take place. Organizations bear a large share of responsibility for creating an environment that *allows* and *enables* managers to engage their abilities and capabilities to manage ethically. But the organization can offer only environment and resources; it is the manager who must provide the competence, the commitment, the energy, and the empathy that makes the fertile work environment into a productive—and ethical—one. If Bellah's assumption is valid, then we must relieve individuals of any contribution to their own capacity since "their beliefs, attitudes, and actions"—which Bellah says result from organizational socialization—are, in fact, simply products of the workplace. So, presumably, if work organizations hold beliefs and attitudes that lead to ethical actions, managers will too. If organizations do not espouse and convey the necessary values, individuals will have nothing to draw on to enhance their capacity for managing ethical dilemmas, nor can we expect them to do so.

This statement seems to me to be nonsensical. The struggles and conflicts described by the managers in these interviews give evidence of the efforts they extend to bring the traditions, the beliefs, and the attitudes with which they were raised and which now shape their lives with family and friends, into the workplace. While some may suggest that such struggles are evidence of Bellah's "discontinuity," I assert that the very fact that those emotional and intellectual battles are waged is evidence that most managers experience and seek to maintain a coherence in their public and private lives.

In the third interview I held with each of the participants, I asked them to talk about their own backgrounds: parents, education, religion, people who guided and influenced them, as well as their present "personal" lives: spouse, children, religion, community. These interviews were conducted after the managers had talked about their jobs, their companies, and the ethical dilemmas they faced. I wanted to see if what they said about themselves, their families, and their backgrounds cohered with what they had reported earlier about who they were as managers and how they handled their jobs.

For example, did a manager raised in a family active in community affairs and concerned with the welfare of others, instinctively define the limits of his responsibility more broadly than the manager raised in the anonymity of a large city or the isolation of a rural area? In the latter cases, where responsibility may have been focused primarily on the maintenance of the family, would the manager define his responsibility quite narrowly? Do family beliefs about "rooting for the underdog" or "always backing a winner" affect the way a manager weighs the different stakeholders to whom she has a responsibility in a given situation? If there is a unity between individual managers' public and private lives, then there will also be a very real difference among managers in how they perceive the corporate world around them and how they handle the ethical dilemmas presented to them. All managers will not respond in the same way to a situation just because they are managers. The background, education, and experience will shape the capacity of each man and woman to manage the ethical dilemmas at work.

THE INTERVIEWS

The three managers in the interviews that follow present a range of backgrounds, jobs, and personal styles that are found in American corporate life today. One is Protestant, one Jewish, and one Catholic. One was raised in a small colonial town in the East, one in a cosmopolitan, urban center of the Midwest, and one in an immigrant community in the heartland of America. As students, one went to the Naval Academy, one was an Ivy Leaguer, and one attended a small, somewhat avant-garde university. One man is the head of an organization, one a high-level staff person, one a middle-level line manager working in a technical area. All are married and have children. And all put in long hours at jobs that they, for the most part, enjoy.

ROBERT
SMITH

Chief Executive Officer
Sixty-four years old

"They felt that this was 'smoking gun' evidence that the balances were being improperly used."

I was born and brought up in a city near Boston, as were all of my relatives and ancestors as far back as you care to go. I had a sister four years older than I was, and when I was 12 she suddenly died of a serious infection, which was a terrible blow to my parents. She was very talented; I remember her a little bit. So I became an only child at the age of 12. My father was a lawyer and a judge; he was very well respected locally. He also sat on the board of a nearby university, which was a very important part of his life. So I grew up in a comfortable home with no serious financial problems in the family. We were pure middle class but comfortable; no wealth but nobody ever had to worry. At least I didn't. Maybe my dad did.

My mother had been a schoolteacher and my aunt was a schoolteacher, very well thought of in the community, so all in all many people looked at me as a young man with a silver spoon in his mouth. Every time I did anything bad at school, the teacher used to look at me and say, "Robert, you're taking advantage." I never knew what that meant for a long time, but I used to hear that all the time, "You're taking advantage."

Like all other young WASPs of the time, I went to Sunday school. I grew up with that, and singing in the choir, and participating actively in church affairs. We belonged to a liberal church which regards Christ as a wonderful man and good teacher but not necessarily divine. Then I went to high school. I was never athletic. I was musical, played in the band, and led the school orchestra. Also, I was in the student government as an undergraduate. Studies came easily to me; I didn't work too hard.

When I was graduated from high school, I was a year too young as I'd skipped the fifth grade at the urging of the teachers who were friends of my mother and aunt. As a result, I barely knew how to do long division. So I went to preparatory school for a year to get older (and maybe a little boost in mathematics). I enjoyed it very much, and I made some good friends there. I led a dance orchestra, and while we were playing on the Cunard Lines going back and forth, I got a letter from my father saying the president of his university had just died, and that he was going to have quite a lot to do with temporarily running the place till they could find a new president, so perhaps I'd rather not go there. My mother never approved of it anyway because it was coeducational. She

· 250 ·

suggested that perhaps I'd like to go to an ivy league college which was definitely all male. I wrote back and said, "Fine." So my father called up a trustee friend of his (of course this was 1937, and you could do that then), and I was accepted. Again, I did not work terribly hard; I had a lot of outside activities; I was a lazy student. I got by comfortably with reasonably good grades, but below the honors level. Later, I went to graduate school and got my MBA.

Going to business school then was fairly easy because you could give up your fourth year of liberal arts, get your bachelor's degree at the end of the first year and your master's degree a year later. So you really only put five years into it. That was a mistake. The mistake was that I gave up the richest year of liberal arts; that's the year when you're old enough to know what you're doing. I've always missed that. Now I strongly advise people against it. Just before I was graduated from business school, the war started and the Navy came up and recruited. I was always a water-type person, so I thought I would join, and I was made an ensign, subject to receiving my MBA. This lasted nearly four years. I had an interesting career. For some unknown reason I decided to be a bomb disposal officer, which of course alarmed my parents. I guess I did it to try to prove something.

In between my two terms in business school I worked for this bank. I was expected to have a summer job and, fortunately, the school arranged for an interview. I worked here one summer; did a very good job. I was helping to answer letters of inquiry from customers about the credit-worthiness of foreign customers. If they were selling goods to an Indian concern, or a French concern, obviously they'd want to know about the credit risk. We maintained files on many of these companies, so we would either use our files or would write to correspondent banks in those countries. I'd have to put it all together. My mentor on the job suddenly got sick toward the end of the summer. I had been planning to go on a commercial fishing voyage for two weeks with a Gloucester fisherman. My boss called and said, "We need you for two more weeks. Can you stay?" And I said, "Sure." So I gave up the fishing trip. I guess something I always did was to subordinate personal and even family things to the call of the job. When I finally left, they said, "Any time you want a job in this bank, you've got it."

I went to war for four years, and when I returned, I didn't want to be a banker. I wanted to be in advertising. I went to two or three advertising agencies, and they said, "We don't hire anybody who doesn't have experience." To this day, I don't know how you get into the advertising business. Finally, through a friend of my father, I had an interview with Lever Brothers, which was then head-quartered in this area and they agreed to hire me. The job was to start in three months, as the fellow I was going to replace wasn't going to leave until then, which is not a very smart way to recruit. So I remembered that this bank had offered me a job, and I came here without saying that I was going to leave in three months. Basically, I needed to have something to do. I started to work doing the same thing I had done that summer four years before. Then I got moved into the credit department. Three months later I got my call from Lever Brothers, and I said, "I'm sorry, I've changed my mind, I like what I'm doing." And I stayed.

It was a rapid growth period after the war, and there weren't too many people to fill the jobs, so I had fairly clear sailing. I guess I made myself useful. I never asked anybody what my career was going to be; I never asked for a pay raise. Whatever jobs were assigned to me I did, my theory being that if I could be as useful as I knew how, the Lord would provide.

My wife is a minister's daughter, and she worked in the bank. I met my wife at work, and, of course, she had to quit because in those days when the employer refused to allow husbands and wives to work, the wife always gave it up. She became a housewife and mother. I switched to her church and we were pretty good about attending. Our children attended Sunday school regularly, and attended public schools until, one by one, they went to prep schools and then college. As they got older and went away to school, they gave up their formal religious life, and after they had gone, my wife and I became less involved. We had too many other things to do on weekends. Nevertheless, we still support the church.

Religion was simply because you did it. That was it. Your parents taught you to do it; we taught our children to do it. But they made a choice—an adult choice—that religion didn't mean that much to them. All three of our little WASPs married Catholic spouses. I don't think any of them—except my youngest son, whose wife, I think, still goes to church occasionally—actively attend church. But they seem to be insistent about having their children go.

My family, my parents and grandparents and great grandparents, were very much a part of the church. The church was a social center—just about the only one. Now that's changed. Our children have found a much broader menu of choices. I have to say that you probably cannot be very deeply, formally religious if you choose all these other things, rather than church.

Q. *Who influenced you as you were growing up?*

Both my mother and father had quite a lot of influence, particularly my father. I looked up to him, I admired him, he was a pretty important frog in our little puddle. I believed him to be a man of strong ethics and am reasonably sure a lot of my present ethical standards are inherited from him. Oddly enough, the few times I have had an opportunity to talk frankly with my kids, or they talk to their mother about me, which is usually where I get it, they say the same thing: that I've been a role model to them, that a lot of the standards they hold for themselves, they think they learned from me. I think it's somewhat the same.

My mother was a housewife. She had been a school teacher teaching kindergarten and first grade before I was born. She had a maid, who she finally let go when she got to $21 a month. She belonged to one or two women's clubs and was perfectly satisfied making a home and taking care of the children, with the help of the maid. We had a modest summer place, which was typically middle class in those days. My mother was little involved with my father's work; she was a housewife without a lot of imagination, but she provided a good support for him, and she never gave him a bad time. They loved and respected each other.

You can imagine how difficult it is for someone of my generation, my upbringing, to understand the women's movement. My mother never questioned her role. My aunt was a schoolteacher who never married. You simply did what was expected, and once you married, you took care of the children and the house, and that was fulfillment enough.

My wife was somewhat the same. She is pretty active now with the symphony, things like that, but she's basically a homemaker. Very happy with the role. She's always busy; in fact I never saw anyone so busy as she is. But I think she's happy. She doesn't understand, herself, why women yearn for careers. She's proud of her financial ability. She used to work at the bank, so she understands what the bank's culture is. And of course, she's traveled a great deal; I've dragged her around the world so many times—she's been to just about every country you can think of. It's often a very difficult situation. She's had to stand in reception lines and meet as many as 500 people, and be the gracious hostess. Now that's just second nature to her, but it certainly wasn't when we were married. She would be quite uncomfortable. When we have the bank Christmas party, nearly 4000 people with all their children and babies, she stands there for three or four hours and "oohs" and "ahs" over every one of them. And of course all the secretaries know her. She's considered to be one of them, so she's been very helpful with human relations here. In a lot of ways that she probably doesn't even know about, there are a lot of people around here who know her and are proud to know her. She's very nice to them. They describe her as just adorable. She's like a friend to them.

When I started out, a bank was a much simpler place than it is now. It was really just a bank. And the principal career path was through the lending area. That's just the way it was. If you came up through the credit side, you were elite. Most of the senior officers came through that route. And of course you knew that as long as you were competent and pleasant and didn't upset people (either the people you work with, or your customers, or your bosses), you would get promoted. Somewhere along the line one of your superiors, usually the president or the chairman of the board, who realized that one of his responsibilities was to begin to think about succession, noticed you. Something happens to call yourself to his attention, and all of a sudden he would say, "I like that young man." Then what I think would happen is that in talking with some of his peers outside the bank about their mutual duties, he'd hear them brag about how great they were at identifying young people, what great people they had working for them, and so on. So, if you happened to have been the object of affection of one of these people, pretty soon he would start to talk about you. And then, all of a sudden a myth would start. The myth being that this is a young man you have to keep your eye on. Who's going to be the next president? That's a game. And sometime when I was a vice-president (there weren't so many then as there are now), someone would come up to me at a social event, often a friend of my parents, and say, "We hear they're looking you over."

I was assigned to work with customers in northern New England. My boss, a somewhat older man, was related by marriage to the chairman. He and I became good friends. He introduced me widely, we fished together with customers, and, I think, did an effective job for the bank. Obviously, all of this helped. At any rate, I was then given a number of assignments for cross-training and rather suddenly became an executive vice-president. Actually, they created two executive vice-presidents to provide for more depth and to give them choices. Then the chairman decided to step down as CEO two years early so we could all move up. And that's when they called me in and said, "You're going to be the president." I always felt that the chairman imposed me a bit prematurely on his successor, but, of course, I never quarreled with that decision—then or now. I became chairman and CEO when my predecessor retired at the age of 65.

It's quite something when you suddenly realize you have the final responsibility for the conduct of the affairs of your company. You're also responsible for leading and working with the board of directors. They are strong, capable individuals in their own right, and they have to be dealt with at their level candidly and fairly. But you mustn't let a board run away with you because they will if they have an opportunity. You have the job of nominating new directors as others retire. That was one new responsibility I had never had before. A lot of thought and a lot of time must be devoted to the board, not only in teaching them your business but in keeping them fully informed. Then, of course, you have the continuing responsibility for being involved in all of the important decisions that are going on, such as investment decisions. Although we have a capable staff in our investment division, when we make a decision to go out and borrow $100 million at market rates, or a decision to shorten the maturities of our investment portfolio, or whatever it is, which are significant shifts in direction that can have an important effect on the bottom line, I must become involved. Also, people simply must have access to you. They'll come to see you sometimes a couple of times a day, and sometimes a couple of times a week, and you have to be available to them to discuss personnel problems, policies, personalities, whatever they wish. The people in the international division may wish to discuss the advisability of a new joint venture in Africa. So these are the things that go on in the really routine operation of the organization.

At first, while you're in a learning phase, you want to give all of yourself to everything, much more so than you probably should. And then as time goes on, you begin to think about the organization; you begin to think about assigning more and more responsibilities to others; you begin to think about your own successor, which you are supposed to do fairly early in any tenure. And you make decisions and assign responsibilities, and sometimes you find you've gone too far, you've moved too many responsibilities away from you and don't really know what's going on. Sometimes you find out you haven't done enough. I would guess that conferences with associates take perhaps half of my time and the rest is spent on a whole variety of external activities, such as community responsibilities, whether it be helping with the United Way, going to meetings in the art museum, or the committee on racial problems, or business-oriented organizations. And a lot of time is spent interfacing with the political sector, both here in the state and in Washington. In Washington, usually it's on an industry basis; here you're representing the business community for the state. And that takes a lot of time. Then you have the problem of marketing—dealing with customers. That's because a lot of our customers simply want to see the boss. So I have to make time for this or time to go to other cities and call on different accounts. That's terribly important. The rest of the time is spent on outside boards. I'm on several of these and they take increasing amounts of time because of the growing complexity of corporate affairs, the threat of litigation, and so on. And you justify that by the fact that it's terribly important. I learned a lot about how to run this place by seeing how other CEOs run their organizations. Also it forges a closer relationship between our organizations. It's something I do because my predecessors did it. I guess I would advise my successors to cool that a little bit. It's good to be on a couple of boards, but not on, say, five. That's too many. Probably you begin to cheat the stockholders a little bit in terms of the time you spend.

As a result of all of this involvement, it became apparent to me that I had to work as quickly as I could to develop a strong person who could become "Mr. Inside," and who, in effect, would take over many of the day-to-day operating responsibilities. It was probably important to develop that person as quickly as possible. Also, I think I knew enough about myself to know I sometimes shied away from detail—probably an essential laziness that I won't admit because I don't understand the detail. Therefore, it was important to have somebody who was really going to spot these things, and to let the organization know that this is being done. This led to the fairly rapid assignment of a myriad of duties to our president. He, fortunately, had the personality and the drive and the inclination to take any responsibility, except when he was told not to take it. He'd take whatever there was, and I rarely told him not to take it. He was prepared to make the decisions that had to be made during my absence. Also he was equally quick to keep me fully informed at all times as to what he was doing. He obviously had the intuition to know when something really had to have my involvement. We developed a wonderful working relationship over the years.

A few years ago we spent a morning together at his home. I told him then that when I became 63 I thought we should have everything in place so that he could become CEO and I could step aside with a fancy title but considerably less puissant. If I didn't do that, he would only have two years, following my normal retirement, to run the show as he's only two years younger than I. It just wouldn't be right to have somebody run this big bureaucracy for only two years. "So," I said, "this is what we must plan for. And furthermore," I said, "it's going to be good for us, because it's going to allow us to identify a new president, move everybody up a rung, and it's going to force us to do the job. Otherwise, we'll wait 'til the last minute." So that day we developed a plan calling for various people decisions every six months for about five years. Promising executives would be sent to run important foreign branches, other cross-training shifts would take place, and gradually we would arrive at our choices in time to meet the various deadlines we set for ourselves. At least six "fast track" people were identified, and we knew that the new president would come from this group. We followed that document almost to a T. And while there were a few changes in the players and their roles, there were not many.

A year ago, I established the office of the chairman, which was new for us. Now four of us meet once a week. And certain functions now report to the chairman's office instead of to individuals. This will give us the opportunity to really train those who will follow. In the past, the president and I used to sit down at 5:45 at night and make decisions. That's the way we'd always done it—even the big decisions. I decided that we simply had to discipline ourselves so that we stopped making these bilateral decisions. Not that we were abdicating our responsibilities, but we decided we would not make important decisions without discussing them first with the members of the chairman's office. And so we got in the habit of doing that; the main purpose of that was to make sure all four of us knew fully what the other ones were doing. Therefore, one could substitute for another one at any time. And each one of these officers has his own network reporting to him directly. So, it's a kind of communication; four of us know what the others are doing and information goes out immediately through each network if it is appropriate.

One thing I've never mentioned during this whole conversation is how much time I spend on leadership. You don't consciously spend any time on leadership. But you learn over a period of time that you have to be a leader. There are different ways to do it. But it means setting standards. There are a lot of qualities which I can't describe but it's part of the job.

I like the whole process of banking. I like dealing with a lot of different problems. I like to have something to do each day that's challenging. One of the great things is that in our business we deal with our customers' executives at a very high level. In other words, we deal with the policy-making people, the presidents and financial vice-presidents of corporations. We dig deeply into their financial affairs. One minute it's a furniture manufacturer, then, say, a sardine factory, and some time later, an aircraft manufacturing company. But at all times you are dealing with people who are intellectually your equal or your superior. It's an elitism that I like. If I were selling soap for Procter & Gamble I would only be dealing with the purchasing officers of all the companies I did business with.

The least appealing part of the job, I guess, is making personnel decisions, particularly unhappy ones. The thing I most dislike is telling someone he is not doing a good job. It's the hardest thing to do. Most managers don't do it well, or don't do it at all and I can understand why. They just don't like to do it. I also thoroughly dislike loan reviews. I hate them. You're reviewing your mistakes, the terrible mistakes you've made in retrospect. We sit down every quarter and review a large group of loans that have been reclassified as substandard. So I guess it's simple: I like to deal with nice things, and I don't like to deal with bad ones. I suspect most people are the same.

The toughest thing about my job is the time factor. You simply do not have time to do well everything that should be done well. I have to go to a lot of meetings. I find that unless I'm really getting good staff work, I'm not that well prepared and don't have time to really get into it and do the best job I know how. I sort of show up, or I'll have somebody in the car with me who will brief me rapidly about the next meeting: this is what you ought to say, this is what they are going to ask. I feel like a puppet, sitting up there, being told what to do and what to say and what to look out for. But there's no other way. You have to be briefed as well as you can, and you go and try to act knowledgeable and intelligent but you really don't know half of what's going on. I don't like that; hate it. But I don't know how to avoid it except to severely reduce these commitments. I do understand now why people in public life, senators, congressmen have such a short attention span. There are just so many hours in a day. You can just do so many things. I can understand why Ronald Reagan will say some dumb things because he has not had time to be briefed yet, and doesn't want to say, "Gosh, I don't know." I'm sure this is why it happens.

I think though that I would advise my successors to be a little more discriminating than I was in taking on all these outside activities and responsibilities. When I started doing it, life was a lot easier. It was a lot simpler running a bank. In the early days you did not necessarily have to be brilliant, and the work was not as complicated as it is now. You had to be in the right place at the right time, you had to have the right sponsorship, you had to keep your face clean, you had to have good human relations so you didn't make any enemies. Now, I'm almost positive that I would not repeat that under today's conditions. It's so much more complex; so much more professionalism is required. You've got to have much more brain power than I think I have to manage this job. The people working for us, the professional people working for us, are so bright; they can see through a fraud in a minute.

You have to train yourself to meet people well. I took a course in public speaking at college. It was a gut course. But it was one of the best things I ever did. Public speaking was very easy for me. I never had any problems with it. That course was tremendously valuable to me. I've done some high-level business around the world and became president of two premier banking organizations, one domestic and one global, both considered somewhat prestigious. And I've been on nominating committees for these things over and over again, and I know how people are ruled out in the preliminaries. "Oh, yeah, he's abrasive," or "He'll get people into an argument," or "I don't like him," or that sort of thing. You rarely stop and say "Does he really have the intellect to do this kind of thing?" So I guess I have been lucky. I've been available. I have learned how to avoid unnecessary confrontation for the sake of confrontation. There are some people who say "Well, you have leadership qualities." I don't know what they are. My impression generally is that people here in the bank have considered me to be a leader, that they look up to me; they're not ashamed of me. But, you know, this place is getting so complex, the world is so competitive, there are so many changes taking place that I sensed we really needed a new door key—professional management.

I just came from a meeting of our leasing company, and they were talking about leveraged leases of six airplanes to a major airline at $30 million apiece. God, here were these bright computer guys sitting there having figured out all the yields on the lease from the best case to the worst case and so on. You know, there were times when I hardly understood what they were talking about.

After I retire, I'll stay on the board for two or three years, which is our custom. I'm on several other boards, and I run two nonprofit organizations with large budgets. I'm going to be pretty busy, but I'm trying to design it so that if I want to go away for a week with my wife I can go and I don't have to worry about these other things. I've peeled off some layers of the onion already; there are a few layers left.

Q. *What is the culture of this bank?*

Well, I'm not sure I know now. In the first place it has always been, since I've been here, simply by virtue of its size, a very large bank in the region. It happened during the Depression. A lot of banks failed and we were able to buy them and suddenly make a quantum leap into a big-time bank. For many years our deposits were greater than all the other banks in our clearinghouse. Most people around here take a certain pride in that. We're in the catbird seat; we're the king; we're the best. That's pretty good for an organization; it will cover up an awful lot of seams. So there is a fundamental pride in being connected with the biggest. And our society says that the biggest is also the best. So that's probably the most important glue we've had in the whole culture of the organization. We've always tried to be innovators and tried to instill a sense of pride in this. I think we may have slipped somewhat simply because we've gotten so big. We've always tried very hard to allow a lot of freedom of action other than in very large loan decisions. We've had a pretty informal management structure for a long time. We didn't have a current organization chart 15 or 20 years ago. We had ready access to the senior officers. People would wander in to talk about something or just to meet me. I think that's helped. And for some reason, I don't know quite how we've done it, we've had less empire building or back-biting than a lot of organizations. Of course, there's been some, but there's been less of it.

Obviously the most important thing that drives the place and predominates is the people in power. There are times when they run it miserably; there are times when they run it very well. I want people to be proud to be the best. That's important. My son, who was graduated from business school about three or four years ago, went to work for an organization that got into a lot of trouble. You could just tell it really bothered him; he was losing his pride in an institution he had been very proud of for that short period of time. You could tell how very disappointed he was. I'm sure that was true throughout the whole organization. They were embarrassed to tell somebody where they worked. I talked with him on the phone and asked him how things were. He said, "One thing I've learned is that we still have many of the same people here who made me think this was a great company. They're still here, and," he said, "we've gotten through this mess and we're going to get out of it. We're still the same company." He said, "I've gotten over it." That's important.

Q. *When does ethics come up here at the bank?*

Well, I guess it comes up a lot. There are a lot of obvious things. It's inconceivable to me that the head of our Latin America division would come to me and say, "Look, if we're going to have a branch in Peru, we've got to pay someone for it." I can't conceive of that happening simply because I'm sure the manager of the Latin America division knows very well we'd simply say "no." We just wouldn't do it. Life's too short. We have, on the other hand, paid gratuities for telephones, but that was the only way you could get one in several countries. But fundamentally our managers know we have a set of standards. We have a written policy on the subject. It's circulated once a year to all the officers and we all have to sign it. It's very well understood. So those problems don't arise. Obviously, like everyone else, we have liars and cheats from time to time.

I was very disappointed in an incident with a young man we hired away from another bank. We needed a manager for two years in one of our developing country branches and he seemed to have the experience. We hired him and he started to run the new operation. When I went to cut the ribbon I met him and his wife, an absolutely charming woman with two or three kids between five and nine years old, just a typical American Norman Rockwell family, just an absolute straight arrow, probably too straight. Turned out he was not the right one because he was insensitive to blacks; he was too white himself. We brought him back here because of his lack of sensitivity to the people in the community where he worked, and put him in a lending division. I saw him once or twice, asked him how his wife was, and so on. Then all of a sudden, while I was on vacation, I read in the paper that he had been indicted for asking a customer for a personal gratuity for a letter of credit. I showed it to my wife and said, "I can't believe it." He was intelligent, he had a good future, he was a squeaky clean young man with a picture book family. I don't have all the facts yet; obviously he hasn't been tried. When we heard from the customer that this was happening we informed the FBI. Then we wired the customer and the transaction was completed. Apparently the FBI caught him in the act. The boy's career is destroyed. That was bad. But it happens once in a while.

The real things are I guess much more subtle, and they have to do with fairness to other people. Am I really leveling with an associate when I say we're going to make so-and-so a senior vice-president, and don't worry about it, we'll take care of you later? Maybe I won't take care of him later; maybe I'm postponing the problem, trying to keep him happy and motivated but I have no immediate intention of making him senior vice-president. That's a thing that you find yourself doing and should resist.

Competitive pricing and marketing can be an ethical minefield. Obviously we want to get all the business we can, and obviously we want to do it at profitable margins. But competition stands in our way. Discussing price with competitors is unthinkable, but studying their price lists and trying to figure out their strategies is essential. Then the new product is priced and marketed in a fashion slightly more to the consumer's advantage. But, do we penetrate a market with cheap prices and subsequently raise them if we are successful? I guess we would if we could, but, alas, the world of financial services doesn't work that way. Providers of these services hang in there, ready to devastate you the minute you appear to be less competitive. In any event, is it ethical to even attempt such a strategy? I really don't know.

I'm not at all concerned about what the proper standards are; I think I have taken the leadership role and set high standards. Everybody knows where I stand on these matters. But it's the subtleties that I'm not so sure about, like borderline areas. When do you tell bad news to the stockholders? To the directors? How much do you tell the stockholders? How much do you tell your directors? The stated reason for holding back is to make sure you have all the facts. The real reason for holding back, however, could be that you hope it will go away before you have to say anything about it. These questions come up all the time. My future successor taught me that the easiest thing to do is to get it out in the open as fast as you can and get the bad news out of the way. From then on it's a lot easier. Usually when you begin to hide something in your life, it gets worse. But it's a question we wrestle with a lot.

Let me talk about a situation we went through, the ultimate result of which was that the bank was censured by the SEC. The newspapers called it a slap on the wrist, something like that. What it amounted to was intensely embarrassing, and I just didn't like it at all. We were lending money to a growing conglomerate of financial service companies in order to finance acquisitions including mutual fund managers. Now you understand that a mutual fund is owned by its own shareholders. While the management company may be owned by others, they get paid to manage the funds. But the mutual fund is pure—it's supposed to be. It has its own independent directors and it hires the management company, even though the management company may have started it. The SEC is very fussy about making sure that a mutual fund is maintained purely for the benefit of those who buy its shares.

One of our very capable officers handled that account, which was extremely complex. We used to insist on compensating balances for a loan which were part of our standard pricing—between 10 and 20% in demand deposits. This, of course, was traditional in the banking community. There were probably eight or nine different subsidiaries, affiliates of this company, and every now and then their treasurer would allow his deposit balances to drop below the agreed level. In those precomputer days we assigned someone to keep track of the total balances to make sure they lived up to the agreement. In settlement they would either increase their deposits or pay a fee. So, in one instance, our officer went to the treasurer with a list prepared by his assistant of all the balances that we were counting against the loan. The treasurer said, "You included on that list the balances of the mutual fund. We can't count them. Those funds don't belong to us. They belong to the shareholders. That's a no–no. I'll have to make it up to you in some other way." And our man said, "Fine. I guess the person who prepared the memo didn't realize that these had to be excluded from the list. I'll remove them, but you've got to give us more balances from another source." At that time I think the company was coming under an SEC investigation as a result of shareholder disagreement. Anyway, the treasurer said to him, "If I were you, I would destroy that document and substitute a correct one," which was a perfectly normal thing to say. For some reason my associate forgot about it and returned it to the files in his desk. He gave instructions to his assistant not to include these in the balances any more, and that was done. Then the investigation began in an attempt to see if the company was using mutual fund assets to its advantage. As part of the probe they subpoenaed all the pertinent records in the bank.

Now, when there's a subpoena, we have to disgorge everything in our files; there's no holding back. All of a sudden our lawyers came upon this document and said, "Oh my God. That's damaging. It says that you know your borrower, the conglomerate, is using those balances to help compensate the bank." And our officer said, "But we didn't do that. This document is wrong." Then the thing was bucked up to me. I could have said to the lawyers, "Sorry, we're going to destroy that document as it is not correct. You'll simply have to defend us. We're not going to comply." What I actually said was "What's the right thing to do in the case?" And they said, "The right thing to do is to turn it over. You will have a chance to prove in court that these documents are no longer valid." So I had the decision to make. I could have quietly torn up the documents and made them disappear. But they told me it was the wrong thing to do. I gave them the documents. And we had a terrible time persuading the SEC of the truth during the hearings that took place. They simply didn't believe us. They felt that this was "smoking gun" evidence that the balances were being improperly used. We negotiated. They wanted to bring strong action against us to make an example. So we finally negotiated a compromise. The compromise was to accept the censure without denying or admitting any guilt. That was the end of it. Nothing happened. It was in the papers. The competition loved it. I felt a little embarrassed. Most people didn't say anything to me, which was even worse. I knew what they were thinking; they just didn't want to bring it up in front of me. But, that was a decision that had to be made. I could very easily have squelched that paper.

One thing that goes through your mind when you are deciding whether or not to do something that might be wrong is "Am I going to get caught?" That is erroneous thinking but it does come up as an option you are considering. The law calls for the submission of *all* documents and under some conditions of cross-examination you would either have to lie or say that you had ordered them destroyed. Once we learn that one option is to lie, the option is obliterated.

Incidentally, I was mad as hell. It was dumb to keep that document, especially when we could have changed it, which would have been a legal act, then. Few people around here would have known had we decided to destroy it. Our in-house lawyer would have known. Probably our outside counsel would have too. And, certainly the young man who was involved with this whole thing. But even more important than a few people knowing that I had made a decision to stonewall this one, was the fact that it was a violation of the law. When you respond to a subpoena, you are giving your word that you have turned over all evidence you have.

Another aspect was that I felt that if you're really going to run an ethical institution, and set high standards, you have to set them from the top. A lot of people, I think, knew of the decision and how it was made. I can't help but feel that they said, "Well, you know, we leaned over backwards." And I'd like everybody to lean over backwards.

Dealing with the media can be a minefield and often presents many ethical questions. Outright lying, while tempting at times, is useless and, of course, wrong. On the other hand, refusing to comment in order to protect the confidentiality of a client relationship is promptly publicized by the press as "stonewalling"—and sometimes shown on TV as an empty chair. There is very little protection in going off the record as the ethical standards of eager reporters and their editors are less than the highest, particularly when they feel a higher responsibility to the public.

We had a very troublesome situation involving a corporate borrower who, for 10 years, used the court system to frustrate our taking of collateral which had been pledged in good faith. Numerous appeals and changes of venues strung out the process interminably, even though we won our case in every single proceeding. Then the borrower went to the *New York Times* and pleaded injustice, harrassment on our part, big bank against little guy (his company owed us many millions of dollars), and just about every banking crime in the book. In accordance with our policy with respect to client matters (good or bad) we would not comment. The newspaper did a front page major story accusing us of everything the borrower fabricated. There was no examination of the legal proceedings and no attempt to do research on the credibility of the complainer. We could not defend ourselves in the media without violating a policy, but we did visit a few publishers and editors to set the record straight—this time off the record.

The story finally died of its own accord and later on in a discovery proceeding, we found a letter from the borrower which clearly indicated he was going to plant the story with a *Times* reporter to bring maximum pressure on us.

Q. *Going back to the SEC case, if there had been no legal constraint, would you have destroyed the document?*

Oh, I think so. I think if there had been no requirement to do so, and in effect to make a statement that I had turned over everything, I'm not sure I would have. The ethical thing, as far as I'm concerned, was that the law said to do it, and the law implied that I was swearing I had done it. So, even though you can break a speeding law, and you can break a lot of little laws, you don't like to break the law when you swear that you've done something. I think if this had just been a case of a lawyer coming to me and saying, "Look, be a good guy and give us everything you know about this," I would have said to myself, "That's not relevant, I'm just not going to do it." But, if I had to promise that I had given everything—and hadn't—then I've told a lie. I don't think that's so much a moral issue. I just don't think it's right for anybody in any position to go around swearing falsely that he had or hadn't done something.

Our fellow could have made a note on that document that said "John Jones said don't count these, so we won't count these," but he didn't do that either. He just stuck it in his file. We are very conscious of that now. We try very hard to reduce the amount of documents we have on any transaction. We're dealing in such a litigious world. So, we're always sending things off to the shredder. Or, quite often when our lawyers write us a memorandum on some issue that could become a contentious issue, they write across the top of it something like "Privileged Memorandum," "Privileged Client Memorandum." And the law does allow communications from your lawyers which are privileged to be kept out of a subpoena. But any document can be taken out of context, and then you have the burden of having to try to prove that it's not an incriminating one.

Actually, one of the biggest problems in management is cowardice, particularly in the area of performance evaluation. It's very difficult to sit down with someone and really criticize him. Fairly and honestly criticize him. You want to be liked. I'm sure there's self-delusion. Yes, maybe things will work out. Maybe he or she will really turn around and become highly productive, and might be able to be promoted. So you don't bother to sit down and ask yourself honestly, is Joe really ever going to be a good lending officer or whatever. And, if you do, the right thing to do would be to go to Joe and say, "You're just not going to make it." I'm sure that there's some self-delusion. We have a protective mechanism here, and the minute we start to do something that feels a little wrong, that protective mechanism surrounds it and makes it appear to be all right. And, you don't bother to break through that shroud— that protective mechanism. Everything will come out all right in the end. And, every now and then—two years goes by and here comes Joe!

There are a lot of ethical compromises made in the whole area of human development, dealing with people's lives and their careers. We say, "I don't want to discourage you; we need you to continue doing what you're doing. I hope that you will find a way to work your way up to the next rung of the ladder." What I'm really saying is that I really don't want you to move up at this point. In fact, for the jobs that you may be aspiring to, I can see some real difficulties because I happen to know there are a couple of other people who may be better for those jobs than you are. But, I don't want to lose you. I want to keep you in the management pool. And I want to motivate you. It's not soft-soaping. But I don't say to you, "I have other people that I think are going to be better for this job. I know you want to be an executive vice-president. Peter and Joe want to be executive vice-presidents. It's just not time for you now. And, I don't know when it is going to be." In other words, I am trying to persuade you to gamble further. Stick it out and stay with us. Hope that something nice will happen. Maybe you may have your own protective mechanism. Our egos do a lot for us. There've been a few cases where we've done this, and the person eventually became an executive vice-president. So sometimes something nice happens. But even for those who don't go higher, I believe that the job they now have is a good one. I have seen a number of cases where people have left because they weren't promoted and have been very unhappy. They suddenly discovered the outside world isn't quite as nice as it was in here. And I guess part of it has been my own philosophy which is that I never planned a career pattern. I just felt that if I do whatever is expected of me and do it the best I know how, the Lord will provide, and, somehow it will work out. And it always has.

ARNOLD
ROWAN

Director, Public Affairs
Thirty-seven years old

"I hate the whole notion of issues management. It lets people off the hook for what's an obvious gut ethical feeling and you can't do that."

I grew up in the Hyde Park area of Chicago, and as I got older we moved to the South Shore, and then to Kansas City. By the time I got to high school, it was the suburbs of Chicago in Skokie. My father was in the photographic business. Originally he, an uncle, and relatives started a very good chain of camera stores in Chicago. Then he went on to work for various photographic distributors. My mother started working part time when everybody was finally in elementary school. I think she did secretarial work. But she was always there when we returned from school. I have two younger brothers. We're all three years apart. Both are married and both have children. One sells pearls on 47th Street and the other is a lawyer in New York.

My parents are first generation Americans; my grandparents were not born here. Neither of my parents are college educated. They grew up in the depression. They worked very early. They're both sort of intellectual Jewish parents: always listened to FM radio and had play-reading groups and book clubs and that sort of thing. They went to concerts to see Jascha Heifitz, and to museums. Very normal. They liked Studs Terkel. I think they believed in doing things for their children before themselves.

I went to public schools. I don't remember much about school, though. I remember things like classes were always divided up. There were the people who they thought would probably go to college and those who wouldn't go to college. And they had different levels of learning and levels of placement. I remember in high school that senior and junior year were totally directed toward taking advanced placement tests for college and that sort of thing. I think that suburban Chicago schools were very competitive. It was very important to them to place a lot of college-bound graduates. There were many schools there that were well known, like New Trier and Evanston. But I remember being with very nice people, almost all professionals now. Pretty normal.

I had religious training, but my parents were not Orthodox at all. I went to Hebrew schools and had a bar mitzvah. And I went to confirmation class. I remember going to services on Saturday because you had to as part of the bar mitzvah preparation. I think once I got a little older that ended very quickly.

My home was fairly matriarchal. My mother ran the place, it seemed. Maybe she didn't, but she organized it. And I think she was the person who did most of the child rearing. My father worked right in town, was always home, worked nine to five. I don't remember him ever taking work home from the office or anything like that. The family always ate together. They always had a lot of friends, friends with children who were our ages. They've kept those friendships to this day; most of their friends are people they met when I was in co-op nursery school. It's so unbelievable to me, but that's the way it was, I guess. I don't think work was the central obsession. It was just making a living, and something that they enjoyed. The focus was the family, and an extended family too. Always a lot of cousins, always relatives and aunts and uncles. Most of them lived in the Chicago area. But that was the last generation, because now all the cousins are spread all over the map. I remember always having a lot of friends as well.

My early sense of "right and wrong" was that it was just so natural: some things were right and some things were wrong. Honesty was right and dishonesty was wrong. It was wrong to be late for class and all those kinds of things. It was wrong not to do well in school. I remember it being fairly easy; no great enormous lessons. You could go through life being intellectual about it, and being rational was better than being irrational. Being sane was better than being insane. We went to Pete Seeger concerts and the Weavers, and all that stuff. And it just happens. I mean the Weavers don't lie, right? They can't. I have the record of their reunion concert. My children love it—that's their favorite record. I was just in New York and I happened to be reading the paper and Ronnie Gilbert, who was a Weaver, had a concert at Lincoln Center. It sold out in a half a day. It brought back so much. The nuclear freeze movement seems very reminiscent of SANE and Benjamin Spock; the whole nuclear freeze movement seems to be made up not of young people at all, but people in their thirties and forties. It's really interesting to me. It seems to be a revival of that kind of mood in which I remember things. I don't remember the early fifties, I don't remember Joe McCarthy or anything like that. But I remember things like SANE. I don't think many people at this company have that background, to tell you the truth. That particular urban Jewish background. . . . Basically I think there was a positive value in the way I was raised. There certainly was a celebration of some of the kinder human instincts and things that made human beings heroic.

I think my children are being raised slightly differently than I was. They go to private school. I'm a lot wealthier than my parents were, but I think my children are being raised probably in a similar way, except without the religion. My wife's not Jewish. There's no religion in the household except the holidays. We celebrate all of them. Denomination doesn't matter to us. My children seem to be being raised very admirably. They go to a very good school, good values; they're being raised to be gentlemen. It seems very similar to my own upbringing in many ways. My nine year old is more worried about nuclear war than I'd ever been. The issue was fallout shelters when I was younger, and he's more worried about it than I ever was. He thinks about it and talks about it, and of course he sees news much more graphically than I ever did. And he seems very ethical in his thinking. He doesn't like injustice. I mean he talks about not liking racism. He's being raised in a liberal intellectual tradition. I don't know if that's good or bad, but that's pretty much what it is. We're moving from the suburbs back to the city so he's really going to get a heavy dose of it now. I don't like the suburbs, to tell you the truth, and always wanted one of these grand old city homes. I finally found one. It's beautiful, and it's exactly what I always wanted.

My world's very different from my parents'. My parents were never wealthy at all—never, ever. They grew up when times were tough. It never mattered. It's like, if you had some money you spent it on college education. It was very unmaterialistic. I'm much more materialistic than they ever were. Franklin Roosevelt was one of my parents' heroes. I remember when I was little, my parents over and over again telling me how much they cried when Franklin Roosevelt died. And Leonard Bernstein was their hero. My early life was very rich in values, very rich, and you can make fun of it because it is kind of funny, but I'm really very appreciative of it. I don't know how much of it was just natural or if it was a conscious effort on their part. It was pretty much a celebration of: it's nice to be alive.

I went to college at Brandeis, 1964. I remember applying to two schools: the University of Wisconsin and Brandeis. I had no idea what Brandeis was like, nor did my parents. I just assumed that Brandeis was a good school and a small school. And that's all I knew. I never even went for an interview.

I remember my first day very well. First of all, it was a very hot day, but I was wearing this tweed three-piece suit because I had no idea how I should dress. And I realized that that was really not appropriate. First of all I was sweating like a pig. When I got there I went to find my dorm. There was a beautiful little pond in front of the dorm, so I remember changing my clothes and just sitting out there. Then I remember this girl coming up to me. She came up and she said "Hi," and I said my name, and she said, "I'll let you sleep with me if you read an Ayn Rand book," which I thought was kind of strange. But I said, "Why not?" And I went to the bookstore and I found the smallest one I could find. I think it was *Anthem*. I read it real quick and she gave me a little test and it was terrific. And I thought, "What an odd place this is. This is not at all what I expected."

The school got odd indeed. It was quite an eye opener for a young Jewish guy from Skokie, let me tell you. I mean just very different, very New York. The girls all came from Dalton or the Walden School, and they had known drugs since they were three, and all that. Very different, very urban—and also very activist in politics and drug culture. There were folk singers; Angela Davis was there and Herbert Marcuse was giving a course. I think I sort of drifted toward the same kinds of people that I'd always drifted toward. It was more of a fun-loving counterculture, you know: sit-and-tell-jokes-and-drink-coffee types. Of course, then all the courses kept changing too. "Sociology and Ethics" became a meditation course; the school got very different.

But I was still quite an achiever. I placed out of my first year when I came because of all those advanced placement tests they had geared me up for. I thought I was going to go into the sciences. I remember getting the sense that I was always pretty bright in school, but never the brightest. But here there were a lot of bright people. And I remember being the only freshman in the organic chemistry class, and it was really too much for me. It was very difficult. I got through it, but realized that it wasn't for me. When you're in the lab on Friday afternoons and you look down and you see all these people rolling around naked on the grass, you realize that maybe science is not the right thing to do. Maybe I should be doing something else on Friday afternoon. So I quickly changed into sociology, which at Brandeis was one of the major majors. There were some wonderful professors. There's one that's still quite a good friend. And even a few English professors were very pleasant.

Near the very end of school I hadn't decided what I wanted to do. I'd applied to grad school and I got a fellowship at the University of British Columbia. Why there? I'd never been there. It just seemed like another nice place. I never went. Instead, I went to California and lived in a commune. It started out mainly with people who were friends of mine at Brandeis. That was interesting. There were 30 people or so, and we got this very big house in Berkeley, which was supposed to be temporary. We were going to buy some land in northern California and live in a commune. It was terrific. We used to send five people out at a time to look for land. They'd never come back. So five more would go and they'd never come back. And we'd send another five, and they'd never come back. So we realized it probably wasn't working, there were so few people left. But it was very nice being in Berkeley. Mario Savio and the People's Park and Haight-Ashbury were in their prime then. I was politically sympathetic but not active. Of course, the draft came up then. I brought a note from my psychiatrist saying I was in therapy and took a Minnesota Multiphasic Personality test, which you can't cheat on. It has questions like "Do you like to play hopscotch?" But if you answer them truthfully, really truthfully, you come out delusional schizophrenic every time. There's a little computer readout that says "delusional schizophrenic," and so they gave me a deferral. That was at the big recruiting base in Oakland.

What did I do in this commune? I don't know. You don't have much of an individual role in that kind of situation; you have to share things and you have to try and communicate. I did not enjoy that aspect very much; I remember just hating all this eye contact, this trying to communicate silently. I hated Gestalt therapy. I hated all that crap. Totally. But I quickly came to enjoy the West Coast. So I left the commune with a friend of mine. We were going out with the Blumberg twins. So the four of us went to a wilderness area in northern California for a month, the Marble Mountain wilderness area—very beautiful. We walked in and stayed for a month and walked out. And then the Blumberg twins said we didn't communicate enough, and they kicked us out. I never could figure any of that out at all. In order to be accepted, you had to get angry in public; you had to cry; you had to scream, and I never felt like doing any of it. I never felt that way. I was not made for doing all this interpersonal stuff. I'm a pretty private person; I just didn't feel like it.

My mental attitude now is not very different than it was then. Those days were filled with adventures. You could go to the supermarket and wind up on some archeological dig. So, aside from the eye contact, I remember it being quite lovely: walking in the Berkeley Botanical Gardens and going fishing. But working was not on my mind. I don't remember having any money. I remember cashing in some Israel bonds and they gave me a very hard time, just horrible, even though the bonds were way past maturity. They called me a traitor. I guess I had some money. I don't remember needing any, to tell you the truth. It was interesting. It is different now because there's a lot of fear about money. But I didn't worry about that at all, so when I talk to college students today, I can't understand why they could possibly want to go to work right after college. It doesn't make any sense to me.

After Marble Mountain, I went to stay with some friends in Palo Alto, and one of them gave me a motorcycle, a nice beautiful old BMW. I remember riding it up a skyline boulevard and I pulled into this estate to ask directions. There was this lovely women there. It turned out that she was manager of a place that did weekend sensitivity training for teachers. She offered me the job of caretaker and I moved in. I did some chores and cleared some trails, but I wasn't very good at it at all. I didn't know how to do all that.

A company was forming to produce counterculture publications. They asked me if I wanted to do an educational magazine and I said, "Sure . . . But I don't know anything about it." But they said, "That's fine." The magazine went to teachers and dealt with educational resources. I did other things too. I was very much part of that San Francisco community for years. There were all sorts of things, independent publishing, all the small crafts publishing, and poets. I started the first San Francisco Bookfair. Famous typesetters like Andrew Hoyam would hold classes on Saturday morning and let people print their own broadsides and handset type and letters. Very nice, very nice time. Great writers. I got associated with great writers from whom I really learned how to write. Wallace Stegner was out there teaching at Stanford, and they had a crop of these charming Kentucky writers. I really learned how to write from them, and learned to enjoy publishing. That became much more important than the education field itself. I was terrible at it to begin with. I had to learn how to do all these things, to write and to design and paste-up and print.

I was thinking more about writing and publishing, and a lot of East Coast publishers at that time felt that the West Coast people knew something that they didn't know, so there were always a lot of book contracts dangled in front of me. Then, after three years, the people who ran the Aspen design conference asked me to become director of resources for one summer. So I went to Aspen and just stayed. I think this was in 1971. I lived there for about a year and a half to two years. I still hadn't had a job, but I had a book contract and I had some money from the advance.

Whenever I was totally out of money, I would call up my agent who worked in New York. He's a very good agent, and I'd beg for— just give me—send $300. Finally he said, "Look, you don't make any money. I can't do this anymore."

I was very heavily in debt and times were changing; that same kind of magic that I remember was pretty much disappearing. It was getting to be a harsher life. I also got married at this time. And my wife, who worked for my agent, said, "OK, but I know about your earning potential as a writer and I think you ought to change your line of work." And I agreed. So she was still working, and I was looking around at publishing and things like that, but it didn't seem like it would pay very much. Finally I remembered that my father was in the photographic business, and I talked to him, and he made a few calls and found me a job at a company in New York in the photographic business doing sales promotion. I never had done any of that before. It was a distributor, a fairly big company. It was about a hundred million dollar company. I went to work there, and liked it. Then I went to a small company in New Jersey and got more money and a better position in a marketing job, and then after that this place found me.

I came here in the marketing department. They said, "We're not sure what the job is. Does it matter?" And I said, "No, it doesn't matter," so they sort of created one. I remember coming here and my boss at that time was the vice-president of advertising, who has since left the company. He just was thrilled with my background. He made me tell the stories over and over again. He thought it was hilarious that some people actually did some of these things.

My job here now is director of public affairs. I have an odd mix of responsibilities; it's just an accident of organization structure that these things fall together. There are about 35 people working in these areas, plus secretaries.

The 35 people I mentioned work for me, and I work for an executive vice-president. But in a sense, this company tries to operate on some kind of consensus basis, so although I report to him there are different key officers who I feel a need to keep informed and to talk to. It's done on a fairly informal basis. The company has resisted formal ways of doing these things. There are times when that is very frustrating. I'm trying very, very hard to get the company to set up a public affairs committee of senior officers and board members. It's not because I don't think we can do the job; but I feel a little dumb speaking for the company on issues on which the company has a position, without any mandate. I try to state what I think is *best* for the company and what I think is *right* for the company at the same time, but our senior officers have very different perspectives on what obligations the corporation has.

If the company had no history my job would be even more difficult. But the company's history drives it. We've had articulate presidents, who could articulate some of the obligations we felt industry had to its employees, to the world, to the product, and that's so deep that even if others in the company don't agree with it, it's part of their subconscious. What you may have to understand, to understand this company, is how much it's changed. There have been a lot of significant changes in the last three or four years organizationally and philosophically—in the nature of our business, and in the mood of the company. Like most of American industry, this company is definitely a company in transition. The world is changing. There is a generation now that doesn't marvel at technology in the way people much older than you or I might marvel. We are moving to broaden our technological base these days, broaden our marketing base, and broaden our business segments to become more diversified. That seems pretty normal from an outside point of view, but inside it's meant a tremendous upheaval for a lot of reasons. There's been a shift in the population of the company. There are less people and they have become more senior and higher paid on average. There is a lot of cross- and inter-disciplinary activity that never happened before. I think you'll find that in any industry in America these days, the technology has changed so fast that there's no way anybody can do it alone. You have to work together. So the other change that's happening here is the realization that, in spite of the fact that most of our products came from our own invention, we may indeed have to go outside, either through acquisition or some kind of arrangement, to close some gaps and do the kinds of things we want to do. We can't do everything.

One of the things I really like about this job is being able to be both inside and outside the company. The challenge comes in dealing with the necessary conflicts that happen between a lively constituency on the outside and what I have to do to represent the company. I can't satisfy both the inside and the outside all the time. I can't satisfy *Business Week*, for instance, with an interview with the chairman if he doesn't want to do it. I can't tell them what they want to know because in many cases I don't know or the company doesn't know. I can't always be close friends with the financial press. There's an adversarial relationship as well as a cooperative relationship. That's difficult. Sometimes there are things I don't want to tell them. Sometimes the answer is "I don't know." But "I don't know" sounds terrible if you say it. Accuracy is something we're looking for, as well as reasonable expectations from the press.

I'm not sure how best to deal with the press. I'm of two minds, and I vacillate. One way is to avoid contact; nothing wrong with that. And the other way to deal with it, though, is really to try and have a lot of informal communication that can help convey the situation, help outside people to better understand. There are problems with both of these. You've got to sort of use your intuition and walk a tightrope. The biggest areas of stress for me though are not in the job but in relating the job to my private life; much more stressful than the job itself. I get called at three in the morning. I'm the person they call if somebody is stabbed or there's fire. You have to call somebody, and I'm the person the company has designated to get called by our own internal security. Then if I think it's important I'm supposed to call the chairman or whomever. They need someone who can make a judgment of how to follow up. It's stressful.

More routinely, stress comes and goes depending on how close it is to a deadline and how unclear I am about what I should be doing. If I'm not clear, if I haven't figured out what I should do or what I should say, then it's more stressful. Once I know then it becomes less stressful. And I think dealing with control issues inside the company either with other people in the company or within my own group is also stressful. For a long time it was very stressful to see people who worked for me doing things very differently than the way I would do them. It would just drive me crazy. But I've gotten over that to a point.

I don't feel very insular about the company, and I think I know about how a lot of other companies work and how people are, and even as discouraged as I get sometimes, I think it's probably a better place to work than any other company I've ever been exposed to. It's an extremely supportive environment. It's supportive professionally and personally, and I feel I can take some risks and experiment, and if it doesn't work out, then there's no harm done. Of course I know when to stop it; I mean, I don't let it go too far. But I feel I'm given enough support to try things. I feel they reward creativity, that that's an admirable quality. There's a reward for intelligence. I think the old criticism that the more creative side of the house used to get about spending money has gone with the wind in the last four years because everybody's pretty conservative with their money. I think that's a natural criticism in any company from the technical side. They say, "Oh, look at these people. They stay in hotels in New York; they take trips." You've got to imagine yourself a scientist not doing anything but schlepping in and schlepping out.

I think the company has products we can be proud of and a product philosophy we can be proud of. It has dedication to some of the finer things in life we can be proud of. It has a sense of social responsibility you can't find anyplace else. Doesn't have much of a bonus plan. But otherwise. . . . I think, in spite of population cutbacks, that unless you're doing something kind of flaky your job is secure. We're not overly populated so that everybody has more than enough work to handle. If you look at those qualities that deal with the job, I think this place has really got it.

We've got so many different types of people here. There's no corporate mold. We've got a chairman who rows in regattas, we've got other people, engineers, that slip on the ice, and eccentric scientists and—honest, you've never seen such an odd collection. The people don't really socialize with each other outside of the place. It's also a very asexual place, not a lot of affairs, not a lot of flirting or anything like that. Some people are extremely articulate; some people are not. The question is, are they good businessmen or not? And I think that in many ways they are and in many ways they're not. You have to build a company on your strengths. I think that's one thing this company wants to do, and keep its flavor. You want to make it an enticing place to work. We've got the best technical people here. It has to be a creative research environment for them or we won't get them.

There are ethical questions that come up and there are legal questions that come up; there's a fine line. And then there is the question of how to deal with an issue in a way that is proper for the company. Of course I'm super-sensitive because I feel I have to maintain the image of respectability of this place.

I think the company has a kind of superego so that people are conscious of it if they are doing something in a slimy way. I think they think of that first before they think about what the correct business decisions are. I think there are a lot of people in the company who make the business decisions and then they think about how they can implement them in a way that's right. And then there's another group of people in the company that shoot from the hip and then suffer the stings of the superego. I think it does come down to this: you might have made the best business decision in the world but if you do it in a sleazy way, I think that's really held against you by your peers. People in this company are very good about learning from each other. Not in any formal way; people just look around and learn from each other. And that superego has to be passed on. It's not just a written tradition or an oral tradition; it's a cultural phenomenon that happens. I'm not sure how it happens, but it's really there. If you went down the halls and you heard derogatory things about people, you'd hear less "What a stupid idiot, he just made a bad decision" than "Do you believe the way he handled that?" That's what you'll hear more of. It's interesting.

It comes from executives that we've had. They've all had one philosophy that was always the same, and that is: never separate style and form from content. I think it may have been the first thing that was drummed into my head when I came to work here. And the product reflects that. In a way, we've packaged an attitude the way we packaged the product. It has to do with the way you treat people, not embarrassing them, not humiliating them. It has to do with not knowingly doing harm to the environment. It has to do with dignity between people. In a business situation, the ten commandments is not enough any more. There are different kinds of ethics. And, tolerance is one of the things you have to add to it. Very important. Tolerance is a key component of this company's ethical makeup.

Now let me try and describe three situations in which, I think, ethics comes into play. One situation involves what a company does when there is a charge of negligence on its part, but the case is removed from the company's hands since it is an insured claim. The second case concerns what happens when someone's supervisor requests some personal publicity that may not be in the company's best interest. The third situation concerns the obligation of the management of the company to represent and advise employees about matters they think have consequences for them, even though it's not their particular responsibility or there is no connection with the company.

Okay, let's talk about the first case which concerns a personal damage suit against the company.

[Author's insert: An employee who had been receiving counseling in the company counseling program physically attacked another person whose family brought suit against the company. Despite the company's claim of innocence, the insurance company ultimately agreed to settle out of court, rather than risk higher damages through a trial. The company felt the settlement, and public announcement of it, implied guilt on its part.]

This company is a company that, when it thought it was right in a situation (not just legally right but ethically right), has a long tradition of defending itself vigorously, even if the defense of the situation would cost more than the claim itself. Certainly there is a practical reason. It discourages further unnecessary grievances or litigations if you stand up for what you think is right. It's like negotiations over hostages and whether you give in to ransom demands or not. But what happens when a company puts its reputation in the hands of someone else (the insurance company) whose interests are not the same as the company's? What do you say about it to your employees, and what do you say about it publicly? In my mind, this whole situation involved a number of interesting ethical questions. Do you insure claims in which you feel your ethical interests will be ignored by that third party who doesn't have those same ethical interests? Do you talk about a case publicly, even if the court asks you not to talk about it? Do you talk about the technicality of not being involved in the case when, in fact, you're the defendant in the case and represented by the insurance company? You read about a lot of malpractice cases in the papers and you never read that the insurance company has decided this, or the insurance company has decided that. It's always the defendant, even though, my guess is, the defendant never tries the case; it's always the insurance company, if they're insured. There's no insurance company in the world that will insure you unless they have control over the claim. It doesn't make any sense for them. So, how do you complain when the full story is not coming out, even though the reporting may be accurate? And that was the case here, because there was pressure to complain that the reporting of the trial in the *Record* wasn't accurate, when in fact, they were literally accurate. There was nothing they said that was wrong, except they did not mention the decision to settle the case wasn't ours to make.

People felt it was inaccurate, because they were reacting emotionally. I consider it a very serious matter to accuse the press of inaccuracy, which they take fairly seriously if they are not. If you have legitimate claims later on, they don't have nearly the impact if you have already complained just because you didn't like the way a story was written. In this particular case I refused to complain, and a senior officer in the company did write a letter to the *Record* saying their story was in error. He wrote a letter to the editorial director of the *Record*. Afterwards, he felt very embarrassed because he realized that indeed they were not inaccurate, and he had just responded to his own impression. After the fact, I was able to go back to the *Record* and explain the situation. It really was quite difficult. If a company feels it was ethically right in the first place, it's got to carry that kind of integrity through the whole process. If you don't, then your original claims for integrity start to get diluted.

My sense is that the lawyers for the claimants brought the *Record* in. Lawyers who try these kind of personal damage cases seek a lot of publicity. Both the claimants and the company had been directed by the court not to talk about the case. The first day, we all adhered to the decision not to talk about it. The next day, the lawyer for the claimant talked to the paper himself. The reporting was not inaccurate, but it only told one side of the story. All I could have said was "We did not make the decision to settle the case." Everybody in the world knows that insurance companies get involved. The follow-up question is "Oh, you mean you wouldn't have settled the case, you mean you thought you were right?" And then, I'm on tricky ground, because I'm not involved in the case, and I don't know everything. There was no way to get out of that situation, as far as I was concerned. The only way out of that kind of situation, if you feel strongly about personal injury cases, is you don't insure them. And if you do insure them, then you have to accept the stipulation that you put the case in the hands of someone else whose interests are not necessarily your own. This particular case involved the reputations of some members of the company more so than the company itself. But the reputations of the good programs here were challenged. My sense is that we have a pretty good counseling program—it works well with stress and alcoholism and other things. I have no idea if they were negligent in this particular case.

There is no way, after the fact, to tell your side of the story, except to say that it wasn't your decision. It wasn't your decision isn't good enough for the world. It's like "I was just following orders" or "It's not my job." It really is quite a lame thing to talk about. So, there's a situation that was very difficult. The number of these cases around the country is increasing, so much so that I'm afraid that a lot of companies are dropping their counseling programs because they can't take the risk, which is a terrible shame.

You have to remember that these cases go to juries; these are not common sense situations. In fact, one of the reasons why our insurance company settled the claim is because they had lost four cases in a row. When it's a jury trial, you're dealing with a jury feeling very sympathetically toward the little guy as opposed to the big guy.

My ethical dilemma in the damages case was: do I react quickly to emotional people who have some authority over me or do I think it out and assume that I know my job better than they do and offer some advice back? Fortunately, no one ever gives direct orders around here, so I wasn't feeling under great pressure. And I felt pretty confident that there was nothing I could do about it. In this particular case it didn't even involve any compromise. Whether the insurance company was right or wrong, or whether we would have defended it differently, or whether we did or did not agree with the insurance company were different questions than whether the reporting was inaccurate. It's hard to keep it in perspective. But I think most of these ethical considerations involve future credibility as opposed to immediate consequences. My sense is that you can cheat somebody and make some more money; you could do that, but in the long run you can't keep doing that. So my sense is that in many of these ethical things, the immediate consequences are not nearly as serious as the long-range damage.

The second case is about a situation in which an executive in the company wanted personal publicity because she wanted to put pressure on the company by having the "outside world" agree that what she was doing was right. She had asked me to highlight her work and her, personally, when describing the company position. That's a very serious problem. There is a tremendous amount of power I have as to who is quoted, and if not quoted, whose point of view gets across. So that's a very serious problem. There were personal motivations on her part that weren't necessarily in concert with the company point of view. I have to tell the company story in a way that reflects well on the whole company and everyone involved in the company. In this particular case the executive wanted to use the corporate function to promote herself and her own particular business activity. I had to put that activity in perspective of our total business and put her as a manager in perspective of a total management team. Obviously I couldn't do what she wanted. That wouldn't have been very responsible.

I have a corporate function and a responsibility to the interest of the company and to the interest of harmony in the company. It doesn't serve me or the company well if I don't have a total perspective on what's going on. So in this particular case, I did promote her and her business, but in the perspective of the whole company, with everyone else involved. And at the same time, when the demands were outlandish, I pointed that out to her: "That's ridiculous; we can't do that." I did it in a way that didn't make it an ethical question for her. I didn't impugn her motives. I said things like "If you get all this publicity, they'll think you're grabbing for power and they'll put a lot of hindrances in your way, so I don't think that's a wise decision." So I didn't pose it as an ethical consideration. It was easy enough to handle; however, I was put in an uncomfortable situation, at least intellectually.

If you're asked to do something that's not in the company's interest, then that's very uncomfortable. Of course, there's the question of who decides what the company's interest is and that's me, based on my own observations. In this case it could have been in my own interest, too, but it could have also not been. I have made the decision that it is in my best interest that I be perceived as fair. In this case, though, I never felt the threat of personal consequences. I think I agonized personally, but there was really no choice in the matter. There was a right way to do things, and a wrong way to do things. It's like there's a right way to do the job, and there's a process and a duty and a responsibility involved in doing the job right; and there's tremendous satisfaction in doing things in that manner. That's what you get by striving to do the job right and making it a work of art. I rarely think of personal consequences. Maybe it's the nature of this firm that I don't have to. I guess there are other companies where, if the boss doesn't like you, he'd kick you out. I don't feel that would happen here. If it did I'd be shocked.

I've had to be very careful. I can't make mistakes as easily as other people, because my mistakes are very visible. So I have to be extremely cautious about things. Other people react, shoot from the hip, or emotionally react from all kinds of motives, but for me that could lead to mistakes that become very visible, and I can't do that.

Q. *How do you think through a dilemma?*

I first play out the scenario of what would happen if I did it one way and what would happen if I did it the other way. What would be the followup? What would be the next move? What would be the response back and what would be the consequences? That's the only way you can tell if you're going to make the right move or not because I think something that instinctively may feel right or wrong, if you analyze it, may not pan out that way.

Often a company gets itself in a box and can't get out. There are two ways to handle it. You can get out by doing something that may be a little unethical but may be the right thing to do in this particular situation, or you can let it die down and see what happens and tell your story privately to whomever wants to hear it. I look at my job a little differently from other people in my profession. I don't consider my job one of solely showing the company in the best light, but of presenting it accurately. I believe the company can live with the consequences of its actions as long as they're reported accurately and without bias, so that's how I approach it. If I lose my credibility, it would be hard for me to get things done. I think the difficulties I've had with my career over the years, the major difficulties, both personal and professional, have always stemmed from situations where I wasn't very credible. In those situations you get deeper and deeper into holes. So by experience I try to avoid them. Obviously, like every human being I can't sometimes.

People who are in positions of authority have a tremendous need to convince themselves they're right. I've seen it over and over and over again. I've seen every rationalization under the sun; they believe they're right when they're wrong. Now, when it comes to a business decision, that's the way it goes, that's their job. But if it comes to a question of reporting, where there's some fiduciary and legal responsibility, you've got to be there and tell them that there's no way to say this. That is an ethical question. You can't lie to your shareholders because it serves your interests. Besides that, you'll get sued.

Of course I'm not a lawyer. But I've used that sometimes just as a device. I don't know what people can sue for. I have no idea. But you know, companies are very emotional places, and a lot of people probably run into moral dilemmas particularly if they react very quickly to emotional instructions or give emotional responses. I still wind up promising some things I can't possibly do. But far less than I used to when I was younger. There are still many people here that promise outrageous things, whether it's to the world or to vendors or to customers; they promise things they can't possibly come up with. I think that's ethically reprehensible. You know there are people that promise employment when they can't possibly come through. People base their whole lives on these things. I try hard anyhow not to do things like that, but I still occasionally do. It takes constant attention to the details of what you're saying to deal with ethical situations, and that's very hard for people to do, to constantly be aware of what they're saying.

I don't know if the next situation is really an ethical question. I thought it was, but now that I think about it, maybe it's not. The company is in a situation now that's coming to a head. It involves the company stores. These stores are independent from the company. Many use the company's name, and most of their customers are our employees. Most employees think they're part of the company, but they're not. The store right now wants to embark on a very ambitious expansion program to other companies. Management has no say over that but has decided to act in the interest of the employees and try and block this move. So the management has had to make a decision—and this has nothing to do with business, remember, nothing to do with this company's business—whether it can act in the employees' interests on a matter that's unrelated to the company. And this management feels it does have the right to do that. It's kind of a parental view of things. I felt the whole issue of whether the management of the company should decide what's right and wrong for its employees on matters unrelated to the company is an ethical situation. It's like forcing people to contribute to political action groups or charities that management says it should. That I think is an ethical situation, where the management makes a decision for employees and expects employees to act on it. If a decision is made in a business context, then that's appropriate for the managers to decide. Their job is to decide what employees should do and not do. They don't ask employees to vote on whether to introduce a new product or not. But this is a situation that doesn't involve the business. The management of the company feels an ethical responsibility to inform and influence employees on something they think is in the employees' best interests, even though they haven't polled the employees whatsoever. In many ways it's a carryback to company towns and company stores. From the other side, you can go on the assumption that most employees are not sophisticated enough to understand the consequences of some complicated financial interactions. The store's board is made up of about two-thirds fairly low-level and middle-level employees. It's an independent board. If the management of the company tells these middle-level employees they think what they're doing is wrong, I don't know how the board can make a clear-cut decision. If they think they're right in terms of their job as independent board members, and yet they're getting all this pressure from the management, it's going to be pretty hard for them to make an independent decision, I would think. The second thing is, of course, it will be my job to communicate this decision if it ever happens. This situation would be like a proxy fight. Oppose the board, and all this kind of thing; it will be very uncomfortable.

At the time this was coming up, my wife and I were trying to make a major purchase. I needed the store to get the deal I wanted, and I felt very personally that there might be some conflict of interest involved in that situation. I inquired whether there was a legal conflict of interest and was told there was not, but I felt there might be. In this particular situation, which is a labor and management negotiation, I'm the management side. But I'm poor too, and I need to buy from the company store and use their credit. So I did think of that, and whether there'd be consequences.

It's not a question of whether the management is right or wrong in this situation. Probably right, as a matter of fact. But, in this particular case, it is my job to convey the management point of view. There's no ifs, ands or buts about it. That's part of my job. If it affects me financially, there's nothing I can do about it. If it gets messy, and it could get weird, I don't know what would happen. But if financially I'm personally affected, that just goes with the territory. There's nothing I can do about it, for the same reason that I can't buy and sell company stock, because I know too much. I could be a lot wealthier if I did it, and there's no legal reason why I can't. I don't feel it's the right way to do things. In this particular case it felt like a personal responsibility versus a professional responsibility. It's a situation where I could be personally damaged by doing my job. But I had no choice in the decision. I couldn't say "I'm sorry, I don't want to do my job because of some private transaction." That would be silly.

There is still a large section of the world that considers us to be a nice bunch of people with a lot of integrity. But because of that they think we don't make good business decisions. They think the two are opposed to each other. I can tell you that they're not opposed to each other. If you make a decision at the right time to manage your industrial wastes properly, you'll save much more money than if you don't decide to do it. There's a danger in this culture of being perceived as not being good business people. The unfortunate thing is I sense that many of the senior managers here are becoming so sensitive to that that they may change the way they think because they're embarrassed by this point of view. I think that is a shame. I see more people playing devil's advocate than I have ever seen before. Very odd. But I'm totally convinced that if you follow your actions and the consequences of your actions from inception, all the way through, eventually you'll save money and you'll do things a lot better.

Long before there were any EPA regulations about companies being responsible even after the stuff was dumped, we were responsible. We'd follow up, even when it wasn't legally our stuff anymore. And in the long run, I think we saved money that way. So if you take that attitude with everything you do and you pay attention to the details along the way, I think you'll function a little better. I can't say how many people still feel that way here. I have managers that delegate work, and it doesn't get done right, and when I confront them, they say, "I told this person to do it and it just didn't get done right." But I refuse to accept that. They just have to follow through every step of the way.

I think the consequences for unethical business decisions are enormous in the long run. And for your personal career as well. I'm not even talking just about ethics. It applies to everything. It's very hard to find merit—I don't know how many American managers there are who are paying attention to all these things. They do in Japan, for example, and I really think that's the key to success. But there are many people, including people who work for me, who consider so much of their job unimportant that they don't pay attention. But as soon as the base of the pillar starts to crumble, the whole pillar will start to crumble. There are still people who feel as I do, like our chairman. If there's a phone call or a letter that comes to him, even if it's a form letter like he gets all the time, and he passes it on, if you don't answer it within a couple of days, he gets furious.

I think the public sees business leaders as dealing with some calculating certainty, when the fact is they rarely know everything that's going on in their own company as well as outside. It's all calculated guesses and risks and assessments and things like that; there are no predictions. One of the biggest rash of stockholder suits in the world in the last five, six years is around claims that management knew things would or would not work. There's an assumption that business people make unethical decisions. It's incredible to me. I'm just astounded. I can't think of any *Fortune* 500 company that would make such decisions as "Let's make this car that's going to explode; that will be good."

Most managers are very professional, and unethical decisions are not very professional. The other thing managers have, is they have all these people who work for them who are concerned with the business. There are all these people who constantly check you and double check you. A built-in jury. It's really quite hard to make any decisions in any company that doesn't involve a lot of people's input along the line, and in those numbers of people, there will be an ethical point of view, as well as a legal point of view, and a public relations point of view. It's very hard to find a decision that doesn't involve all those things. How will it affect the community? Is it going to take away housing and stuff like that from low-income people? All those factors are in there. That's what I hate so much about "issues management." In a sense it is trying to make these things very amoral decisions. I hate the whole notion of "issues management" for that reason. It's letting people off the hook for what's an obvious gut ethical feeling, and you can't do that. If business becomes that way, it won't be very interesting or creative or good for the world.

The seductive part about ethics is that there's either a lot of self-deprecation or a lot of self-satisfaction involved. "Look how good I am," "Yeah, I've done my job," "I feel pretty good," when the job hasn't been done at all. I swear that is my biggest management problem. I have got people who, once they've made the right decision, think the job's done, rather than doing it. People are obviously looking for some kind of moral satisfaction in their work, which is a terrible mistake. Moral satisfaction is one part of doing the job right; the whole part gets you all your satisfaction. But it's very seductive because a lot of people can stop there. The whole problem of ethics, of course, is that it causes people to be defensive. I wish there was a better word. But I guess there isn't.

RICHARD
MANZINI

**Manager, Engineering
Forty-five years old**

*"It was a point that bothered the hell out of
me . . . hiring people to lay them off
in a couple of months."*

I was born in Omaha, Nebraska. My mother and father were both immigrants. They were the only members of their families to come to this country. My mother had seven sisters and a brother, and my dad had two brothers. They're still over there. My father came here in 1916. If he were alive now, he'd be 92. He brought his first wife here with him. They had three daughters; then she died in childbirth with what would have been a son. My half-sisters were placed in an orphanage in Omaha while my father worked. He was a gandy dancer. All the Italians worked for the railroad. They lived that way for five or six years, and then my father struck up a correspondence with my mother. My mother's family was very large and very poor. Around the First World War, an aunt of my mother's had gone to Paris with her husband, an itinerant barrelmaker. My mother, pretty much against her will, was shipped off to live with her aunt. During the war her aunt died and she left because she didn't want to live with her uncle. She became a seamstress in Paris and eventually went back to Italy where she started her own business in her hometown. She was in every respect that age's liberated woman. She did not marry my father, who had come back to Italy, until she was about 37. They came to this country and I was born when she was 39. My half-sisters were taken out of the orphanage and we went on from there.

It was not a happy marriage. The relationship had been developed by mail and, from my mother's side of the story, there was some misrepresentation—my father was almost totally deaf, which she didn't know. My father was deaf and my mother was a liberated woman, so to speak; there were lots of fireworks in our family. My father was a very old-world person. He was something of an autocrat. He was an excellent provider. He made his wine every year; that was kind of a family thing. But I never saw him drunk. He didn't run around; he was a typical, conservative, Italian fellow. He didn't go to church, didn't want to have anything to do with the church. He went to church on Easter, though, because I think there was something that said if you didn't go to church on Easter you'd be damned forever, or something like that. He wasn't taking any chances—he was keeping one foot in there anyway. My mother I would characterize as a believer, but she could very easily accept new ideas. For example, this 80-year-old woman has absolutely no trouble believing that somewhere back in our ancestry there might have been an ape. To most 80-year-old Italian women that would be a sacrilege. She is really a great lady. She's had a tremendous influence on my life because my father was deaf and left the day-to-day upbringing to her. I had very little to do with my father. I played basketball all through high school, and my folks never saw me play. I don't think it was because they were old-fashioned. We didn't have a car. We lived in something like the North End of Boston—a little different in Nebraska because you don't have tenements and narrow streets, you have wide streets and houses. But everybody spoke Italian. We spoke Italian before we spoke English.

I went to Catholic schools in the neighborhood, and then went to a Jesuit high school, all boys. It was probably the best four years I've ever spent. It helped me make decisions that got me into adulthood. I went to Catholic schools because that's what everybody did; everybody had to go to the nuns. There's a book about a Chicago kid and his experiences in Catholic grade school, funnier than hell . . . *Why Do Patent Leather Shoes Shine Up?* or something like that.

I remember almost all of my grade school teachers. For better or for worse I think they had a terrific impact on me. My first grade teacher was a very young nun who has since left the convent at a relatively late age, 52, and married. She was a fantastic artist, a sculptress, and found the constraints on her talent placed on her by a religious society eventually intolerable. She was in an order that was not Jesuitical. The Jesuits say "Do your own thing," and they become astronomers, psychiatrists, whatever. This order was not quite that way. They said that everybody has to conform and she had some problems with that. My teachers were very demanding. They pushed, which in my case was very good, because I think I am a wee bit on the lazy side. They demanded things I think we don't demand of kids any more. You simply didn't turn in a paper with poor penmanship. It wasn't just content—it was everything. When I got to the eighth grade, there was no question that I was going to go to Creighton Prep, the Jesuit high school. There were a lot of Catholic high schools in Omaha, but that was the one everyone wanted to go to—at least, that's where your parents and the nuns wanted you to go. There were three of us from my class who took the exam, and two of us made it.

The Jesuit experience was probably the best experience of my life. Jesuits are a unique breed. My Greek teacher had been an all-state football player. There were a lot of good role models. All during grade school and into my first couple of years of high school, I was going to be a priest; that's important. As far back as I can remember, there was never any doubt that I was going to be a priest. I remember the priests at that grade school; they were Franciscans. In my eyes they were really super guys. We had a lot of priests in the family. My mother's side of the family had four priests who were first cousins of mine, sons of sisters of hers. My father had a younger brother who had a son who was a priest, same name as mine. I had been to Italy and met all these people, so there was a whole body of influence working on me. At some point along the line, that whole idea of being a priest faded away; that was probably early in high school. I started thinking about law, about the professions, because that's the way the environment pushed us. The Naval Academy came up. I had the opportunity to go to four colleges, tuition free. Three besides the Naval Academy— Colorado, Creighton, and Kansas State. I never seriously considered the secular colleges. Creighton was a very good university, and I would have been very happy to go there, but the Naval Academy intercepted. So I didn't go to a coeducational school after the eighth grade until I was 28. And then all the people in my MBA class were guys. My wife believes that from the time of eighth grade to when I was graduated, my social graces were stunted by the fact that I didn't have social intercourse with ladies.

Of course, there was Mercy High School—the Creighton Prep of girl's schools in Omaha. They were our cheerleaders at basketball games. Their prom king was from our school, and our prom queen was from their school. Socially, it was one school; but during the week it was on the other side of town.

Q. *Who influenced you when you were growing up?*

The Greek teacher influenced me quite a bit. His name was Bill Sullivan; he was a Scholastic in those days. He was a training Jesuit, in that three-year period of regency, field work, prior to ordination. Bill taught me two years of Greek, my last two years. He taught me speech, and then I think I had him for theology, too, for a while. He was really my hero. He is now the president of Seattle University, so there had to be something in it. Just a super guy. I see him every once in a while. He's still a relatively young man. I don't know how to explain my affection for him. To me he was a guy who could teach you Greek and yet during the noon hour could beat the hell out of you on the basketball court.

I've always enjoyed the classics. I still read Greek literature quite often, and the Greek epitome of the athlete, the student athlete, or the Renaissance man, or whatever you want to call it, has always fascinated me. Studies that the Navy has done say that the high ranking officers in the Navy today were not only good students, but also good athletes. I've always felt the two were synonymous. One by itself does not give you what both of them together do. I think there's a synergy there. To me, Bill Sullivan was just that whole thing put together. It seemed to me that he had taken self-actualization to the extreme. The guy was completely at ease with himself. Obviously that's an outward appearance— that may not have been the case—but it's what I saw. There were a lot of fellows like that. They were just not an uptight crowd. They were very confident, very relaxed, very sure of themselves. They were the kind of people I said I would like to be like someday.

During my junior year in high school I started getting letters from a number of colleges. One of the letters I got was from the Naval Academy, and it awakened this thing in me from when I was a little kid, about being in the Navy. I was really excited about it. Of course, I had gone to a liberal arts high school, and the Naval Academy looked at me and said, "You've only had a little physics and math. You won't last five minutes in an engineering curriculum." They wanted to send me to school for a year, a prep school. I absolutely refused. Still, I got an appointment. The appointment gives you the opportunity of taking an exam. What really got me into the Academy was a competitive examination. In those days it was a special civil service exam, not the SATs. So I passed the test, was sworn in on July 1st, and spent the next four years in Annapolis.

The four years at the Academy were four very unique years. I grew up in that time. But I think my four years in high school were the years that really influenced my thinking.

I completed the four years, and somewhere along the line I got very interested in aviation. My orders out of graduation were to Pensacola. I was commissioned and became an aviator about a year later. Between my junior and senior years I was home in Omaha and a buddy of mine fixed me up with a blind date from the other side of town; all the Italians were on my side—they were mostly Scandinavians and Danes on the other side. I met Anne; she was in nursing school. She came down to Pensacola with a girlfriend while I was going through flight training, and about six months later we went back home and got married. Then we went back down to Pensacola, after which we went to Corpus Christi, where our son was born. I was designated an aviator there and got orders to the Philippines, where we lived for about a year. Then in '63–'64 the Vietnam thing heated up. The Department of Defense made a sweeping statement that the Navy would no longer have dependents in the Far East. So we came back to San Diego. Our second son was born in August of '64. I went back to Vietnam twice over the next 18 months. During that time I made the decision to leave the service. There were a lot of reasons—none of which I can point to as being the major reason. The biggest thing I can remember was: I was looking at my commanding officers and at being an aviator. I saw that I was slotted into a fairly narrow career path, and what I saw ahead of me for the next 20 years just didn't turn me on. I didn't particularly want to be in my commanding officers' position, and if I stayed in the navy, that's exactly where I would be in 15 or 16 years. The other issue was that the Vietnam War was a very distasteful episode. So somewhere around '65–'66, I handed in my letter. I had no more than done that when they came back and said, "We're going to keep you in an extra year." We argued, but that's the way it was. All it meant was a year in San Diego as an instructor. I was home every night; I lived five minutes from the hangar; it was really a nice year. In that year our daughter was born.

We went back to Nebraska and I went into an MBA program there. I got my masters degree in the summer of 1969 and had my choice of three companies. All three companies felt my age and experience were an asset; some companies did not. Some companies were looking for the 22- to 23-year-old MBA at that point. This company had a program that really appealed to me. They called it a high-risk, high-reward program. Essentially they said, "We're going to grade you for seven years, and you have to hit certain milestones, milestones in your assignments. If you fulfill that aspect of it, we will guarantee you promotion." The guarantee was a third-level position in seven years, which is the position I have right now. In the middle of '74, in my fifth year, the company was forced to disband the program because our growth had stopped. It was a small program; there weren't that many in it; but they just could not keep it up. We were going into a monstrous downturn in '74 and the company could not promote everyone who was due for a promotion. So they gave everybody three choices: you could quit, with 90 days severance pay to go out and look for another job; you could just stay at the level you were, join the universe and be on your own; and there was one more option. I don't remember what it was, but it was not attractive. I decided that I had a good reputation, so I took the second route.

We ended up staying in Omaha for eleven years. I traveled all over the city in different divisions, which really gave me a lot of experience. In the middle of 1979 I was asked if I wanted to go to the management training program which had also been cut in '74. The management training program was a six-month program that had a long tradition of success in the company. Virtually every one of the high ranking executives of the company was a graduate of the program, going back to about 1947. The only problem with it was that you didn't know where you were going to go after the six months; it was an open-ended deal. Anne and I talked about that. We knew we were going to have to move or I would be staying where I was forever. That didn't appeal to either of us. Our first boy was just finishing high school. The problem was the second boy who would have to leave at the end of his junior year. So I actually went to the management training program for the first half of my son's senior year and then lived in a motel for six months after that until he graduated. It was not an easy time for the next couple of years, but now things are really coming together.

Q. *Can you tell me about your present position?*

My title is work service manager. Work service is a euphemism for all of the building and fixing that goes on in this place. Everything we do can be classified as either construction or maintenance. I have all the trades; we have millwrights, carpenters, sheetmetal workers, welders, electricians, CSTs. CSTs are control system technicians. They are a hybrid between electrician, mechanic, and electronics technician. These are the fellows who will eventually handle things like robotics. We also have garage mechanics. Eventually I will maintain all the computers and miniprocessors in the building. So that's it in a nutshell. Fix and build, that's my business. I'm purely a service organization.

This is a very interesting job. There are a lot of labor relations problems, not because of a poor relationship with the union at all, but because in this particular place, the trades have always seen themselves as the elite of the bargaining unit. If you talk to some of them, and you talk to some of the people in the shop, you'd think they were working under two different contracts. It's the same contract. I've been on the job for about six months. I have talked to our operatives and urged an increase in productivity. That entails breaking down some long-standing work rules. For instance, I have to send two guys to remove a pump. I have to send the electrician out to unhook the electrical connection and the mechanic to unbolt the pump. That's the sort of thing that really is killing American industry. That's the interesting part of my job—virtually 95% of my problems have been people problems, nothing to do with keeping the building running, because they're all qualified to do that.

I am a third-level manager. I am responsible for four departments. I report to the general manager for no good reason whatsoever. It's just one of those things. We've been in a lot of turmoil here in terms of the organization chart. Everything is always defined as an interim step. We've been in interim steps since the day I walked in here. The big rumor is that next Wednesday the final step is going to occur. The only thing I can say is that I am reporting to the general manager simply because I once reported to a director who got moved and so the box above me disappeared. I don't think I could go back far enough to figure out how it all happened. But it's a very workable situation, my reporting to the general manager, because, obviously, the guy could care less about what I'm doing in work service. It's great in that I don't have my boss ringing me every five minutes and looking over my shoulder. But from a practical point of view, it's tough. My expenditure approval authority is limited and, consequently, anytime I have anything of a lump sum nature that costs over $2000, I have to get somebody to sign for it. I have to take it to my general manager, and he's never available. If I had a boss he would be more intimately involved with the details. I can't go into my general manager and expect him to have a work service hat on. In the scheme of things, I am a little pimple on a wart of progress. So it doesn't work well. We've been doing this now for several months, ever since the director went out. It seems like every time we get together he asks me how things are going, and I say, "Not very well, boss." So we talk the whole thing through. Every time we meet we go through the whole thing. I really do need a boss. It is not that I want to be managed, because nobody wants to be managed. But I need some horsepower above me to get something done.

I would say that virtually 90% of my time is spent communicating. When I came on the job, I came on with a specific mandate to turn things around, and "things" meant productivity. We have no way to measure our productivity. We don't have time standards or work standards. Our estimate of how long it takes to do a good job is simply in the mind of the first-line supervisor. The philosophy in work service over all these years has been just get the job done. Get it done and get it done quickly. There was very little concern with how the job got done or how effectively we had utilized the resources to get it done. Consequently, over the years we have been overstaffed. In fact, what is symptomatic of work service is really symptomatic of this whole place in general.

This company has had some extremely volatile ups and downs, and when we're going down we do a marvelous job of slashing. We will lay people off at the drop of a hat. But on the way up we tend to forget how to run the business, and anything goes. The problem in work service is, even when there were downturns, the work stayed the same. That's why I've had so many labor relations problems. I look at the contract, and the contract is essentially a limit on my prerogatives. It does not say what I can do, it says what I can't do. Consequently, I look at the contract and say, "Well, it doesn't say I can't do that." So we do it, and the next thing you know I've got a union grievance. They are sitting there saying "You can't do that." So I say, "Where does it say that I can't do that?" And they say, "We've always done it *this* way." And a lot of time, unfortunately, we go back and check and they're right. The arbitrator would never sustain my case in a situation like that. If they can show that regardless of what it says in the contract, we've been doing it a particular way for a long time, that's a very strong case.

I haven't had many of those situations, but since I've come on the job there have been probably six or seven major grievances that I told the union in a very calm, rational way, ought to go to arbitration to be settled once and for all. It really is necessary, because we get the union coming in arguing one side, and the next week they're in here arguing the other side, all depending on who the grievant is. It is simply because the contract does not cover every circumstance. The union would never admit to their constituents (though they do in private) that the contract is solely a limit on my prerogatives and not something with which they can initiate action. So when I say that communication is the major part of my job, I mean that on this job I have literally had to turn around the supervisors who have been here all these years. I think I've got them convinced and things are working pretty well.

We're going into a productivity improvement program that is going to use something like quality circles. I've gotten everything from open acceptance to open hostility, depending upon which trade feels the least secure about how they fit into the future. There is a lot of emphasis on wage incentive programs. I am very much against wage incentive programs. I'm one of the few in this place who is. I don't think they work very well. I don't think the average person in the plant can tie his or her productive effort to the bonus. Therefore, the system cannot do what it's supposed to do. It's a group incentive plan. To my mind, once you get away from individual piecework, where a person can see the 300 widgets an hour he or she has made and know that that is 100 more than the average, and move to these huge departments that have 400 to 500 people where the guy at the beginning who takes this thing and this thing and this thing and puts them together is paid based on what goes out the door down there, it's difficult. Also, the wage incentive must be based on extremely sound work measurement studies and that is a continuing process of keeping things up-to-date. If you introduce a new product or a new method, technically it has to be time studied. Over the years we've cut our wage incentive engineer force to the extent that there's a smearing, a use of averages to handle things. Another problem is the type of person we have out there today. Many people would disagree with me, but my dad worked better under a wage incentive system than my son does or would. When my father went to work in the morning, his obsession was to make a lot of money and to get home at night. My son doesn't feel that way. My son will earn just so much and then he's going to have some fun. I'm not saying my son is a worse worker than my father was, but the monetary incentive is not as powerful as it was.

I think the fact that we are trying so many new things and stepping into a fairly uncertain future is exciting. I can't wait to spring this productivity improvement on the troops—that will be hair-raising. It's going to be very touchy and we're going to have to sell it with kid gloves. We're going to have a real selling job to do there.

When I first came on I saw a million things that I wanted to change. If I had changed them overnight, I'd have had the troops out on the pavement. You just can't do that. As much as my boss would say, "Go down there and straighten out that mess," you're not going to do it overnight. It took years and years to break down. But that's an exciting part of the job. I haven't had that feeling in a long time. However, between you and me and the lamppost, there's a very big rumor that next Tuesday I won't be on the job anymore. I'm a little disappointed about that, but that's neither here nor there. I think I'm going to engineering; they need engineering support. That's unfortunate, because although I have an engineering degree, I've never been an engineer in my life. I'm just not an engineer.

One Month Later

My job now is engineer for the majority of high-volume products at this location. I'm still a support organization for the general manager. I also have responsibility for eight or nine new products that are being introduced. If there's a problem manufacturing a product on the floor, I'm the engineer responsible for it. All the engineers that service the floor belong to me. We can do some things on our own. Any time we're talking about a basic change in the design parameters of a product, however, I can't do that. I have to go to R&D, even if a product is 20 years old. We'll change some of that eventually. We are getting more and more control over old products. We don't want R&D Mickey-Mousing around with 20-year-old products, because they are scarce resources. On the newer products, they pass on the design parameters to me and then I determine the product's manufacturability. I'm the guy who says yes or no, we can make that or we can't make that.

I have a 126 engineers in five departments. I report to a manager who reports to one of two directors, who now report to a vice-president. That leads me to believe we will eventually have a general manager on the engineering side of the house. Things are in a real state of turmoil. We're not at the final iteration; it's got to go a couple of more times.

This company was a heavily engineering dominated company. When I joined the company in 1969, virtually everyone who had a degree had an engineering degree, and virtually every senior officer in the company had come up as an engineer. We have always had a reputation for being a very cost-effective producer of quality products. Cost reduction is a sacred cow in this company. Cost reduction is almost described as the prime function of an engineer here. Once we figure out how to build and mass produce a product, our primary mission becomes figuring out how to manufacture the thing cheaper. Instead of using gold, you may use silver; instead of solder, you may use epoxy because it's a couple of cents cheaper. It can get ridiculous—but pennies can add up to millions. I think in the mission we had we were extremely successful.

I think we're changing. We're not changing as fast as I would like to see us change, but I've got to be honest and say that I don't know how we could change any faster without taking the trauma level so high it would just demoralize everyone. My message to my people is: we have to change, and change is coming. It's easy to verbalize that. But when your ox gets gored or your job security is on the line, then the message gets fuddled a little bit. The key question is: will we change in a way that will enable us to survive and go ahead? That's really the crucial point—how fast can we do it and how well? Our general manager comes on very strong and would like to make changes tomorrow. I shudder to think what would happen if he did some of those things because he would so demoralize our work force that he might as well close this plant and start one in the sunbelt. Maybe that's the idea.

Sometimes I walk away from here at night really pessimistic, after a particularly bad day. I don't think basically I'm a pessimist; my wife says I'm a fatalist. I think we're going to have a lot of problems. I think we're going to have a bloody two or three years. Maybe longer. But I think eventually we will pare down. I think we're going to become a much smaller company. A lot of these people are going to lose their jobs; that's the part that we may have to struggle with because those are very hard decisions to make. I think they're going to do it the way they've always done it—with an ax—based purely on dollars and cents.

Q. *How is ethics dealt with in this company?*

Explicitly, I think the only place I have seen it is in a little booklet that the president will come out with periodically. It will talk about our ethical relationships with people with whom we deal; it's oriented, as I recall, to our purchasing contracts. Once a year, everybody who makes so many dollars a year has to sign a questionnaire stating there is no conflict of interest. Those are the only times I can think of that I have ever seen something about ethics. It's not a word you hear spouted around.

Implicitly, I think this company, if you want to give the company a soul for a minute, probably regards itself as a highly ethical company. I would say that by and large, if I can make an intuitive guess about what the rest of business in America is like, we probably are a very ethical company. My experiences have been very good.

When I sit down with my union president, he always pounds on the table and says that layoffs are not fair. I tell him the union contract isn't supposed to be fair, it's supposed to be equal. You would have a hard time making a connection between layoffs and fairness to him. But most of the people who have been around here for a long time take for granted the fact that when the business is good we hire people, and when the business is bad, we lay them off. That's been part and parcel of our being for the last 40 to 50 years. I think that most of the issues that center around layoffs and everything associated with them are raised more frequently by management and by my peers than by the people themselves. I think the issue of layoffs is talked about from an ethical point of view at my level because in many cases we see management actions that may either exacerbate the layoff or bring it on prematurely.

The average person out there on the floor obviously is concerned with being treated fairly. But my guess is that if you were to talk to most of the people out there, you'd get a consensus that this company is a very good employer. We certainly pay well; we have the highest wage scale in this area. Our benefits plan is probably second to none. So in the things that are important to the average person, we come off looking quite favorable.

Quite honestly, I've never been put in a situation where I thought I was being compromised. But there was a situation that caused me some concern. Let me explain. My first job was out in the shop. I had an apparatus shop—an apparatus shop means little "widgets," like microchips and such things. I wasn't responsible for putting systems together. The information systems that govern our loading (that is, our scheduling) in the shop, while not exactly antiquated, were built on a couple of false premises in the early seventies. The system that runs the computer is about 12 years old, and the basic premise of the system is that there is unlimited demand and unlimited capability in the shop. In reality we don't have that. So this is what happens. If I am making a hybrid integrated circuit (HIC), a circuit that takes seven weeks to make, I should be scheduled, loaded, to deliver that circuit seven weeks later. In actuality, I am loaded for whatever I have to deliver within the current week. So I may be ready to deliver 10,000 HICs this week, but if 5000 HICs were scheduled last week (for delivery seven weeks later), those 5000 will be added to my schedule for this week. Well, unless I had had the foresight to start those 5000 way back then (when I started the rightly scheduled 10,000) for no reason whatsoever, I am going to be back scheduled, that is, overdue on delivery of 5000 HICs. Now, when an equipment shop is building a piece of equipment, they have a stock list from which the computer automatically orders all of the parts that are needed as new product is scheduled. The shop simply puts in a request called a draw ticket. But the computer doesn't operate on the seven-week schedule. It just says: "I want it now," and that contributes to the current week add or current addition. Now, as business goes up you tend to get more and more current week ads. That is generally a function of the fact that every supervisor wants to make sure he or she doesn't run out of anything, so he or she keeps on writing draw tickets. What happens is that if a program continues to grow pretty steeply—as mine did for two years—you end up building up a fictitious base of product that isn't needed. But nobody knows it isn't needed, because the company says you are still back-scheduled.

In the middle of 1981, my program began to decline. All of a sudden I began to see that I was back scheduled for eight or nine weeks on some of my components. But for some reason, the shop that I supposedly owed them to wasn't yelling for the stuff. So obviously something was wrong. Some of the old hands around here were warning me. They said, "Watch all the worms come out of the woodwork when we go downhill. What you think you owe is mostly fictitious."

Our vice-presidents have a bonus that isn't discussed much. But it is generally known that there are certain parameters on which a vice-president is measured for the bonus, and one of those parameters is overall back-scheduling of their shops. We had a new vice-president and, obviously, my back-scheduling was not contributing to his bonus evaluations. So my boss said, in no uncertain terms, "I want you off back schedule." I said, "Let's just sit down and analyze this. You know and I know that most of that shop back schedule is fictitious. Do you really want me to drive that number to zero?" He said, "Yes. No question about it." So what we began to do was work outside the system.

To use a word I don't like, we prioritized everything and started taking care of what we saw as the legitimate needs of the shops we served. These needs were based on verbal communication, no reports, no systems. Around August the heat got bad on everybody—my boss, my boss's boss, my boss's boss's boss—because the vice-president wasn't seeing a reduction in back-scheduling. At that point we got a dictum: You are going to drive to zero. And I was told to start hiring people. Well, obviously I was not in a position to want to start hiring people. I was trying to figure out what I was going to do with the people I had there who were, in all likelihood, going to be out of work in a couple of months. Adding people was just going to exacerbate the problem. But that's what we did. We added people. I tried to argue with my boss. "You know that come October or November we are going to fall off a cliff and we're going to have a thousand people out there with nothing to do." Now the company is not bashful about laying people off if we're losing money. But this situation was different. We had a long series of discussions about the situation. Eventually I lost because the point of the matter was that we were going to drive to a zero back schedule. In the background I continued to do all the things I could to avoid the hirings. What I was trying to do was to get the numbers to come down because that would save the situation more than anything else. But the problem is you're working with a system that is extremely complex. I am talking about maybe 20,000 codes of products I was responsible for; you could not do that manually. We really do rely on the system, so when the system gets messed up the way it did, we are very vulnerable. My answer was to say, "Let's sit down and admit that the system does not cover us in this situation. Let's ignore what the system says my backschedule is." At that point, if we had ignored the back-schedule report, and not hired additional people, we would have ended the year maybe five or six weeks back-scheduled on items that weren't needed. But you can't explain those things to a vice-president.

It was an interesting exercise because I was trying to find all the arguments I could to bolster my point of view. I remember one of them was "You realize that in December we're going to lay all these people off." Well, it wasn't December, it was October. I've been in the business long enough to know that layoffs in a cyclical industry are a part of life. But to hire people when you have evidence that you're about to be in deep trouble ... I wasn't the only one who realized it. There were a number of guys in the same situation; for instance, the fellow who had the magnet shop. He worked for the same boss as I did, so I wasn't carrying the banner myself. Now I have to be honest. We would have had a layoff anyway because the downturn in business was real. In my organization, we started with 1800 and a year later I had 800 people. So some would have gone out the door sooner or later. But maybe we could have done it in February or March instead of October. So it's not that I could have saved a million people's job; that's not the case at all. But here is an instance where the subject of ethics was clearly on the table. It was not right to do.

The argument I made, though, was primarily a dollars-and-cents one. My boss was asking us to add people. You don't add people without training. Even if I put somebody down in front of a silicon bonder, I've got to give him enough training so he's not butchering the product. We were in a semiclean room atmosphere, so we had to be careful. We were going to train people; training is very expensive; then we were going to get them off the roll. The biggest argument I made—this was the real kicker—was: assuming that I could deliver all those products, where were they going to go? They were going to go into the storeroom! The problem was that our investment was as high as it had ever been, and one of the vice-president's bonus measurement is investment. I remember making that argument. I said, "It's going to sit in the storeroom; we're never going to get rid of it; the programs are going down." So what happened? My vice-president's counterpart in production service refused to take it. Now all the shop investment was on my floor. And guess who had to report why my floor investment was so high?! It was a real Mickey Mouse situation.

I did not make arguments to him on an ethical basis. I remember we talked about laying people off. I don't know what my exact words were. But I didn't pound on the table and say "You can't do this to these people." That's accepted as a way of life around here. The nature of the ethical problem, though, was adding people who, two months later, would be off the roll. But we did add people. I think they were surplus from other shops. I think we added 80 or

90 people, with a force of 1800 that's no big deal. But it was a point that bothered the hell out of me, you know, hiring people to lay them off in a couple of months. I don't want you to get the idea I was a white knight. That wasn't what I was thinking. I just thought in all honesty that it was wrong to do. It didn't make any sense, and it was stupid. But you fight it as long as you can, and then you realize you've gone as far as you can go, and then you kind of ignore the question. Obviously, it's dependent on the kind of individual you are and the depth of the question as to how you live with it from that point on. I didn't lose any sleep over it, but it was an issue in which the question of ethics came up and the question of whether or not we were doing right by people came to mind.

The problem came from the way information systems were developed in the beginning. We had gone to these huge, all-encompassing systems that no one person knew everything about. All the subsystems were tied together. They were the rage of the early seventies. They were thought to be the systems that would really run places like this, but we found out that there are all sorts of little keys to doing things, and we've lost track of all the things we did to the systems in the first place. You get really frustrated. You sit down with one of the guys who originally designed the system and he'll tell you, "Hell, you're not running the system the way I designed it to be run." So we're forced to these verbal communications. We end up bypassing the system and using little pieces of paper. That was really funny. Everybody would walk up and say, "What do you *really* need?" It got to be a joke. Here's all that information and we're asking each other "What do you really need?" I think people who get themselves into uncomfortable situations like that, who understand that something has to be done, but who are working with few or no resources that allow them to do something rational, often strike out and do something that is strictly a gut reaction.

We have a tendency to ascribe motives to people in the shop that are not subhuman, but close to it. For example, say a person in a shop has an accident, whether or not she gets hurt. Now we have a nice medical department, but we have a safety meeting once a week, and the first question is "What kind of disciplinary action was imposed on the person?" It's always assumed to be operator carelessness. I'm a handyman. I consider myself a carpenter of sorts. I beat the hell out of myself when I get home. But, if you have an individual who has had more than one or two of these reports, someone in that room will ask what kind of disciplinary action was taken. I happen to be a firm believer that most people who bang themselves with a hammer don't need a letter of warning saying don't do it again. I may be wrong. I know there are people out there who are accident prone, and I know you can make the mistake of hiring someone who simply shouldn't be in an industrial environment. But we find those people and try to weed them out. By and large, most people out there are fairly attentive to what they're doing and our accident statistics compared to any other industry are superb.

I have some real questions—what I call mega-questions—that go through my mind all the time, like "What am I willing to pay to get somewhere in this company?" That's always an ethical question. I don't think I'm the most competent guy in the world, but I do have a sense that there aren't many things I can be exposed to at this level that I can't cope with. I think if you really don't have confidence in your ability to do a job, you can be put in a compromising situation—you'll have enough pressure on you to blame the other guy or blame this or blame that, and not simply say "It's my fault." You know, I don't have a problem saying "That's my fault." That's really what I guess we're talking about.

Around here we make a big deal about the word "commitment." You sometimes hear people say "You really didn't commit to that." They mean you didn't sign your life's blood away to doing something. Well, the answer is, "Yes, I am committed." But I ain't going to get unbelievably excited if something goes wrong, because I almost expect something to go wrong. I honestly think a manager's job is unravelling the things that go wrong, because if things ran smoothly, you wouldn't need all these offices up here. So, something is wrong! What comes across my desk are usually exceptions of some kind— something went wrong. I'm not taking a pessimistic view of business; that's my job. If someone is going to ask me "Do you guarantee that nothing will go wrong?"—that's the idea of this commitment thing—I tell them they're full of hot air. I almost guarantee that something will go wrong. And yet you get the sense in this kind of atmosphere that when something goes wrong you're going to be tarred and feathered. I don't buy into that; I just really don't; I tend to ignore it, just don't get involved. Life is too short.

I'm waiting for the day when I won't have to worry about getting ahead in the organization anymore. I won't ignore it anymore. I'll open my mouth and I'll be like a lot of these guys out there who, when I tell them to do something stupid, say to me, "What do you want me to do an idiotic thing like that for?" They can say it because they have no prospects of going any higher than they are. What I'm saying is that as long as you have the prospect of going higher, you are in a position where you have to compromise yourself in one way or another. I think that's a fact of life. How people live with that is obviously their own business. I can honestly say that I have never been put in a position where I was in an agonizingly ethical or moral situation: a situation where I just churned and churned and didn't know what to do. I tend to view people who react like that from the perspective—if that's the way you want it, fine. I am a bit of a libertarian in a way, although I don't like everything I hear about libertarians. As I get older, I tend not to worry about how other people take care of their problems. I just take care of my own problems and think about how I react to any given situation. That's part of the libertarian philosophy that appeals to me, although there's a lot of it that I view as garbage. As far as ethics are concerned, I really feel that way. It depends on how it reaches my gut at a particular time, and what I do is my business, nobody else's. Right now, if I don't like something, I usually ignore it. Ten years from now maybe I'll say something.

I sometimes wonder if things would be any different if I had stayed in the Navy. I think when you get people together in any kind of an organization you run into these sorts of things. Let's face it, this company is somebody's personality, the personality of the guy down the hall or the vice-president. If you get rid of those two guys then somebody else will come in here with a whole different outlook and this place will change. Somebody once said, "History is biography," and I think that's true for this place.

I have always been amazed at the term "management ethics." I thought that was a big misnomer because the two words are mutually exclusive. I saw a woman on television the other night, on "60 Minutes," who I met when I was a young midshipman many years ago. She is a Navy captain by the name of Grace Hopper. She was one of the first women to ever program a computer—the big Univac. Now that Rickover has retired, she is the senior officer in the Navy. She's 76 years old and she's still on active duty. She said something to me 23 years ago. She was a captain then. She's been a captain for a long time. She said, "We always try to manage people the way we manage things. We haven't quite learned that you manage things, but you lead people." I never forget that. That really is the core of the Marine Corp's dictum: a leader has two jobs—get the job done and take care of your people.

When you go to a place like Harvard, or in my case, the University of Nebraska School of Business, you walk away from there with the feeling that there is a rule or code, and if you can learn it well enough, you can go out and manage. We tend to think in terms of dollars and cents; we tend to think in terms of resources; we always lump people and machines together as resources. I think business has gotten into a frame of mind that says "We can manage anything, if we just do the right thing," whatever that is. If we had talked in terms of leadership, of what can nebulously be described as an art—and it is an art—I think that ethics would be a part of it. Ethics is a part of leadership. I don't think ethics is a part of management. Management, to me, implies that there is some scientific way of doing everything, that when you "learn" management you will have the wherewithal to manage any situation to its successful conclusion. I think that's what the business schools teach. With the case study method we're told, "Here's this company, here's the executive of the day, now what are you going to do?" And after two years of those you're supposed to go out and attack the world because you've been exposed to every conceivable situation. And yet the person who really understands people, and the interaction of people and situations, would be foolish to believe that he can manage his way out of every situation. I think we've tried to teach people that there are easy ways to do things. If you learn A and you learn B and you learn C and D, and take a sum total of that, and apply it to every situation, then you can solve any situation. I think that when you teach that, and you teach it in a very scientific, logical A, B, C, D way, you have taken the human element out.

As I get older, I think I find that not only are there no right answers, but half the time we don't even know what questions to ask. I do really think that I regard ethics as a very individual thing. I subscribe to a theory that a society is built up of individual people and the norms and ethics are dependent upon those individuals. I'm not a liberal. I don't think I'm a liberal. I think I'm very middle-of-the-road. I have a real problem with censorship in any form. I have a real problem with anyone defining what is right or wrong. I know we have to have some norms of behavior if we are going to hold it all together. I think the norms come together by themselves; I don't think they have to be defined.

I've always made a distinction between ethics and morals. It's my distinction. Ethics, to me, is how I deal with my outside environment. You've got to have two people for ethics. I think you need only one person for morality. That's the only difference I make of it. No big deal, just that there's more of a connotation of soul with morality. Ethics is obviously governed by some moral code, but it's more secular. And I do think you have to have two to tango on ethics.

My idea of right and wrong was formulated by the religious upbringing I had. I don't know how they are now, but in those days most Catholic grade schools were fairly dogmatic. There was a right and wrong that was predicated on things like the Ten Commandments and what the Church said. We accepted the fact that you didn't eat meat on Fridays; we accepted all the dogma as being very real and very true. I think when you do that, your definition of right and wrong becomes very narrow. To me, a dogmatic person is one who has the unique ability to put himself into a lot of rules that exist and, therefore, make life easy on himself.

My ideas of right and wrong have been tempered a lot since my childhood, because I don't consider myself a dogmatic person at all. I am a doubting Catholic now. I still go to church. I consider myself an active Catholic, but the difference between me now and me then is that then I accepted everything that I was told at face value. I don't answer questions that easily anymore. I'm a searching

Catholic now. I don't believe a lot of things that Catholics should believe, and I don't find that wrong. I don't know how to rationalize it. I don't think I can. I think part of being an adult, part of growing up, is all of a sudden finding out that all those answers for which we had complex questions aren't all right. I think it's part of man's nature to question. From a purely Catholic point of view, I would say that I hope God will give me the grace to see things as He thinks I should see them. I'm not sure I'll ever be there, because I have some severe problems with Catholic dogma.

I don't think my idea of right and wrong has changed. I think I would say my idea of right and wrong has changed from when I was a kid, from reacting to external constraints to reacting to what my gut says is right and wrong. You can't completely divorce the two, of course, because those constraints made me what I am. But I don't see things as being as black and white as I did when I was younger. And, as I get older, I will see things even less as black and white. That may just be the process of growing up.

I can see many times where someone in a managerial position would make a powerful argument in his or her soul on a moral base, but would win the argument in practice by focusing on business issues. I think that's only natural. The business of this business is business. It is not ethics, and it is not morality. I'm not sure that's wrong. I don't want to leave you with the impression that I think it's wrong to do it that way. But assuming we are in business to do all the things that businesses are supposed to do, you should be able to rationalize every decision on some dollars-and-cents quantitative base. But it's not a moral business, so I don't know if you have to answer things on a moral basis. The nub of the problem is—when the two conflict, what happens?

COMMENTS

There are many dimensions along which we can consider the effect of family background, traditions, beliefs, attitudes, or experiences on the manager's approach to his or her work and the ethical dilemmas that occur in its practice. We will look at four of these in relation to Robert Smith, Arnold Rowan and Richard Manzini. The four dimensions reflecting factors that contribute to ethical decision making and implementation are responsibility, competence, empathy, and capacity.

Robert Smith

Responsibility and Competence

In looking at the themes in Bob Smith's life that shape the man and the manager he is, it makes sense to pair the responsibility and competence dimensions. For Bob, the sense of responsibility he feels derives from two sources. The first is his recognition of the principles and comforts with which he was raised. Because of his family's education and professional status, he acknowledges that his community viewed him as "a young man with a silver spoon in his mouth." But he tells us that from an early age he was guided toward appropriate humility and recognition of what he had been given by the frequent reminder, "Robert, you're taking advantage." The twofold message was clear: (1) don't take advantage of the bounty you have been given, and (2) such advantage entails responsibilities and obligations to contribute to society.

The theme of "ease of acquisition" (and the responsibilities that that entails), carries into a discussion of Bob's competence—or more precisely, of his public presentation of his evaluation of his skills and abilities. Bob Smith is a bright and competent man, and yet speaks somewhat deprecatingly of his capabilities and talents. He refers to himself as "an average student, ... intellectually lazy," and tends to downplay the intellectual abilities that contributed to his success in college, graduate school, the navy, and ultimately the banking world. One gets the sense from Bob that he has defined much of himself in terms of the "advantage" he has received as opposed to the effort he has made. His frequent reference to heavenly support, for example, "I'd be just as useful as I know how, the Lord will provide, and somehow it will work out. And it always has," is not so much an expression of religious faith as it is an acknowledgment of the good fortune, the external determinism by which he believes his success has been governed.

Bob's rise in the organization, his analyses of the problems he discusses, his obvious charm and skill at both public and interpersonal relations are clear evidence of the competency he has brought to and acquired in his positions in the bank. Nonetheless, the early notion of advantage—its privileges and its obligations—has remained a guiding theme in Bob's life.

Empathy

The notion of empathy is important in the scheme of ethical behavior because it enables the decision maker to understand and empathize with the positions of the many stakeholders in a situation. No one can begin to understand another's perspective unless first recognizing and accepting that others may not see the world in the same way he does. For Bob, the understanding of the advantages with which he was raised required the awareness of the comparable positions of others. His empathy for his employees is most clearly apparent when he tells us that the young manager caught in the SEC dilemma did not suffer career consequences for mistakes he had made. Whether we can accurately call this behavior empathetic rather than tolerant is not clear, but his ability to feel a situation from other than his own perspective is evident, and evidence of the effect of early values on his present attitudes as a manager.

Capacity

Where Bob Smith differs from many of the managers in this book is in the capacity he has to get done what he believes ought to be done. Simply by position as CEO he can design or change policy, marshall resources, and get action. Being in such a position does not mean that he has no accountability, that he can simply do what he wants. Bob is accountable to his board, to his stockholders, and, less directly, to every individual and group that does business with the bank. But the fact of the matter is, his role accords him the capacity to do what he believes to be the right things to do.

The capacity power inherent in high position is enormous. In the case of ethical dilemmas, it does not provide the answer to "what is right?" but once the decision on "right" is made, capacity power makes *doing* right, probable. The possession of such power demands the recognition of the responsibilities and obligations of "advantage" that have guided Bob Smith's life.

Arnold Rowan

Empathy

The empathy dimension is a good starting point for looking at Arnold Rowan because of the strong "urban, Jewish, intellectual" environment in which he was raised. That encouragement and the values it represented were usually labeled "liberal," and in the days of Arnie's youth, before the word "liberal" took on the negative connotations of recent years, the liberal ideology encouraged an empathy, a concern for one's fellow man, that Arnie recalls when he says "There was a celebration of some of the kinder human instincts." Clearly, for Arnie, the ideological tradition of his early years, the belief in "liberal causes," a general concern for the underdog, a desire for what might be called "a better world" remains critical to his self-image. And he talks, as well, of passing that "liberal intellectual tradition" on to his children, so they, too, may grow with a tolerance for others that he, Arnie, values.

Of course, Arnie is not naïve in his upholding of an ideology. He recognizes the challenges to a belief system brought by reality when he wonders how his oldest son, who "talks about not liking racism" will react when they move to the city and he gets "a heavy dose of it." He also recognizes changes in life style and values from his parents, particularly in terms of materialistic values. (Not an inconsequential change, since the ideology of Arnie's childhood usually included some pride in a lack of materialistic concerns.) Arnie recognizes both the continuity and the change in the somewhat poignant comment about his son's upcoming exposure to a racially mixed population occurring, not because Arnie and his wife want to encourage their children to know many kinds of people, but because they want to acquire a "grand old city house."

Responsibility

Born of the liberal tradition in which Arnie was raised is the notion that one is responsible for moving toward the achievement of those "good" and "right" things in which one believes; that, above all else, one is responsible for caring. One of the changes that has occurred from Arnie's youth to the present, is the awareness of the responsibility for implementing the beliefs that one holds. In a film made of that Weavers' reunion concert that Arnie mentions, Weaver

Ronnie Gilbert, referring to that earlier time says, "We really believed that if we could just sing loud enough, we could change the world." She, of course, is ruefully recognizing that simply holding the "right" values and shouting them loudly is no longer the fully responsible action. Responsibility, as Arnie recognizes it now, entails getting the job done. As he says, "I have got people who, once they've made the right decision, think the job is done, rather than doing it. The seductive part about ethics [and, I think he would add, about the liberal tradition of his youth] is that there's . . . a lot of self-satisfaction involved: 'Look how good I am,' . . . when the job hasn't been done at all."

Competence

For Arnie, competence, like responsibility, is part of the overriding value system in which he was raised. Being smart, being able, being competent are the right things to do and be. "Honesty was right and dishonesty was wrong. It was wrong to be late for class. . . . It was wrong not to do well in school. . . . Being rational was better than being irrational." While academic achievement was valued, and while clearly Arnie and his family took pride in intellectual achievement, brightness and competence were not the special goal. They were expected.

Capacity

As director of public affairs, a high-level staff position, Arnie has a great deal of autonomy in what he does and flexibility in how he does it. More importantly, because he is the public face and voice of the company, the designer of its public image, the protector of the people within, the manager of outside unpleasantness, he is, for the most part, accorded the capacity and the support to do his job as he deems appropriate. (There is a pleasant coherence to the tradition of caring in which Arnie was raised and the position of company protector which he now holds.)

His generally broad capacity is somewhat constrained, however, in two types of situations. First are those situations in which he must speak on behalf of top management against either what he believes or what goes against his own best interests. The company store dilemma is one such case. Arnie's concept of his role responsibility allows him to deal relatively comfortably with these types of situations: he believes he is the conveyor, or communicator, of management's position. Yet he does recognize the limit to his capacity to do what he might wish to do.

The second kind of situation that challenges his capacity occurs when he is trying to recognize and act appropriately on the distinction between "what is *best* for the company and what is *right* for the company." In these cases, he reports he is either supported or constrained by a company history that has been clearly articulated by a series of presidents. But despite these few constraining situations, Arnie has a remarkable amount of freedom to get the resources and the support he needs to carry out his responsibilities and implement the decisions he makes and tasks he is assigned.

Richard Manzini

Competence

Our discussion of Rich Manzini begins on the competence dimension because Rich's sense of himself as an ethical person seems to have grown as he recognized, during his youth, that he was a bright and capable individual. It is striking that when he talks about the important influences of his Jesuit education, in general, and of Bill Sullivan, his Jesuit teacher, in particular, he does not identify religious or moral teachings, which must have been a critical part of the curriculum, as the important learnings. What he values is the respect and drive for excellence of mind and body with which he was inspired, and the fact that "self-actualization," that is, being the best and most fulfilled that one can be, is almost a prerequisite to being a valuable, moral contributor in the world. We see Rich's sense of self-assuredness as a theme through those parts of his adult life that he shares with us. In attempting to countervail the vice-presidential dictum to his apparatus shop, he is confident of his understanding of the situation, the problems with the computer system, the way the system is producing an inaccurate outcome, and everything else he needs to make a cogent argument. There is not a quiver of self-doubt. The issue of capacity to affect what he knows is right is another matter which we will discuss below. But Rich's sense of his own competence is secure.

Even more telling is Rich's strong sense of himself that allows him to be a "doubting" but an "active" Catholic. A strong, and as he says, "dogmatic" religious tradition is more likely to produce one of two effects on those raised in that faith. Either they remain relatively true believers, or they reject the religious organization (if not all its teachings) for want of being able to find a place for their own individuality within it. Rich Manzini falls into neither pattern; he has found where he belongs.

Responsibility

For Rich, the concern with responsibility, while strong, is secondary to the sense of competence. By secondary, I do not mean that it is less important either in terms of what he cares about or in actions that he takes. Rather, for Rich, his notion of responsibility grows out of a sense that his competence makes him *able* to recognize his responsibilities and to act effectively on them. Like many children of immigrant families, Rich's responsibility to his family, as a child, was to do what the Jesuits helped him to do: be the best he could be. His service to his family was his own growth and development. But what he has gained in his own self-actualization now demands that he use that responsibility for his family, his fellow workers, and his company.

Empathy

Empathy, for Rich, reflects how he views himself. Rich sees others as having the capability he has to be self-determining individuals. Hence, he not only respects the rights of others to believe as they do, but believes that those different views are what makes an ethical society. As he says, "I subscribe to a theory that a society is built up of individual people and the norms and ethics are dependent upon those individuals. I have a real problem with censorship in any form. I have a real problem with anyone defining what is right and wrong [for everyone]."

Capacity

Capacity, the ability, outside of one's own competence, skills, and talents, to get a hold of what is necessary to get the job done is the area which for many managers in this book is the most constraining.

Certainly for Rich Manzini that is the case. Although his sense of himself is as a real "can do" kind of person, he is very aware of the "can't do" roadblocks within the organization that limit the control he can exercise. Rich seems to say there are two sources of his limited capacity. One is, clearly, his position, or level, in the corporate hierarchy. As he describes the back-scheduling situation in the apparatus shop and the arguments he raised to correct both the "business" and "ethical" concerns it presented, one can hear the frustration in his words. But his recognition of his limited capacity has also left him philosophically and psychologically self-protected. As he says, "You fight it as long as you can, and then I think you tend to realize that you've gone as far as you can go, and then you kind of ignore the question." It is a thought that echoes Mark Hoffmann, Charles Warren, and many others to whom we have listened.

The second source of his limited capacity is his desire to move up, a desire that has been part of him since his earliest years. We are not talking here about blind ambition to achieve power but of the desire to continue to grow, develop, and "be all that one can be" that has been part of Rich Manzini's life. He tells us: "I don't want to be an assistant manager for the rest of my life. I would not have come here if I thought I was going to stay at this level. I have thought, 'What would happen if . . . a wrenching moral question separated me from a promotion?' I would dread that ever happening, because I don't know how I would react. It's so simple to say I would do things as I've always done them. What I'm saying is that as long as you have the prospect of going higher, you are in a position where you have to compromise yourself in one way or another. I think that's a fact of life." Rich is not talking about doing anything one can to get ahead. He is explaining why he does not try to "expand" his capacity by saying to the vice-president, like his worker said to him, "What do you want me to do an idiotic thing like that for?"

Summary

By background, education, personal traits, and experience each of these managers has a concept of (1) personal responsibility and the obligations that it entails; (2) the need for empathy, for stepping into the minds and eyes of others to see the world from different perspectives; (3) his own competence—where it comes from, in what areas it lies, and its obligation; and finally (4) his capacity and the mechanisms he uses to handle its breadth and scope with its limits. Each man shows a coherence in personal and professional life that, over time, has shaped the way he meets and manages the ethical challenges before him.

CREATING CAPACITY:
SHAPING THE WAY
THINGS ARE DONE

. . . I felt that if you're really going to run an ethical institution, and set high standards, you have to set them from the top. (Smith)

. . . Our institution has an unstructured environment with unwritten rules and regulations. In order to ethically perform in this organization, a lot is left to chance. (Williams)

. . . Most managers are very professional, and unethical decisions are not very professional. (Rowan)

. . . One of the biggest problems in management is cowardice. (Smith)

H ow many work hours are consumed by managers wrestling with ethical dilemmas? How much leisure time, family time—necessary for renewal and reinvigoration—is devoted to rehashing the ethical problems that arise at work? How many dollars do these hours represent? What is the measure of human creativity, productivity, and growth that remains unrealized? Despite all the balance sheets, earnings statements, annual reports, quarterly reports, and the rest, we have no statistics on the impact of ethical dilemmas on corporate productivity or managerial and executive development. If the managers who spoke in this book are considered a fair cross section of American corporate life, however, the cost of struggling to resolve ethical dilemmas effectively is far from trivial.

This is not to suggest that what is needed is some new accounting tool to measure dilemma-evaluation time; nor should managers be encouraged to spend *less* time with ethical problems. And I am not simply stating that it is worth the cost because "good ethics is good business," which it is, but that is not my point. Ethical dilemmas will always occur in the course of doing business, and managers, therefore, will always have to spend time working them through to produce the most ethical, effective results. So, if the economic and human costs of that time are high, it is essential that time be used well. And the responsibility for achieving this lies with both the organization and the individual manager.

This project began three years ago with my belief that individuals could and should shape and change the organizations of which they were a part, that with integrity—and energy, enthusiasm, and commitment—managers, at all levels, could make their companies into ethically responsible and responsive institutions. Over the next three years, as I listened to the tales of Mike Williams, Charles Warren, Hal Lightner, Rich Manzini, and others, and thought about what they meant, my belief in the power of the individual eroded. Despite the examples of people "managing the system"—Evelyn Grant, Bob McDonald, Jim Gordon, to name a few—it seemed it was the organization that shaped what individuals could or could not do. If a manager had selected a job well and was lucky, her values were congruent with those of the company and she could act comfortably according to those values. If a manager had not found as good a match, however, he was faced with the choice of loyally complying against his values, of refusing to comply at the risk of losing job or career advantage, or of being creative about finding a way to solve a specific problem without having any impact on the conditions that may have created it. The option of exercising effective "voice" (Hirschman, 1980) was not evident, and the sense I had of the powerlessness of the individual was enhanced by the recognition that these conditions were unlikely to remain stable in an environment in which mergers and acquisitions—and, thus, rapidly changing corporate cultures—are increasingly the order of the day so that even the manager with a comfortable "fit" might suddenly find the company values had changed.

The result of this initial interpretation was the conclusion that for business to be ethical, and for managers to be ethical, *organizations* would have to make changes—in the way they were designed, in how policy was made and implemented, and in the processes by which their work was accomplished, and that the individual manager could have little effect. But that interpretation remained inadequate, for what, in fact, is an organization? Its legal corporate personhood notwithstanding, an organization is the people in it. It is designed and shaped and run not only by the top executives, but by every other individual who is responsible for overseeing the performance of others or for serving as a representative of the company to those outside it. While for every one of us who works in an organized setting there is always a "they" who seem to pull the strings and over whom we feel little control, each of us is also the organization to some others; Wendell is the organization to Mac; Frank McGraw is the organization to his supplier; Ron Harris is the organization to his customers. So, after three years, this project has brought me to a middle ground between the naïve (an individual can change the world) and the cynical (we're all victims of the system) (Kotter, 1985).

Given the middle ground on which we now stand, what follows is directed to managers in the two essential roles they play: manager as organization, and manager as individual. It is in fulfilling both those roles that individuals can shape organizations and organizations can create environments in which managers can marshall the capacity to handle dilemmas ethically, effectively, and ultimately, profitably.

THE MANAGER AS ORGANIZATION

... I felt that if you're really going to run an ethical institution, and set high standards, you have to set them from the top.

... Our institution has an unstructured environment with unwritten rules and regulations. In order to ethically perform in this organization, a lot is left to chance.

Taking Responsibility and Being Accountable

Questions and concerns about responsibility and accountability have come up repeatedly in this book. The ability of the organization to determine its own accountability and responsibility, and to accept them is essential to ethical management. As well as looking at organizational factors, the manager as organization must be conscious of three ways in which he will be viewed by company members as the conduit of the organization's sensitivity. One, how much does he want or is he willing to know? Two, what resources does he feel responsible to provide? And three, how willing is he to stand as last resort?

Knowing What to Know*

Fifteen division presidents of a leading U. S. oil company read the Frank McGraw interview and were then asked how they would respond to Frank if he were their purchasing agent. The first answer blurted out was, "I'd fire him." To the vigorous nods of assent around the room, the "terminator" was asked "Why?" In essence, his answer was, "I don't want to know all that stuff. It's his responsibility, not mine. Just tell me the bottom line." He was then asked if he would value his purchasing agent going through the thought process that Frank verbalizes. As he answered affirmatively, but reiterated that he wanted no part of it, a colleague of his across the room fairly shouted out, "If Frank wants to talk about it, let him tell a priest or psychiatrist. The office is no place for that stuff." Later in the chapter I will talk about the necessity of making ethics a legitimate topic of discussion. But for now, the critical

* Many ideas in this section grew out of a discussion with Professor Renato Tagiuri of the Harvard Business School.

questions are: how much *should* the management of an organization know about what is happening in that organization? How much can it be *expected* to know? How much does it *want* to know? In almost every recent report of corporate malfeasance, the leaders of the cited organizations have come forth sooner or later to proclaim their ignorance of the questionable activities. There is then considerable grumbling by the public that the "big guys" always get off the hook. The more thoughtful response usually concerns just how much individuals sitting at the head of corporations, which are made up of thousands of employees, geographically dispersed, *can* know about everything that is going on. Such an argument is made by former Attorney General Griffin B. Bell, in his report on the overdrafting practices of E. F. Hutton, Inc. In exonerating chairman and CEO Robert Fomon, Bell's report (*New York Times*, September 6, 1985) states:

> A corporate officer is, in the performance of his duty and functions, entitled to rely on the decision, judgments, and performance of other officers and employees of the company if the officer believes that such decisions, judgments or performance are with[in] the professional or other competence of such officer or employee.

The report goes on to say that the people employed were competent and, therefore, the chairman was neither responsible nor accountable for what occurred.

I have no intention of questioning Bell's analysis here; he does cite others in the organization who should have known what was happening and who, therefore, should be held accountable. But, what this pronouncement makes clear is that the question of who does or should have knowledge is critical to establishing who ought to be taking responsibility. Since ignorance is easily accepted as a valid release from responsibility, too many managers don't want to know. Since it is close to impossible for any individual to know everything that is going on, the critical question is, How do I know when I should be paying attention or seeking information, and how do I know when it is dangerous for me not to know? A definitive answer cannot be served up, but any time a manager starts to react like the "I don't want to know" oil company person about something, it is advisable that she stop and ask why she doesn't want to know. It just may be that not wanting to know is the surest sign that attention ought to be paid. While we can agree that no one can know everything, the choice to *want* to know more than "just the bottom line" is essential to creating an ethically capable organization.

The Golden Opportunity Versus the Impossible Demand

One of the most exciting things an organization—a boss—can do is offer an employee a "golden opportunity," a chance to tackle a tough problem and show his stuff. One of the most devastating actions an organization—a boss—can take is to place upon an employee an impossible demand, a tough problem that he has no way of doing. What is the difference? It is *capacity* to do the job, and an honest assessment of where that capacity lies.

Ralph Quinn, the new Latin America branch manager in Mike Williams' interview was offered the golden opportunity of retiring in glory as a manager—a job he had never been in during his 40-year career. Ralph, however, did not have the skills to do the job, and was turned down when he asked for appropriate resources. Since Ralph did not have the ability to do the job, what was intended as a golden opportunity became an impossible demand.

Opportunities that may be golden or disastrous can be offered for a number of reasons, from career development for a promising employee to the need to palm-off a threatening situation on someone. Management's obligation is to be clear *why* the opportunity is being given, to accurately assess capability, and to acknowledge its own responsibility in making the golden opportunity a success. Because while it may be that the bright and promising young person will always find *some way* to get the job done, without the appropriate resources and support, that way may, of necessity, be unethical.

"The Buck Stops Here"

What I have been talking about in this section on responsibility is that organizations—and by that I mean managers—must think about the Truman aphorism. Knowing where the buck stops—where responsibility and accountability ought to be located—is essential to supporting ethical activity within the organization.

The organization is not responsible for everything. But, it is responsible for knowing what it should know, for seeing that responsibility and accountability are placed with those who have the capacity to perform what is expected, and for supporting those it has deemed responsible.

The manager as organization is not just the conduit through which others in the company concretely encounter the organization. Managers, in this role, are those who collectively create the elements of the organization, referred to earlier in the book, who make possible the unified labor of many individuals to produce products and/or services effectively and efficiently. These elements are policies, the systems designed to enact those policies, and the processes that implement the systems.

Developing Policy that Works in Practice

Organizational culture is expressed by policies, codes, rules and guidelines which are formal statements of the values held by an organization or by a subunit of the organization. These statements are also messages about how those values should be practiced. However, as many examples in this book have shown, formal and unstated policy as well as other guidelines frequently do not result in their implementation as intended. The awareness of this problem is not new. Argyris and Schon (1974) dealt with it in general terms, when they compared theory espoused with theory in practice. Their concern was that organizations often do not, or cannot, practice what they preach. As we have seen, there are several forms of mistranslation of policy: (1) A policy that is positive, or even simply benign, can in concert with other similar policies result in unethical behavior in practice. Wendell Johnson's dilemma is an example of such a situation. (2) Policies are written to deal with *issues* and, therefore, focus on values and goals outside the context of any specific situation; they are statements of what the organization believes to be "the right thing." However, managers within the organization rarely face issues. Their problems arrive in the form of dilemmas in which, regardless of policy, "the right thing" is not evident. (3) Formal policies can conflict with cultural norms of the organization. Evelyn Grant's dilemma about evaluating her subordinates was the direct result of a conflict between a performance evaluation policy (and system which I shall discuss below) and an organization-wide norm of static ranking.

What can be done? Managers who sit in policy-making positions, whether at the top executive level or as the head of a department or work group, must develop policies, guidelines, rules, and procedures with two considerations in mind. The first is, how do these formal statements hold together as an integrated package? Does the achievement of one affect or contradict another? Do any of these guiding statements, if practiced together, create unintended conditions? The second consideration, following from the first, is, how are the situations which these policies are written to address, likely to present themselves to the employees in this organization? How can we make guiding statements that recognize the dilemmas faced in implementation? To create an environment for the ethical conduct of business, organizations must develop formal and informal policies and guidelines which unambiguously state the values of the organization, while reflecting an awareness of the dilemmas of implementation.

Designing Ethically Responsive Organizations Systems

Just as policy and other value statements must be developed with implementation in mind, so too must systems be designed with careful anticipation of their intended and unintended effects. Too often, "good" systems can have "bad" results. We see this played out frequently in the design of reward systems. It makes eminent good sense to reward individuals (or groups) for achieving desired goals of the organization. Two problems can occur, however. First, often the measures on which the reward system is built are inappropriate reflections of what the organization really wants to get. Worse still, they frequently are measures whose achievement either deflects the manager from the activity necessary for productivity or drives the manager to unethical behavior as the only "logical" way to meet them. Charles Warren talked about having to "fudge" shipping dates so that all orders would appear to be out the door by a particular date. The reason he "had" to do this was because a senior manager, several levels above him, received bonus pay based on zero monthly shipping delays (among other measures). Much has been written already about short-term measures and their detrimental effects (e.g. Hayes and Abernathy, 1980), but beyond such concerns is the fact that these measures do not reflect what the organization wants to achieve, which is to get product to customers in a timely way. If there is to be a short-term measure related to shipping, it more appropriately should relate to delivery since that will reflect customer satisfaction and profitability. Since, as Charles Warren says, they invariably meet delivery date with expedited shipping, the appropriate measure (delivery) would remove the need for Charles (and others, we presume) to find a way to meet the unrealistic and inappropriate shipping measure.

The second problem is that many reward systems are based on measures over which the manager has no control—other than the demand that somebody else do something. Rich Manzini's vice-president, who demanded zero back orders despite a computer system which precluded that ever being achieved *on paper*, is an example. Although Rich's comment, "You can't tell that to a vice-president," may reflect a cynical attitude toward the position, if not the individual, the reality was that the vice-president was located 1000 miles from Rich's plant, dealing with paper and occasional phone calls from a number of facilities, and unable to be involved in managing the processes on which his rewards were based. From such situations do we inevitably get the "Move it!" philosophy.

The design of systems—human resource, personnel, technical, financial—must be undertaken with the same awareness necessary for policy development. Certainly, checks and balances must be brought in, particularly with information systems like Rich Manzini's. But, more generally, the impact of systems in their implementation must be carefully considered. Anticipation of how systems will work together and of unintended results is essential to building an ethically competent organization.

Job Design

In making recommendations about policies and systems, I have focused on elements that can create conditions in which ethical situations develop. When we consider the design of jobs, our concern turns to employees and their ability to cope with ethical dilemmas that arise. Much of the work on job design has dealt with increasing worker satisfaction and growth, both as an end in itself and as a means to a productive work force. One of the key features of jobs designed to achieve these ends is autonomy for the worker in how the job is done (Hackman and Oldham, 1980). However, the need for autonomy, and thus flexibility, in jobs has critical implications as well for organizations that are committed to supporting ethical managerial behavior.

There are two issues of concern, one tangible and the other primarily psychological. The first is reflected in Evelyn Grant's comment that what she likes least about her job is "that there are so many things that are beyond the control of the job, yet the solution is still expected." Her experience, which would be echoed by countless American managers, relates back to the concerns raised earlier about organizations providing the support so that managers have the capacity to handle the challenges that confront them. One definite way of giving employees the capacity to manage effectively is to give them flexibility and choice in how they do their tasks, how they arrange their time, and to whom they have access. Along with tangible control of the work is the issue of perceived power. The less freedom and flexibility individuals are given, the greater is their sense of powerlessness. The concerns expressed by many managers as to whether they *really* have a choice about what they can and cannot do reflect the sense of powerlessness that is evoked by their lack of control over their jobs and their inability to perform as effectively as they would like. Until they design appropriately flexible jobs, organizations will continue to support unethical behavior by people who, as Rich Manzini says, "understand that something has to be done, but who [because] they are working with few or no resources that allow them to do something rational, often strike out and do something that is strictly a gut reaction." And too often that gut reaction has ethical consequences for both managers and organizations.

Building Effective Processes

The finest policies and designs will be limited in their effect if organizations do not develop the processes that both allow them to be implemented well, and allow concerns, problems, and disagreements to be raised and responded to. To do this requires attention to two things: making ethics a legitimate topic of discussion, and developing and supporting effective communication at and between all levels of the organization.

Making Ethics a Legitimate Topic of Discussion: A Matter of Communication

Although more and more companies are stating publicly their commitment to ethics in management, few individuals find it comfortable to raise such concerns (unless they can couch those concerns in other words). There seems to be a sense among managers that talking about ethics is "just not done here." And, unfortunately, they are usually right.

The CEO of a major corporation was addressing the participants at the start of a recent executive development seminar. The CEO offered some general remarks, and then called for questions. After responding openly and enthusiastically to a number of questions about changing corporate policy in several sensitive areas, he was asked what a manager in his company, who had an ethical concern about a policy, practice, or order she was given, ought to do. After a long pause, the CEO began a story about a crazy letter he had once received from an employee. The thought process that led him to this story is not hard to trace. Encouraging people to "complain" about something on the job can certainly tempt "the worm to come out of the woodpile," as one interviewee put it. But it was disconcerting to hear that this admirable leader, whose company stands in the forefront of corporate ethical awareness, could not, in truth, tell his people to discuss such concerns in the workday environment. Although they were encouraged to talk about ethics off-site, the underlying message was, "Keep your mouth shut (about ethics) on the job."

Organizations must consciously act to make ethics a legitimate topic of discussion, not only for those times of crisis when a personal value is challenged or painful competing claims are present, but also to allow employees to fully examine the range of options available, to anticipate pitfalls, and to explore creative ways of resolving their dilemmas. Making ethics a part of the "language game" (Ladd, 1970) of business can encourage all employees to think about what it is they do think about ethics. Jim Gordon said the only reason he thought of his good/bad/right/wrong matrix (which was a strong clarifying device for him) was because he was encouraged to think about ethics for this project.

How does an organization go about legitimizing the discussion of ethics as a part of routine management? One way is by establishing formal policy that encourages speaking out and offers "protection" from possible unpleasant consequences. One example of such a policy is from the Cummins Engine Company Statement on Questionable Practices. It states:

> No employee will suffer a career disadvantage for failing to carry out an instruction which he or she believes to be morally inappropriate or for raising questions about a corporate practice which he or she believes is morally dubious.

A skeptical employee of another company, when shown this statement, said, "Great! But, how do they make it work?" That, of course, is the critical question. A policy is only as good as the process for implementing it. A statement like the one developed at Cummins requires mechanisms to make it work. And it, undoubtedly, must be monitored for possible negative effects. For example, *Newsweek* columnist Meg Greenfield (1978) argues that such policies, while encouraging appropriate whistle-blowing, have the dangerous potential for scapegoating, blame-placing, and general witch-hunting. Such possible outcomes should not, however, deter companies from developing formal statements about building ethical awareness into management practices. (We have already seen that many policies have unanticipated traps.) The challenge is to find a way to implement them that anticipates negative and unintended consequences. A necessary corollary to this statement is the readiness of management to listen and support. No employee in his right mind would approach the oil company "terminator" with ethical concerns, whatever policies existed. No employee would feel supported if told—as Mike Williams was—that "I don't expect to get that call." Management may not necessarily agree that an employee's concerns *are* ethical, nor may it necessarily agree with the considered course of action an employee decides to follow. But management must act to demonstrate that it respects employees' needs and rights to consider ethical concerns as a valid factor in decision making.

Another way to legitimize the discussion of ethics at work is for managers to serve as role models. Rather than making pronouncements about how ethical the company is, or dictating the ethical behavior expected of employees, top managers should publicly discuss some of their own dilemmas. In this way they not only show that it is acceptable and expected that employees voice their concerns, they also acknowledge the complexity involved in dealing with the kinds of dilemmas their employees face.

What I have been urging, of course, is better *communication*. Managers at all levels of the organization and their employees must learn to *express* their ethical concerns and *to listen to and hear* each other as they do so. Without such effective exchange, the ethically best intentions are likely to fall short of effective implementation.

Education and Training

To enable management and employees to communicate their ethical concerns and to act on them effectively requires both education and training—education to help them *think about ethics*, and training to help them *incorporate it into their activities*.

Too often the notion of educating people is to put something *into* their heads. Ethics educators and managements committed to ethical performance frequently fall into this trap. They *tell* people what ethics means (to management) and what behavior is expected of them (employees). But, the origin of the word education—*educare*, to lead out—provides the clue to what is needed. Ethics education requires that individuals be encouraged and assisted in understanding their own perceptions and beliefs about what ethics is and what their own values are. They need to explore their perceptions of the values of the company in which they work to develop an awareness of value differences. They need to exercise their imaginations to be able to identify the ethical dilemmas in their daily work and to create a range of ethically responsive options. In sum, individuals in organizations must be led out of a narrow, simplistic and constraining view of ethics to a recognition and appreciation of the complexity of ethical dilemmas and their own intellectual ability at responding to them.

But training is also necessary. It is probably impossible to "train" someone to be ethical or even to behave ethically (whether or not they "are ethical"). Yet once education has developed an ethical awareness (and once organizations are genuinely supportive of its expression), people do need practice at using it. Most specifically, individuals must be trained to use ethical language as comfortably as they use business language. "Fair" must flow off the tongue as comfortably as "ROI." And not only must the language be uttered with ease, it must also be used as skillfully in making an argument or challenging a decision. And that takes training and practice.

Training must also be provided to develop communication skills in all managers and employees. Not only must individuals develop the speaking and listening skills that have long been necessary for effective management, they must learn, specifically, how to express ethical concerns—and value concerns—in ways that do not raise emotional barriers. Clearly, policy, design, and systems geared to creating an ethically aware and responsive organization are critical to ethical management. But without a work force that can "make it happen," the best environment is all for naught.

THE MANAGER AS INDIVIDUAL

. . . Most managers are very professional, and unethical decisions are not very professional.

. . . One of the biggest problems in management is cowardice.

The challenges to individuals in their routine work activities in organizations are formidable. They must act with integrity in the face of pressures from many stakeholders; they must work for the benefit of the organization in the way the organization deems important; they must manage their careers; they must get the job done because that is what they are paid for; they must do all of

CREATING CAPACITY: SHAPING THE WAY THINGS ARE DONE

these things within an organizational environment which, as we have seen, affects almost every aspect of their working lives. And, most important, their actions will be the basis on which the company's ethics will be judged.

Taking Responsibility and Being Accountable

There is an old joke whose punch line is "the devil made me do it." Too often, for individuals working in organizations the answer is the same—only the "devil" has become "the company." No individual feels particularly proud of offering up some version of "I was only following orders," and yet, because of a number of real and perceived pressures, many find excuse if not exoneration in those words.

Yet, just as organizations must recognize and accept their responsibility and stand accountable when they are, so too must individuals acknowledge their own responsibility and accountability. Doing so is not just a matter of strong moral fibre as many critics of corporate managers proclaim. Moral fiber—character—is, of course, essential to being a responsible person in the world. But the pressures and competing claims under which an individual in an organization labors are very real impediments that must be managed. Taking responsibility and being an ethical and effective manager requires more than simply good character.

Managing Competing Claims: Avoiding the Either/Or

Whether dealing with organizational constraints or wrestling with personal value conflicts, managers in these interviews repeatedly noted that the most painful aspect of dealing with ethical dilemmas was managing competing claims. "If I evaluate Fred's performance honestly, then other people will, unfairly, lose their rankings," "If I protect my informant by 'not telling,' then others may be injured." In every situation of competing claims, the natural instinct is to move to an either/or formulation of the problem, that is, to construct a situation in which there is one winner and everyone else loses. This inclination probably grows out of a basic belief that if one is dealing with ethics, one is dealing with simple "right and wrong," and that doing the right thing is the one right answer. But the tales in this book make eminently clear the fact that ethical dilemmas, by their very nature, have no clear-cut right answers, and that seeking one through an either/or problem formulation may result in the worst of all possible outcomes. Managing competing claims requires the individual to reject the either/or in defining the problem and conceptualizing a situation.

Managing competing claims in this manner is one of the greatest challenges a manager will undertake. So although the purpose of this book is to map the terrain of ethical problems at work and not to discuss the mechanisms for resolving them, it is essential to lay out some broad guidelines for reformulating either/or-driven ethical problems.

First, managers must accept that the problem is a dilemma—the fact that however they look at it they cannot eliminate the competing claims. And they must recognize that their inability to eliminate the competing (or conflicting) claims is not a personal failure but a fact of the situation. Next, they must define what the elements of the conflict are (e.g., being supportive to a supplier with whom I have a 20-year relationship versus equity in dealing with all suppliers) in a way that allows the examination of both *positive and negative elements for each claimant*, rather than defining the problem as a "good" versus "bad" situation.

After defining the problem appropriately, managers must assess their responsibility—for what and to what extent—in resolving the dilemma. Bob McDonald saw himself as the only person who could both prevent further injury and protect his informant, and thus he considered himself highly responsible for resolving the problem. Ron Harris believed his responsibility in regard to blowing the whistle on the municipal contractor versus protecting the company was limited to informing others in the company sufficiently that they could take the full responsibility of making the decision. Everyone is not responsible for everything. Figuring out the responsibility of each participant in a dilemma is essential to resolving it.

Once responsibility is assessed, managers must use their imaginations to both seek out the key factor on which the dilemma hinges and to creatively find or develop a mechanism to turn that key factor. Bob McDonald identified the key factor of his problem as the necessity that he be "ignorant" of the informant's identity. If he could engage his imagination to find a way to create that illusion (and it had to be an illusion since the reality was different), he could solve both pieces of his dilemma. The word "imagination" is used infrequently in discussions of management, and yet imagination is one of the most important tools an individual brings to the handling of the ambiguities of managerial activity. And it is essential to the effective resolution of ethical dilemmas.

Sometimes, however, managers must recognize that despite the stretching of an active imagination, a "key factor" may not emerge. In these cases, they must assess the claim of each stakeholder or value that is in conflict with another, and balance them, choosing to weight one consideration more heavily than another while striving to respond as fully as possible to the less weighty claim. Evelyn Grant's decision to continue the "injustice" to Fred for some period of time because she placed greater weight on the claims of the other subordinates is an example of an effective balancing act. The fact that she resolved the legitimate ethical claims of Fred over a two-year period introduces the final important point in managing competing claims: effective resolution of ethical dilemmas often takes *time*. Certainly there are ethical crises that must be handled on the spot, or by tomorrow morning. But more often, when the panic has subsided, effective managers will recognize that time is a basic and necessary tool of dealing effectively with competing claims.

Knowing Where to Draw the Line

"You fight as long as you can, and then you realize you've gone as far as you can go, and then you kind of ignore [it]."

Rich Manzini's words were repeated, in one form or another, by many of the managers in this book. And there is a great deal of sense in the "I'll try but I'm not going to beat my head against the wall" attitude. Raising ethical concerns in an atmosphere that would rather not hear them can, at best, be frustrating and, at worst, threatening to job or career. So to suggest that every manager challenge with moral rectitude every ethical concern may be unwise.

But there are dangers in applying the "don't beat your head against the wall" attitude too casually. For one, it reinforces the sense of impotence that many employees say they feel, and encourages a laissez-faire attitude which can allow ethical problems to develop and continue unchecked. Secondly, and of greater concern, it blurs the line between that for which it is not "worth" fighting and those things which must not be allowed to go unchallenged. Recall Charles Warren's words: "If it's not grossly unethical, then I feel it's out of my hands." The question that must be asked, and answered by each individual, is, when is something grossly unethical; where do I draw the line?

The complexity of ethical dilemmas and the pains and pressures felt by those who are dealing with them make it difficult for any individual to prescribe, absolutely, where someone else should draw that line. But every individual must be guided by personal standards and conscience. Ron Harris could not submit a bid after being shown the competing bids because to do so would have compromised a personal, bottom-line, principle of his. His choice was clear, regardless of other pressures and pulls. Every manager must commit to standing firm on basic values and beliefs. To do so does not mean becoming a moral Don Quixote, stalking every ethical windmill along the way. What it means is keeping the question of ethical limits clearly in view. Knowing where to draw the line is essential to responsible and effective management.

Beware of Rationalization

When we rationalize a decision we have made, or an action we have taken, we give creditable, although often untrue, reasons for why we have done as we have done. It is an instinctive response driven by a need for psychological self-protection, and no amount of admonition to beware of its effects on the management of ethical dilemmas is likely to abolish it. However, any manager seeking to contribute to creating an ethically responsible organization must be aware of the instinct to rationalize, and must, if not control it, recognize it and recognize the realities it is masking.

The interviews suggest that managers rationalize at two different points in the process of dealing with ethical decisions: before (in order to make a decision that does not feel quite right), and after (in order to live with such a decision). Although it may be splitting hairs to differentiate like that, I am doing so because I would suggest that rationalizing *before* making the decision is potentially more threatening to responsible decision making, than reducing dissonance afterward. (The fact that ethical dilemmas require the balancing of competing claims and often elude a pat and perfect response suggests that there will almost always be some residual discomfort which must be managed, although doing differently the next time is probably a more dissonance-reducing mechanism than rationalization.)

The concerns about rationalizing on the way to making a decision are obvious. Rationalization redefines the problem; it masks the unpleasant aspects and inserts inappropriate motives and goals ("If I don't do it, somebody else will, and at least I'm a good [or competent or responsible] person, so it won't be so bad"). Once the ethical problem has been redefined by rationalization, the possibility for creative problem solving is diminished. The result is that the conditions that allowed the dilemma to arise remain unchallenged and the status quo is reinforced. Only by tackling ethical dilemmas head-on, and applying imagination to creatively solving tough problems, can an individual manager have impact on an organization.

And although it is probably less harmful, postdecision rationalization cannot escape without comment. Rationalizing after the fact is self-defeating for a manager committed to shaping an ethical organization. Diminishing the discomfort by masking the trade-offs or compromises and the stumbling blocks that were part of coping with the complexities of a dilemma deprives both the manager and the organization of learning from the experience. Like pre-decision rationalizing, it denies the organization the opportunity to understand its mistakes and to increase its capabilities for ethical management. In sum, rationalization's greatest sin is not that it encourages individual self-delusion, but that it promotes the organizational status quo.

Must We Do Things the Way We Do Things Around Here?

A major focus of this final section of the book has been addressed to the manager as organization. In other words, a strong message has been that organizations bear the burden of creating environments in which ethical management can be carried out. And that is true. Our passage through the 21 interviews has shown that the corporation—its values, style, policies, rules, and norms—either overtly affect the actions of its manager or are perceived to do so, or are looked to for final recourse by those individuals wrestling with themselves about painful dilemmas at work. So it is appropriate that we demand that managers in their capacity as designers, builders, and guides of organizations take a major share of responsibility for promoting ethical business management.

However, the fact that organizations are so powerful in affecting what happens in them gives a clear message to managers: no matter how comfortable, how acceptable, or how expected, be wary of simply doing things "the way we do things around here." This does not mean that instructions should be ignored or superiors challenged at every turn; it does not mean that the resources, the ideas, the policies, and rules which guided decisions and actions over time should be ignored.

Although it may sometimes come to that—to standing firm, to questioning, to challenging, to refusing—it more frequently means simply pausing before doing "what we always do in cases like this," and asking oneself a few questions: Why do we always do it this way? Are there any problems with doing what we always do? Should we try it another way? Managers' greatest stock in trade is the creativity they bring to their ambiguous task called "managing." That creativity should be contributing to keeping their organizations alert and ethically aware and capable of providing an environment in which all employees have the capacity to act with integrity. And that requires never just settling for "the way we do things around here."

SELECTED
BIBLIOGRAPHY

Andrews, Kenneth R. "Can the Best Corporations Be Made Moral?" *Harvard Bus. Rev.*, May–June 1973.

Argyris, Chris and Donald A. Schon. *Theory in Practice: Increasing Professional Effectiveness*. San Francisco: Jossey-Bass. 1974.

Baumhart, S. J., Raymond C. "How Ethical Are Businessmen?" *Harvard Bus. Rev.*, July–Aug. 1961.

Bellah, R. N., R. Madsen, M. Sullivan, A. Swindler, and S. M. Tipton. *Habits of the Heart*. Berkeley and Los Angeles: Univ. California. 1985.

Biddle, B. J. and E. J. Thomas (eds). *Role Theory: Concepts and Research*. New York: Wiley. 1966.

Bower, Marvin. *The Will to Manage*. New York: McGraw-Hill. 1966.

Brehm, J. W. *A Theory of Psychological Reactance*. New York: Academic Press. 1966.

Brenner, Steven N. and Earl A. Molander. "Is the Ethics of Business Changing?" *Harvard Bus. Rev.*, Jan.–Feb. 1977.

Carroll, Archie B. "Managerial Ethics—A Post-Watergate View." *Bus. Horizons* **18**, 2, Apr., 1975.

Coles, Robert. *The Moral Life of Children*. Boston: Atlantic Monthly. 1986.

Coles, Robert. *The Political Life of Children*. Boston: Atlantic Monthly. 1986.

Donaldson, Gordon and J. W. Lorsch. *Decision Making at the Top*. New York: Basic Books. 1983.

Drucker, Peter F. "Ethical Chic." *Forbes*, Sept. 14, 1981.

Festinger, Leon. *Theory of Cognitive Dissonance*. Evanston, IL: Row, Peterson. 1957.

Gilligan, Carol. *In a Different Voice*. Cambridge, MA: Harvard Univ. Press. 1982

Hackman, J. Richard and Greg R. Oldham. *Work Redesign*. Reading, MA: Addison-Wesley. 1980.

Hampshire, Stuart. *Morality and Conflict*. Cambridge, MA: Harvard Univ. Press. 1983.

Hart, H. L. A. *The Concept of Law, Punishment, and the Elimination of Responsibility*. New York: Oxford. 1961.

Hayes, Robert H. and William J. Abernathy. "Managing Our Way to Economic Decline." *Harvard Bus. Rev.*, July–Aug. 1980.

Heilman, Madeline E. and Barbara Ley Toffler. "Reacting to Reactance: An Interpersonal Interpretation of the Need for Freedom." *J. Exp. Soc. Psychol.* **12**, 1976.

Hirschman, Albert O. *Exit, Voice and Loyalty: Responses to Decline in Firms, Organizations and States*. Cambridge, MA: Harvard Univ. Press. 1970.

House, R. J. and J. R. Rizzo. "Role Conflict and Ambiguity as Critical Variables in a Model of Organizational Behavior." *Organ. Behavior Hum. Performance* **7**, 1972.

Kahn, R. L., D. M. Wolfe, R. P. Quinn, J. D. Snoek, and R. A. Rosenthal. *Organizational Stress: Studies in Role Conflict and Ambiguity*. New York: Wiley. 1964.

Kotter, John P. *Power and Influence*. New York: Free Press. 1985.

Ladd, John. "Morality and the Ideal of Rationality in Formal Organizations." *The Monist* **54**, 1970.

MacIntyre, Alasdair. *After Viture*. Notre Dame, IN: Univ. Notre Dame Press. 1981.

Matthews, John B., Jr. and Kenneth E. Goodpaster. "Can a Corporation Have a Conscience?" *Harvard Bus. Rev.*, **132**, Jan.–Feb. 1982.

Meisand, Joseph, (ed). *Three Plays About Business and America*. New York: Washington Sq. Press. 1964.

Miles, Robert H. "Role-set Configuration as a Predictor of Role Conflict and Ambiguity in Complex Organizations." *Sociometry* **40**, 1977.

Miller, Arthur. *Death of a Salesman*. New York: Dramatists' Play Serv. 1948.

Neibuhr, H. Richard. *The Meaning of Revelation*. New York: Macmillan. 1962.

Neibuhr, H. Richard. *The Responsible Self*. New York: Harper & Row. 1963.

Payne, Stephen L. "Organization Ethics and Antecedents to Social Control Processes." *Acad. Manage. Rev.* **5**, 3, July 1980.

Powers, Charles W. "Understanding and Justifying Intervention." Unpublished paper, Apr. 1978.

Purcell, Theodore V. "Do Courses in Business Ethics Pay Off?" *Calif. Manage. Rev.* **19**, 4, Summer 1977.

Schein, Edgar H. "The Problem of Moral Education for the Business Manager." *Indust. Manage. Rev.* **8**, 1, Fall 1966.

Simon, Herbert A. *Administrative Behavior*. (3d ed) New York: Free Press. 1976.

Simon, John G., Charles W. Powers, and John P. Gunnemann. *The Ethical Investor*. New Haven: Yale Univ. Press. 1972.

Solomon, Robert C. and Kristine R. Hanson. *Above the Bottom Line*. New York: Harcourt, Brace, Jovanovich. 1983.

Toffler, Barbara Ley. "Occupational Role Development: The Changing Determinants of Outcomes for the Individual." *Adm. Sci. Quarterly*, Sept. 1981.

Vickers, Geoffrey. *Making Institutions Work*. New York: John Wiley and Sons. 1973.

Von Glinow, Mary Ann and Erik Jansen. "Ethical Ambivalence and Organizational Reward System." *Acad. Manage. Rev.* **10**, 4, October 1985.

Warnock, J. J. *Contemporary Moral Philosophy*. London: Macmillan. 1967.

APPENDIX A

Interview Schedules and

Post-Interview Questionnaire

The interviews were conducted with 33 managers drawn from four organizations. Represented were financial services, the computer industry, manufacturing, and research and development.

Each participant was interviewed in three sessions, each session lasting approximately two hours. Meetings with an individual were scheduled at least two weeks apart to allow for reflection and, in the case of the second interview, for review of ethical problems experienced at work.

Participants were given the questionnaire at the conclusion of the third interview and returned it by mail.

MANAGEMENT ETHICS RESEARCH PROJECT

INTERVIEW I

Introduction

(1) Review purpose
  Three interviews—discuss general content
(2) Tape recorder—permission
                  —will turn off any time
(3) Review/release procedure
  I. Let's begin by talking about your job:
    A. What do you do?
      1. Position
      2. Where fit in organization
      3. People work with
        a. Subordinates
        b. Superiors
        c. Peers
    B. Can you describe a typical day on the job?
      1. Meetings
      2. Phone
      3. Blocks of time/interrupted
    C. What do you like most about your work? Least? Why?
    D. What kinds of pressures do you feel on the job?

II. Let's talk for a few minutes about [organization]:
   A. What is life like in _____ ?
      1. Feelings (about colleagues, about the company, perceptions of others' feelings)
      2. Attitudes (toward employees; toward others)
      3. "Speed"—things move quickly/slowly—why
      4. How things get done
      5. Explicit values/implicit values
   B. Is there a "favorite" story around _____ that typifies life in this organization?
   C. What about your department/area/function—is it pretty much like the company in style and personality? What's different? (if anything)
   D. Terms like business ethics, management ethics, corporate responsibility are being used more and more frequently by increasing numbers of people and organizations—and the more they are used, the more and varied meanings seem to be attached to them:

When the topic of ethics comes up in your organization, in what ways does it usually surface?
      1. Key issues
      2. Key words
      3. Key areas
      4. Key people
   E. What about in your department? Any different than in the organization as a whole?

III. We've been talking about the company—what it's like, some of its values—let's get back to you now:

We're going to be talking quite a bit over the next two sessions about values, ethics, etc., so let's not try to cover vast territory now, but just *begin* to think about those topics:

   A. When you think about the things that matter to you—your values—which of those are important to you to find in any organization for which you work?
      1. Why?

      2. What if some are not there? Do you feel you could
         work in such an environment? Change it?

  B. Very generally, when you think of "ethics," what does
     it mean to you?
     1. "Always" aware of it?
     2. Come to mind in specific situations?
     3. What ways does it surface?

  C. Have you ever been asked to do anything that you feel
     was against your values? How handled?

IV. Can we talk for a few minutes about this interview we've
   had:

  A. How has it felt talking—rather generally, about ethics?
     1. Easy to do?
     2. Hard to do?
     3. Comfortable? Why/why not?

  B. Did the questions help/hinder you think through your
     feelings, etc., about ethics?

  C. Any suggestions? Road blocks that should be cleared?

  D. Any questions about what we've covered so far?

For next time, please think of two problems you have faced or are now facing which you consider to have an ethical component.

For one—think of a problem you find or found relatively *easy* to handle;

For the other—a problem you found or find *difficult* to handle.

Please think about:

    —Why you consider each of these to be ethical problems

    —The process you are going through—or went through—to
     analyze each situation and move toward a resolution [and
     why used]

    —Whether or not that process is different for "ethical" prob-
     lems than for "routine" management problems

Any questions about what we've talked about so far, or about the next meeting?

Set Date for Interview II

Thank.

INTERVIEW II

I. Any thoughts or questions triggered by our first discussion?
—other thoughts regarding what "ethical" means?

II. Let me review what I had asked you to think about for today.
   A. Two situations
   B. Hard/easy
   C. Why ethical
   D. Why hard or easy

III. Let's talk about the "easy" one first.
   A. Probe details
   B. Who involved
   C. Relationships (to you/to each other)
   D. What did you do?/why?

IV. OK. Why do you call that situation an *ethical* issue?
   A. Values—personal/institutional/conflict?
   B. Person vs. role issues?
   C. Others affected?
   D. Values imposed on you?
   E. Career issues?
   F. Consequences?
   G. Right/wrong?
   H. Feel good/bad
   I. Guilt?

V. As you began to work through the issue—what questions and concerns did you raise (to yourself)?
   —Why?

VI. What "answers" did you come up with? (explore)
   —Who (or what) influenced you (if anyone)?

VII. Refer back to decision—did that decision respond to the questions and concerns you had raised?
   A. Feel satisfied with way you handled the situation?
   B. Feel comfortable?
   C. Would you do same thing now?

VIII. Why did you call that situation "easy?" (Same for "hard")

IX. OK. Now, lets talk about the situation you think of as difficult. [Go through same questions as did for "easy" situation. See III above.]

X. Let's review similarities and differences
   A. Review why both "ethical" dilemmas
   B. Factors differentiating easy/difficult
   C. What about the process of thinking through the two situations: do you feel you analyzed them in a similar fashion?
   —What differences?
XI. Did you work through these problems the same way you go through "routine" management problems?
   A. If different: what and why?
   B. If *not* different: why not?
XII. Let's talk briefly about this discussion
   A. How has it felt talking about ethical dilemmas you faced?
      1. What felt comfortable?
      2. What felt less comfortable?
   B. Did the questions help/hinder you think through your feelings?
   C. Any suggestions?
   D. Any roadblocks that should be cleared?
   E. Any questions?

For the next time no special preparation—we'll talk about your background, education, etc. You might spend a little time thinking about how your background and experience may have affected the way you handled the situations we discussed today.

Thank.

Set Date for Interview III

INTERVIEW III

Any thoughts, questions after last interview?
Let's talk today about your life, your background.

   I. Where did you grow up? What was life like there?
  II. What was your family life like growing up?
   A. Parents' occupations?

B. Parents' roles in household?

C. Siblings—order in family; roles

D. Other relatives or friends who had impact on or influenced you?

III. What were your elementary and high schools like?

A. Teachers/others who had impact on or influenced you?

B. Activities involved in?

IV. What role did religion play in your childhood?

—Can you remember any of your early thoughts about doing "right or wrong?"

V. What was your post-high school education?

A. Where?

B. What was life like there?

C. Was it a comfortable experience?

D. Did your values seem to fit with the institution's values?

E. Did you work while at school?

F. Who had great impact—or influenced you—during those years?

VI. What was your first job?

A. Explore

B. What do you remember most about it—or how you felt about it?

VII. Can you take me through your employment history?

A. Key experiences

B. Key people who influenced you

VIII. What has your relationship with your "first" family been like during these adult years?

IX. Can we talk about your adult immediate family—are you married?

A. Do you have children?

B. What is life like in your household?

C. Key values

D. Values you hope to see in your children

—How are you helping them espouse those values?

X. What is the role of religion in your present life?

—Do you see a direct connection between it and the way you deal with ethical dilemmas on the job?

Thinking back on our second meeting—and reviewing what we've discussed today, do you see any "connections" between specific values, experiences, people (etc.) in your life and how you handled the situations we talked about?

Questions?

Thank.

MANAGEMENT ETHICS RESEARCH PROJECT
Background Questionnaire

Harvard Business School—Spring 1983

Please answer all questions completely. Feel free to make additional comments or to provide clarifying information in the margins.

Please return this questionnaire in the enclosed stamped, addressed envelope.

NAME: _____

POSITION: _____

COMPANY: _____

    A. Your current job:
        1. How long have you been in this job?

        2. As specifically as possible, what are you held responsible for in your job?

        3. What formal authority is inherent in the job?

        4. On the average, how many hours per week do you work (including work done at home)?

    B. Occupational history
        1. Past employment

Approximate Date	Employer	Position
_____	_____	_____
_____	_____	_____
_____	_____	_____

2. Have you served in the Armed Forces? If yes, please indicate date, branch, ranks.

_____

C. Personal history:
1. Birthdate: _____ _____ _____
                    month   day   year
2. Birthplace: _____
3. Parents: Mother   Father
                          _____ _____

   Living?   _____   _____
   Education (highest grade
   completed or degree received)   _____   _____
   Occupation   _____   _____
   Religion   _____   _____
4. Brothers and Sisters:
     Sex   Age   Education   Occupation

   _____   _____   _____   _____
   _____   _____   _____   _____
   _____   _____   _____   _____

5. Education: High School   College   Graduate School
                    _____ _____ _____
   Name of School   _____ _____ _____
   Major Area of
   Study   _____ _____ _____
   Degree   _____ _____ _____
D. Your Family:
1. Married? _____
2. Is this your first marriage? _____
3. Spouse's occupation? _____
4. Children:
     Sex   Age   Occupation (if applicable)
   _____   _____   _____
   _____   _____   _____
   _____   _____   _____
   _____   _____   _____

5. How do you spend your time off the job (hobbies, organizations you belong to)?
E. General:
1. What two or three adjectives best describe your company?

2. What two or three adjectives best describe your department or functional area?
3. What two or three adjectives best describe you?
4. How much tension or stress is there currently in your life? (Circle one)

1	2	3	4	5
None		Some		A Great Deal

Comments:

5. How happy are you with your work life? (Circle one)

1	2	3	4	5
Very Unhappy		Neutral		Very Happy

Comments:

6. How happy are you with your life in general? (Circle one)

1	2	3	4	5
Very Unhappy		Neutral		Very Happy

Comments:

* * * * *

As you think back over our three meetings in which we talked about your job, your organization, ethics in general, specific situations (hard and easy) which for you had an ethical component, and your background and life experiences, what issues, ideas, notions, thoughts, etc. have been raised for you or been important to you?

APPENDIX B

Editing the Interviews

E ach of the managers in this study participated in the three two-hour interviews, with the exception of four people for whom time or other constraints necessitated collapsing the three sessions into two. In those four cases, however, the full range of material was covered. The interviews were tape recorded and then transcribed.

The major challenge for me was to take what in some cases amounted to 150 double-spaced pages of transcription and present, concisely and coherently, what the interviewee intended. As is apparent in the book, in some cases, I focused primarily on the second interview—the ethical dilemmas themselves—and in other cases I drew from the first and second interviews (as in Mike Williams and Evelyn Grant) to embed the ethical problems in their organizational context. For each of the final three interviews (Smith, Rowan, and Manzini) the full transcription was the core material from which the edited version was developed.

Although 33 managers took part in the project, the interviews of only 19 are included. The main reason is that in several cases the situations either duplicated or were similar enough to others so that inclusion of all would have been redundant. Conceptually, it was interesting to find the duplications and similarities, as they further confirmed the finding that ethical dilemmas are part of ordinary, routine management practice and, therefore, occur in the activities which most managers regularly undertake. Some few other individuals and their situations are represented anecdotally at various places in the book.

The actual process of editing required putting together pieces of the interviews to develop the logical narrative intended by the interviewee. Most people, in talking about their work, their company, their family, and specific situations do not move in a clearly linear fashion, but diverge to embellish a portion of a tale, to recall a critical fact, or to report a related idea that suddenly strikes them. My task was to keep the logical thread, using tangential material as appropriate but not allowing it to confuse the narrative. The process also included cutting down—if not out completely—the retellings of stories and the redundancies which are a natural part of any speaker's comments. I did this with some concern, and great care, because as Stuart Hampshire, who is quoted at the outset of the book, suggests, the knowledge gained from listening to stories comes in the "new" pieces that are added with each retelling; that the whole meaning of a situation takes shape from the layer upon layer of new fact and insight at each iteration. If all of the retellings had been allowed to stand, this book would have been beyond most readers' patience. However, I did try to retain some of what seemed to me to be necessry perseverating to allow both the nuance of the situation and the emotion of the speaker to come through.

In attempting to accurately present speakers in their own words while doing the necessary limiting, one runs the great risk of mis-representing or distorting the meaning and intention of the speakers. I made every effort to maintain the integrity of the voices as they wished to be heard. The evidence that I succeeded lies in the responses of the participants after they reviewed their own material. Not only did no one question whether he or she "really said that," in fact, many assumed that their remarks had been lifted verbatim from the transcript. Although the substantial work that goes into bringing such interviews to life is rarely acknowledged, I was pleased that the managers who agreed to voice their experiences publicly felt that those voices were accurately and respectfully heard.

INDEX